The Bottom-Up Simple Approach to School Accountability and Improvement

The Bottom-Up Simple Approach to School Accountability and Improvement

John Carr and Elaine M. Artman

Christopher-Gordon Publishers, Inc.
Norwood, Massachusetts

Credits

Every effort has been made to contact copyright holders for permission to reproduce borrowed material where necessary. We apologize for any oversights and would be happy to rectify them in future printings.

Assessment in the Learning Organization: Shifting the Paradigm by Arthur Costa and Bena Kallick, 1995, Figure 1.1, pp. 9. Copyright 1995, Alexandria, Virginia by Association for Supervision and Curriculum and Development. Reprinted with permission. All rights reserved.

Realizing the Promise of Standards-Based Education by Mike Schmoker and Robert J. Marzano, March 1999, *Educational Leadership*, Volume 56, No. 6, pp. 17-21. Copyright 1999 by ASCD. Reprinted with permission of the Association for Supervision and Curriculum Development.

What Helps Students Learn? By Margaret C. Wang, Geneva D. Haertel, and Herbert J. Walberg, December 1993/January 1994, *Educational Leadership*, Volume 51, No. 4, pp. 74-79. Copyright 1993 by ASCD. Reprinted with permission of the Association for Supervision and Curriculum Development.

The Search for Methods of Group Instruction as Effective as One-to-One Tutoring by Benjamin Bloom, 1984, *Educational Leadership*, Volume 41, No. 8, pp. 4-17. Copyright 1984 by ASCD. Reprinted with permission of the Association for Supervision and Curriculum and Development.

Categories Influencing Change in NAEP Grade 8 Math Scores (1992-96) by L. Darling-Hammond and D.L. Ball, 1997, *Teaching for High Standards: What Policymakers Need to Know and Be Able to Do*, Copyright 1997, by National Education Goals Panel, Washington, D.C. Adapted with permission.

School Culture Scoring Guide used by permission of Accrediting Commission for Schools,Western Association of School and Colleges Self-Study Document.

Excerpt from *USA Today* article, "Old Company Learns New Tricks", April 10, 2000, used with permission.

Excerpts from *The Fifth Discipline: The Art & Practice of Learning Organization*, by P. Senge, 1990. Copyright 1990 New York by Doubleday, a division of Random House, Inc. Reprinted with permission of Doubleday.

Excerpts from *The Fifth Discipline: Strategies and Tools for Building a Learning Organization*, by P. Senge, R. Ross, B. Smith, C. Roberts, & A. Kleiner, 1994. Copyright 1994 New York by Doubleday a division of Random House, Inc.. Reprinted with permission of Doubleday.

Excerpt from *Hope Fulfilled for At-Risk and Violent Youth: K-12 Programs That Work, 2E* by R.D. Barr and W.H. Parrett, 2001. Copyright 2001 Boston, by Allyn & Bacon. Reprinted with permission.

Adapted figure and quotes from *A Comprehensive Guide to Designing Standards-Based Districts, Schools, and Classrooms* by R.J. Marzano and J.S. Kendall, 1996. Copyright 1996 Aurora, Colorado by McREL. Reprinted with permission.

Citations, quotes, and workshop materials by Douglas Reeves appear throughout this book, and are used with permission of the Center for Performance Assessment. Below is a list of works cited by Reeves:

Reeves, D.B. (1998a). *Making Standards Work: How to Implement Standards-Based Assessments in the Classroom, School, and District.* Denver, CO: Center for Performance Assessment.

Reeves, D.B. (2000a). *Accountability in Action: A Blueprint for Learning Organizations.* Denver, CO: Advanced Learning Press.

Reeves, D.B. (2000b). Personal communications and workshop materials.

Works cited from *A Practical Guide to Alternative Assessment,* by Herman, et. al., 1992. Copyright 1992 Los Angeles, by CRESST-UCLA. Reprinted with permission.

Adapted materials from WestEd, San Francisco, used with permission.

Christopher-Gordon Publishers, Inc.
1502 Providence Highway, Suite 12
Norwood, MA 02062
800-934-8322
781-762-5577

Printed in the United States of America

10 9 8 7 6 5 4 3 2 1 06 05 04 03 02

Library of Congress Catalog Card Number: 2001093757

ISBN: 1-929024-38-X

Acknowledgements

We thank the reviewers of this book for their advice, especially Kendyll Stansbury, who offered many pages of recommendations and personal perspectives; Margit Birge, who reviewed the first draft and helped us with an extensive revision of the outline for the second draft; Judy Heathman, who reviewed the first chapter and offered discerning comments; and Sue Canavan and staff at Christopher-Gordon Publishers who responded quickly to our questions and transcended the business relationship to cement a friendship.

Dedications

To Thanad and family in Thailand for their patience and love; my mother, an expert Scottish dance teacher who believes in breaking complexity into simple, teachable steps; Judy Heathman, my dear friend and excellent fifth grade teacher, who has inspired her students and me to experiment and change; and Ann Bickel, a colleague at West Ed who more than once encouraged me to write this book.

—John Carr

To the master teachers who have touched my life, in particular, Ambrose C. Clarke, algebra teacher at Batavia Senior High School (New York), who pushed his students to personal mastery by repeating the admonishment "near enough is not right;" Mrs. Unselt, grade 7–8 homeroom teacher at Pembrook Junior-Senior High School, who challenged mental models until all students believed they had value, the capacity to learn, and the ability to achieve great things; Emily Franclemont, mother and staff member in the Office of the Dean of Boys, Batavia Senior High School, who shared her vision of a common destiny with all "her kids"—her own children, her foster children, and those she supervised in afterschool detention; Bodo Fritzen, soccer coach at University High School (Normal, Illinois), who developed his students' capacity to create an efficient team; and Dr. Robert Bone, Sr., president of Illinois State University, who demonstrated systems thinking and learning organization leadership.

—Elaine M. Artman

Contents

Foreword

By Douglas B. Reeves

You are in for an unusual treat. John Carr and Elaine Artman have injected a splendid mix of common sense, thoughtful analysis, and deep insight into a book that will be of benefit to the educators, school leaders, parents, and policymakers who invest the time and intellectual energy to read it and apply these ideas to their daily decisions. Books that have the dreaded word "accountability" in the title are bound to engender some controversy, and this will be no exception. However, the rationale and constructive focus on standards, assessment, and accountability in the pages that follow is unusual. Those terms are too frequently associated with histrionic diatribes by those who use the club of accountability and standards to berate public education and by the equally irrational critics who find no value in these techniques to improve achievement and equity for students. Readers searching for polemics have come to the wrong place. Those in search of a rational and systematic approach to data analysis and a constructive method of transforming school accountability into meaningful strategies, however, will be rewarded.

The School BUS is designed to be consumed, not merely to be read. The staff development activities throughout the volume will provide challenging opportunities for reflection and constructive discussions for a great many faculty meetings and professional development sessions. The activities focus explicitly on professional practices that are related to local data and provide a welcome relief from one more diatribe from the expert *du jour*. Most importantly, the staff development activities include a focus on the essentials of standards implementation: building consensus on what the word "proficiency" means for individual pieces of student work and what teaching strategies are required for all students to succeed.

There are several analytical insights in *The School BUS* that are worthy of particular attention. First, the authors take academic standards out of the realm of theory and provide practical understanding for the classroom educator through their linking of academic standards to student performance levels. Second, the book recognizes the essential nature of leadership in a successful school without falling victim to the myth of the visionary loner who generates followers based on enigmatic charisma. The leadership model embraced here is less dramatic and far more effective, as it balances guidance and support from the leader with deep and continuous involvement by the staff.

Third, the authors take direct aim at the frequent misuse of Normal Curve Equivalent (NCE) scores and the misleading use of average scores. By demystifying the statistical jargon surrounding these misapplied and misinterpreted statistics, Carr and Artman do a great service to board members and school leaders who have too frequently been led astray by numbers that express guesswork and approximation with inappropriate certitude. Finally, this book provides a splendid balance between causes and effects in the context of student achievement. While student test results are certainly part of the conversation, they are only part of the bottom-up approach. Any discussion of test scores that does not include a discussion of teaching practices, curriculum, leadership support, and classroom assessment is inherently incomplete. Thus, *The School BUS* places test scores in context: they are neither the only focus of discussion nor the subject of ridicule as irrelevant and racist. Rather, scores are but one piece of a complex puzzle, and the other pieces of that puzzle are found not in a district assessment office, but in the discussions among educators who collaboratively fit those pieces together.

Board members, legislators, superintendents, and other readers with leadership and policy responsibilities should pay particular attention to chapters 7 and 9. Here you will find a wonderfully concise explanation of the fundamental principle that accountability is more than test scores. While the production of an accountability report is a formality observed by virtually every school district in the nation, the ideas in these chapters will help to transform your accountability system from a sterile report into a blueprint for progress.

The emotional climate in many educational discussions of standards and accountability has degenerated into an unimpressive combination of whining, defensiveness, anger, and resentment. With each new rhetorical missile, we have contributed to cynicism by our colleagues and the general public. Because Carr and Artman have provided not only intellectual substance, but also a rational, calm, and deliberate approach to the topic, they have made a significant contribution to elevating the tone of the debate. After reading this book, faculties may not agree on every matter regarding assessment, standards, and accountability. Their disagreements, however, will be based upon data and thoughtful analysis rather than prejudice and rancor. For that reason alone, the pages that follow will make the days of educators and school leaders more meaningful and less stressful.

Preface

Teachers and administrators work long, hard hours and strive to respond quickly to the concerns of policymakers, business and community representatives, parents and guardians, and students. Educators must simultaneously resist fads, respond to governmental mandates, and explore innovations that could dramatically improve how teachers teach and students learn.

The current American trend toward public accountability will most likely expand and deepen. A state or national system of accountability may force some poorly performing schools and districts to acknowledge that change is needed. However, we believe the correct response is not to raise test scores to meet some external goal, but instead to develop a local system of accountability that supports best practices and is aligned to state standards. Build a sound local accountability system to address the state systems.

This book is a sensible response to the call for public accountability, one that will empower schools and districts to make well-informed decisions about how best to improve the education of all students. Local accountability and professional development are the true path toward meaningful, continuous, and sustainable improvement. True gains come when teachers work as a team and use a unified approach to overcome challenges one by one.

The School BUS shows how accountability can lead to school improvement and offers a step-by-step approach to help educators do the work at hand. No one approach will work everywhere, but the School BUS features some basic elements that any district can implement from one-school rural district that keeps all student data on paper to a large unified district with a computerized database.

Accountability requires improving student performance in core academics, but that focus should not displace diversity, personal interests, and extracurricular activities that enrich and give meaning to students' lives. Schools should be fun, challenging places where teams of teachers and students work toward common goals and respect individual differences and interests.

We want district and school educators to use this book as a map to help them pilot their course, a sort of in-flight repair manual. Seminar leaders and postsecondary schools can use this book to inspire professional and aspiring educators to think deeply and engage in dialogue about critical aspects of local accountability. We suggest reading, discussing, practicing, and reflecting on each element of the book thoroughly before moving to the next. This book's simple, effective methods for summarizing, analyzing, and reporting data and group agreements can make all teachers and principals data-driven decision makers.

1 The School Bus

The only way we can properly judge where we are is relative to where we want to be.
—*Grant Wiggins*

Things should be as simple as possible, but not more so.
—*Albert Einstein*

Introduction

The School BUS (bottom-up simple) model for school accountability uses local standards-based assessment data to improve schoolwide performance during the year, and from year to year. The School BUS derives its ideas from abundant professional literature about successful school renewal. A local accountability process should link changes in school practices to changes in student achievement. The School BUS's four major components—standards-based assessments, school culture, schoolwide instructional practices, and student results—are called *wheels* because each component moves continually through its own cycle of improvement. A school can use the four wheels to embark on a journey of continuous improvement.

The first component, *standards-based assessments*, focuses on standards and simplifies data collection and analysis. The other three components—culture, instructional practices, and student results—form a causal relationship, or program theory. As the school culture of a learning organization improves, and teachers continually engage in team learning, instructional practices improve schoolwide, resulting in improved student achievement. These teams of teachers can then use student results to pinpoint where and how to further improve teaching, leading to even greater gains in student achievement.

Schools may be pulled in many directions and feel inundated by seemingly unrelated local, state, and federal initiatives and mandates. Change and information are increasing, and school systems must embrace change as a valued cultural norm. Now more than ever, schools need guidance to simplify and integrate a system of education that maintains a clear, calm focus on improving learning opportunities for adults and children.

The School BUS provides one local accountability process, while it addresses many internal and external purposes. For example, the School BUS can address the accountability requirements of Title I, state program reviews and pupil promotion/retention policies, CSRD (Comprehensive School Reform Demonstration) projects, and local district accountability demands. This book gives schools in any district all the ideas, tools, forms, and processes they need to begin using a local accountability process that will serve their students, yet meets the demands of state accountability systems. The tools and forms are not used just to generate reports, but to help educators generate professional dialogue and make timely decisions about best practices.

The School BUS model simplifies assessment, data management, and data analysis. Schools with no local student assessment data as well as those "inundated with data" can learn to identify a good assessment, summarize data and make reasonable decisions about what is working, what is not, and the direction needed for further improvement. For standards-based assessments, student data can be summarized as the percentage of students at a few performance levels. The results at each performance level can then be used to directly inform decisions about the school's instructional practices.

Districts large and small can implement the School BUS with or without sophisticated computer applications. Data results can be recorded on a few pieces of paper with an inexpensive calculator or by using database and query/report software. Data analysis can progress from basic to sophisticated as the school and district build capacity over the years. Everyone in the district can speak the same "accountability language." District leaders can guide, model, support, and provide the coherency needed to drive systemic change in the schools. The district can expect continuous school improvement, and each school can decide how improvement will happen.

The following sections describe part of the model's name: School, Bottom-up, and Simple.

The School

Much professional literature supports the claim that the unit of change is the school, not individual teachers or the district or the state. This means that *all* teachers in a school are committed to a shared vision of excellence and a shared plan of action toward that vision. Districts can support change and lead large-scale efforts, but true change in the educational system percolates upward from each school in the district. Schools need district and state support to begin and sustain meaningful change, but each school must be the locus of the change effort. To create change in a district, all schools must work in flexible unison on common as well as school-specific goals.

One teacher working alone has little impact on schoolwide student results or on the total education of a student. If only one teacher in K–12 works on student writing, the graduating student will unlikely be an accomplished writer. However, the combined effort of all teachers in a school leads to schoolwide results, and the articulated effort of teachers in elementary, middle, and high schools leads to districtwide results and truly educated graduates of the system.

Meaningful schoolwide improvement in student achievement requires that teachers work as a team. Each teacher must say, "These are *our* students, K–12," and not "These are my students this year, and those are yours." Teachers in improving schools share a common vision of each student becoming a wise, thoughtful, caring adult. These teachers know it takes a team effort to accomplish that vision, and they engage in personal and team learning to continually improve as a learning organization. The School BUS is a vehicle for making progress in unison; the principal drives and the staff maps the journey.

A large district might begin the School BUS as a pilot project in a few ready-and-willing schools and phase in remaining schools over several years. Staff from the pilot schools can later help other staff implement the School BUS model in their schools. Small districts may be better able to start the School BUS in all schools at once.

All schools in the district can work on districtwide or school-specific goals. In one small district, for example, math results were lowest in one school, but staff agreed to join the other schools and work on reading the first year. The district office was too small to support different initiatives, and no school wanted to go it alone. Teachers and administrators understood that once they learned how to use the School BUS to assess and improve one area, they could extend the process to other subject areas with relative ease.

Bottom–Up

The School BUS is a bottom-up approach to making decisions about which strategies best improve instruction for all students. The process starts at the individual teacher level and continues by grade or department teams, the whole school, the district, and, perhaps, the state (see figure 1.1). Because teachers are closest to the students, they should be the closest to decisions that affect their students.

FIGURE 1.1
School BUS
Primarily a Bottom-Up Flow of Information and Decisions

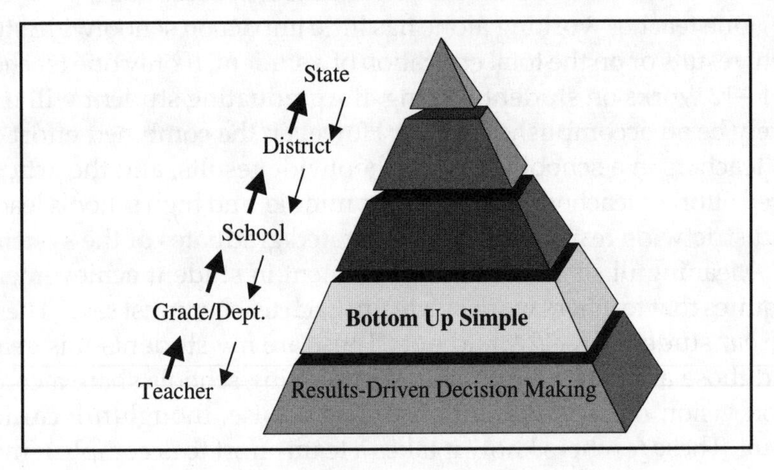

Experience shows that top-down management generally does not work, yet a totally bottom-up approach can lead to chaos and a dysfunctional district. A balanced top-down and bottom-up management seems to work best. "There should be guidance from the top and bottom-up innovation," stated O'Neil (1993). Figure 1.1 shows heavy arrows pointing up and light arrows pointing down. These arrows signify that decisions are made primarily at lower levels, but each higher level has the responsibility to review and accept lower–level decisions. When a decision is unclear, the school and district must agree on a sound decision; co-leadership exists between the district and the schools, the principal and the teachers.

At an elementary school, grade level teams examine student achievement results and make decisions about their next course of action. The school leadership team can question the decision of any grade level team before summarizing the results and common actions into a school report. Likewise, the district can question a school's decision before it summarizes results and common actions into a district report.

Simple

In the School BUS, a school's comprehensive instructional program consists of three simple elements: core classroom practices, school moderate and intensive interventions, and family/community partnerships. Data management, number crunching, analysis of results, and results-driven decisions can be very simple. All reporting forms have a similar format, should be about one page in length, and capture the essence of teachers' professional discussions during a staff meeting. The School BUS allows a school staff to learn *from* the process, not learn *how to do* the process.

Reporting student achievement data is simple: Student results are summarized as the percentage of students at each of five performance levels. Student results can then be used to inform staff decisions about what is working and what needs improvement in the schoolwide instructional program. Figure 1.2 shows these five performance levels and five resulting instructional program decisions. Student results at the Advanced level indicate the effectiveness of enriched, challenging instruction; results at the Proficient level indicate effectiveness of the comprehensive instructional practices (program).

Because teachers have the primary impact on students' reaching proficiency, classroom instruction is the key to improving achievement for students who have not yet met the standards. As stated earlier, student results—the percent of students at each performance level—should inform program decisions. The following three decisions about a school's instructional practices were based on student results:

- Improving classroom instruction should help students at the

Figure 1.2

General Performance Levels		Instructional Program Decisions
Advanced	Above grade level understanding	Effectiveness of an enriched, challenging program in all classrooms
Proficient	Solid grade level understanding	Effectiveness of the comprehensive instructional program (core classroom practices, school interventions, and family and community partnerships)
Approaching	Understanding of most concepts and skills	Improve core classroom practices
Partial	Understanding of some concepts and skills	Improve core classroom practices + moderate interventions
Minimal	Understanding of few or no concepts and skills	Improve core classroom practices + intensive interventions

Approaching level become fully proficient on the grade-level content standards

- Improving classroom instruction plus *moderate* school interventions should help students at the *Partial* level accelerate to proficiency. Improving classroom instruction plus *intensive* school interventions should help students at the *Minimal* level accelerate to proficiency.
- Families and community members and agencies can support the school goals in many ways. The school, families, and community can integrate efforts and learn how to capitalize on one another's strengths.

Figure 1.3 illustrates the three elements of a school's comprehensive instructional program: *core classroom practice, school interventions*, and *family/community partnerships*. These three elements are ranked in terms of their degree of teacher control and relative impact on student learning. *Core classroom practice* is the most important component because a) teachers have the most control over classroom instruction, and b) classroom instruction has the most leverage, or impact, on improving student learning. School staff can first focus on schoolwide core classroom practices and then work outward to improve the remaining two components in the comprehensive instructional program.

FIGURE 1.3

Three Elements of a School's Comprehensive Instructional Program

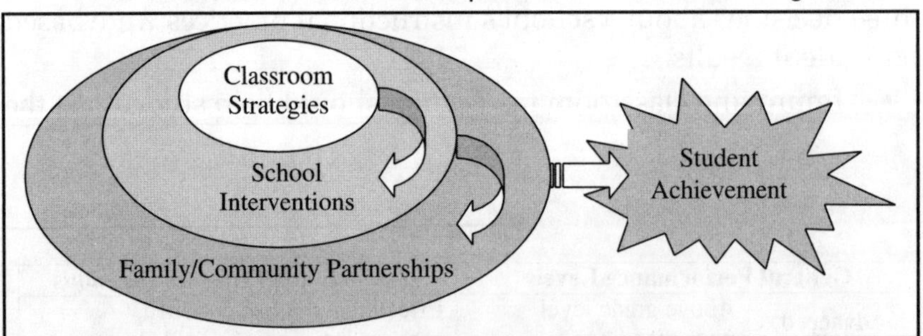

The Four Wheels of the School BUS

Figure 1.4 shows the four wheels of the School BUS, which comprise the main elements of a system of standards-based accountability. The four wheels revolve around results-driven decision making. Before the four wheels can be set in motion, the district must establish academic content standards and "get them into the hands of teachers, students, and parents." The district must provide ongoing professional development in standards-based lesson planning and a toolbox of teaching strategies. Assessing students about what they have learned and using those results to reflect on how students were taught necessitates that all teachers provide some core instruction at each grade level.

FIGURE 1.4

Four Wheels of the School Bus

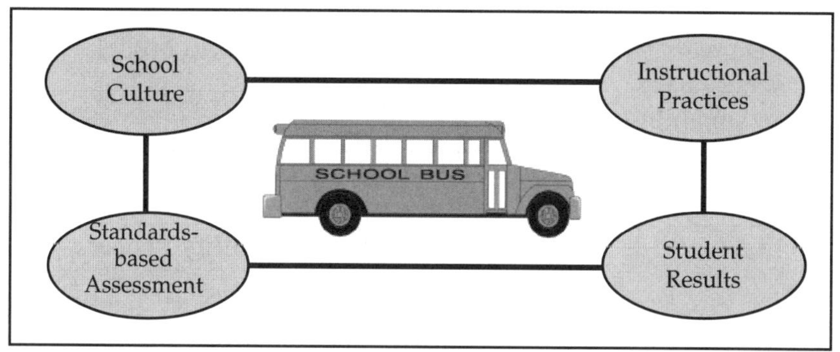

The first wheel of the School BUS involves establishing standards-based assessments that measure the priority for schoolwide instructional improvement and accountability. The second wheel requires that staff assess the school's culture and use that information to improve the school as a learning organization. For the third wheel, teachers self-assess their level of instructional program implementation and plan action for schoolwide improvement. For the fourth wheel, the staff uses the results of standards-based student assessment during the year to celebrate success and plan improvements.

Improving school culture fosters instructional program improvement. When all teachers in a school teach more students more effectively, student achievement dramatically improves. The causal relationship between culture, instructional program implementation, and student results is the simple program theory of the School BUS.

Sample School BUS Schedule

Figure 1.5 presents a sample schedule of meetings for a school district that uses the quarter grading period system. When using the School BUS, certain events must precede the cycles of assessment and use of results. First, district administrators and school representatives participate in a School BUS orientation meeting to learn about the model and agree on implementation. Second, a district committee establishes quintessential standards, or at least one standard, as the focus for improvement. These standards can be common to all schools, or each school can select the standard most in need of improvement based on school assessment results. Third, a district committee establishes quarterly standards-based assessments for all students. These three steps occur before the start of the school year.

FIGURE 1.5
Sample Schedule of School BUS Meetings

Precursors to School BUS accountability process		Orientation to School BUS Model
		Quintessential Standards & Focus
		Standards-Based Assessments
Quarter/Mth		**School BUS Accountability Process**
1	1	School Culture Rating
	2	Classroom Practices Rating
	3	Student Performance Level Results (Grade/Dept → School → District)
2	6	Student Performance Level Results (Grade/Dept → School → District)
3	8	Option: Minimal Level Results
4	9	Culture & Classroom Practices Ratings
	10	Student Performance Level Results (Grade/Dept → School → District)

In the first month of the first quarter, each school's staff rates the school culture and develops a mini action plan during a regular staff meeting. Teachers at each school rate their level of core classroom instructional practices and the staff then develops a mini action plan during their next meeting. These ratings become the *baseline* ratings—they mark the school's beginning performance and will be compared to year-end ratings.

At the end of the first quarter, teachers note the percentage of students at each performance level and develop a mini action plan during a grade level or department team meeting. The school leadership team then writes a report to summarize grade or department reports, and facilitates a whole staff meeting the following week to give feedback and discuss action. The school report is then submitted to the district office. Finally, the superintendent conducts a principals meeting the following week to provide feedback and discuss districtwide action.

At the end of the second quarter, the process of using student results to make school and district decisions is repeated. Particular attention is given to improving learning for the subgroup of students at the Minimal and Partial performance levels. Schools may skip the third quarter or assess students at the Minimal level and make decisions based on the results.

Near the end of the fourth quarter, a staff meeting is scheduled to rate school culture and core classroom instructional practices. Results are compared to the baseline first-quarter ratings to determine if meaningful improvement was made. At the end of the fourth quarter, the cycle of grade/department, school, and district staff meetings is again repeated to review student results and determine if meaningful progress was made. Staff celebrates when culture, instructional practices, and student achievement all improve significantly. Schools operating in a trimester system would follow the schedule outlined above for the first, second, and fourth quarters.

Chapter Overviews

This chapter has thus far defined the School BUS and described its elements and process. The remainder of this chapter presents an overview of the book's remaining chapters, each of which describes a particular topic, presents the appropriate process and tools, and follows with examples of a small rural district in its first year (Basic School BUS Model) and a larger urban district in its second year (Advanced School BUS Model) of implementing the School BUS. Each chapter ends with a section of staff development activities for more practice or deeper exploration of certain key concepts. Some chapters contain activities that would be essential in some schools and districts.

Figure 1.6 illustrates the elements of a local system of accountability. Professional development and the culture of a learning organization—the two threads interweaving all other elements—are part of the illustration's background or foundation. The main topics in chapters 2 through 6 address the elements presented in Figure 1.6 and join a few minor elements to the School BUS's major components: standards-based assessment, culture of a learning organization, instructional practices, and student results.

FIGURE 1.6

Flowchart of a Local System of Accountability

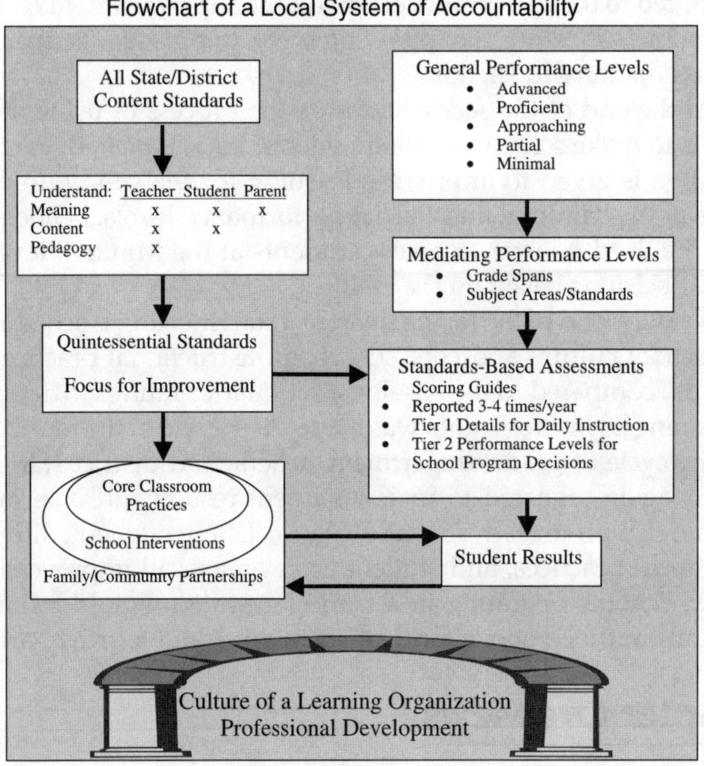

Chapter 2—Content Standards

Academic content standards define what students are expected to know and be able to do (concepts and skills). Teachers must understand the standards statements before they can help students and parents understand the expectations. Teachers might guide students to translate the statements into kid-friendly language. Teachers must also understand the standards' concepts and know *pedagogy*, a variety of instructional strategies, so that all students have the opportunity to learn the standards. Professional development plays an important role in helping teachers understand the meaning, content, and pedagogy involved in standards-based instruction.

Some states have a multitude of content standards (sometimes called benchmarks or indicators) and require districts to follow suit. Teaching all standards well so that all students can succeed is a daunting task. Many find it unrealistic to attempt to teach in depth standards in ways varied enough for diverse learners while offering interventions for students who need extra help. Some schools resort to pacing schedules that are unrealistic for many students. Other schools decide which standards will receive the most attention, giving standards of less urgency lower priority; these schools apply triage to systematically address an overwhelming condition.

When a district is required to adopt state standards or establish local standards closely aligned to state standards, it may be advantageous to cluster standards into levels of priority. Schmoker and Marzano (1999) and Reeves (1998a, 2000a) call for teachers to teach a few enduring standards well and deeply, leaving other standards to be taught in the time remaining. A district with a multitude of standards might set three levels of priority for teaching and learning: *quintessential* standards, *essential* standards, and the remaining *important* standards.

Quintessential content standards are the few standards that endure across grade levels and are the most important content standards (or benchmarks) in the local district. Quintessential standards are selected by delicately balancing what is most heavily tested (e.g., on state tests) with what is most highly valued, that is, skills all adults should possess throughout their lives. Because all students are expected to master the quintessential standards, the school must focus its comprehensive instructional program first and foremost on these few standards. If a district cannot concentrate on teaching, assessing, and using the results for all quintessential standards, it can set priorities and focus on one or a few quintessential standards for local accountability in a given year.

A district might not be ready to identify the full set of quintessential standards across all subject areas and grade levels. To begin the School BUS, a district or school might select one quintessential content standard as the focus for professional development and accountability during the first year. After gaining experience and success with one quintessential standard, the district and schools can expand their selection to include all quintessential standards as well as the essential and important standards. However, the School BUS's "focused" accountability process can be applied to just the quintessential standards.

Next, the district can establish a set of meaningful *performance levels* to evaluate how well students have mastered the (quintessential) content standards. A district might adopt state performance levels, if they exist, or modify state levels to fit local context while maintaining reasonable alignment with state levels. The intent is to create performance levels that are directly matched to types of instructional program decisions at the school and district levels. Figure 1.6 shows that the district begins by defining *General Performance Levels* (GPLs) that broadly address all grade levels and subject areas. *Mediating Performance Levels* (MPLs) narrow the descriptors to grade spans and/or particular subject areas or standards. MPLs form a bridge between GPLs and very specific scoring guides for assessments at each grade level for each standard or a cluster of standards.

Chapter 3—Standards-Based Assessment

The first wheel of the School BUS helps establish at least one *standards-based assessment* to periodically measure student progress toward learning the content standard targeted for improvement and accountability that year. If assessments already exist, they may only need adjustments to fit all students' needs, measure specific content standards, and yield performance levels. A district's standards-based assessments will likely be continuously enhanced in an ongoing cycle of adding, deleting, updating, and modifying parts or whole instruments. The assessment may need accommodations or alternatives to provide accurate results for all students. Multiple, diverse assessments may be needed. A person with assessment expertise can help establish a set of good assessments.

Standards-based assessments are established after setting GPLs and MPLs (see figure 1.6) and are used to measure a content standard and yield a score as a performance level. Performance level data is used in the school accountability system.

Chapter 4—School Culture

School culture is the second wheel of the School BUS. The culture of a learning organization fosters and sustains changes in the schoolwide instructional practices that benefit all students. Developing a school culture of a learning organization is the foundation for school improvement. Team learning that shares a vision of high expectations and uses consistent strategies to reach that vision unites all teachers in the school. They have a singular commitment to improve instructional practices and articulate common standards of learning across all grade levels.

After school staff rate their school culture based on descriptors of a learning organization contained in a scoring guide (rubric), they discuss ways to improve their culture. The ratings might be done at the beginning and end of each year, and results are used to plan improvements. The results are recorded on a summary form that may or may not stay at the school site. Figure 1.6 shows the culture of a learning organization as the foundation for continual improvement, particularly in classroom instructional practices.

Chapter 5—Improving Instruction

Instructional practices, especially core classroom strategies, are the third wheel of the School BUS. The *will* to change, exemplified by the school culture, supports the *means* to change, that is, professional development to learn better ways of teaching. By focusing on core strategies—those most important teaching practices that all teachers have agreed to implement—staff can support each other in team learning, and students experience a coherent classroom management and pedagogy throughout their years in the school system.

Figure 1.6 uses three concentric circles to illustrate the three components of a school's *comprehensive instructional program* in order of importance: core classroom practices, school interventions, and family/community partnerships. All three components are important, but teachers have the most control over classroom instruction, which has the greatest effect on student achievement. Teachers rate their own level of proficiency implementing whatever core pedagogy has been the focus of professional development throughout the year. Teachers compare year-end results to those from the beginning of the year and used to plan improvements. The shift upwards in the percent of teachers at proficiency indicates a supportive culture, effective professional development, and teacher commitment to excellence.

Chapter 6—Using Student Results

Using student achievement results at key times during the year to inform instructional program decisions about what is very effective and what is the next improvement is the fourth wheel of the School BUS. School staff examines the percentage of students at each performance level each quarter or trimester (whichever grading periods exist). Decisions center on improving classroom instruction, then extend out to include school interventions and family and community partnerships.

Figure 1.6 illustrates how student results from standards-based assessments are used to inform decisions about what is very effective and what could be improved in the instructional program. The looping arrows between the comprehensive instructional program and student results show that school practices affect student results, and student results are used to inform ways to change school practices.

Chapter 7—Accountability Reports

States, districts, and schools often set goals for improving student achievement results. Goals should be measurable but might not specify the exact test score gain expected. A school or district might set the goal, "Every student will be a proficient reader by the end of third grade." Each year they measure the percentage of students reaching or exceeding grade level standards, and they continue to work on improving instructional practices until the lofty goal of 100 percent proficiency is realized.

Goals can be inspirational to a school staff and can create a shared vision of school excellence. The will to change drives exploration and experimentation. Maximum goals about all students reaching proficiency can be energizing and beneficial, but only in a system that acknowledges meaningful progress toward such high goals.

The second part of chapter 7 describes elements of an annual comprehensive accountability report, which includes data from the School BUS report forms discussed in chapters 4 through 6. To present a complete picture of the school and its progress toward excellence, the report also includes information about school context and resources; attitudes of staff, parents and students; and the school's unique academic and nonacademic qualities.

Chapter 8—Deeper Analysis

In the School BUS process, data analysis can become more sophisticated as schools gain more capacity to analyze and use student results. A school staff can examine patterns across years and student subgroup differences in relation to closing achievement gaps. This chapter provides a systematic approach for digging deeper into achievement data using methods that do not require sophisticated computer software capability, however, standard spreadsheet or database applications can facilitate the process. Longitudinal analysis—following the achievement level of the same group of students across years—can be very informative but is not always possible due to the lack of a student database or a group's rapid shrinking from high mobility. This chapter presents a method of quasi-cohort analysis, using the annual results that many states produce for schools.

Chapter 9—Accountability of a Higher Authority

The district's role is to guide and support school accountability and improvement while it engages in its own accountability process. This chapter includes scoring guides and forms about culture and practices similar to those used by schools.

All stakeholders should be included in a state's accountability system to ensure that schools, districts, and the state work together to build and sustain change. All stakeholders must commit to stay the course for the time it takes to reach proficiency, not switch to a different program or initiative each year or election term. Some districts have a strategic plan for involving parents, the community, and local universities and businesses in a concerted initiative to improve teacher and student learning (e.g., Navarro and Natalicio, 1999).

What the Professional Literature Says. Well-intentioned state accountability programs meant to encourage school improvement and produce better-educated youth may have no impact or may instead have serious negative consequences when a school's staff feels too much pressure to raise state test scores and receives too little support or direction for change.

McNeil (2000) cited examples from Texas that could apply to any state where sanctions are swift and serious. Standards-based accountability will fail if schools react to external systems by spending an exorbitant amount of instructional time on test-prep activities and narrowing the curriculum to those areas measured by the state test. McNeil suggested asking whether the school's curriculum and teaching methods are the same that a person would want for his or her own children.

Rallis and McMullen (2000) wrote that no research base supports the claim that popular external accountability policies achieve the goal of real school improvement. They advocate instead an approach that balances external (state) and internal (school) accountability systems by emphasizing inquiry about improvement. A cycle of inquiry about what works and what needs to be improved bridges external and internal accountability. Schools need the will to change, the capacity to change, and the support of parents, community members, businesses, and policymakers.

Fullan (2000) used the inside-outside metaphor to describe the multiple methods of educational reform. In this model, three stories must work as one for sustained school improvement. The inside story about reculturing—developing a professional learning community within a school—helps teachers make improvements by focusing on assessment and pedagogy. In the inside-out story, a school insulating itself from fragmented external forces selectively chooses and applies what is helpful from the outside to improve the inside. The outside-in story, which tells how external agencies can organize and assist large-scale school reform, focuses on decentralization, building local capacity, using rigorous external accountability to ensure that high standards are implemented in schools, and stimulating innovation to continually improve teaching and learning.

Tacheny (1999) stated that "accountability is as much a culture as a system." Through the words and actions of key leaders, accountability becomes a value with clear, measurable goals. Accountability works when a passionate team uses data as a means to achieve common goals. Accountability wrongly applied lays blame or tries to force change from the bully pulpit. When true accountability exists, everyone within the organization feels responsibility for—and defines contributions toward—measurable goals.

In a school where staff does not want to change, it is futile to discuss changing the instructional program as a reaction to external sanctions. The staff will likely reject each option. Accountability is not a cultural norm in this school. Accountability is about taking charge of the change process and publicly showcasing the learning and progress being made within the school's classrooms. School change is about, as Fullan (2000) puts it, "reculturing."

Sirotnik and Kimball (1999) went a step further, outlining eleven standards for standards-based accountability systems. Their system must include multiple indicators, not just test scores, to evaluate each school within its own context as well as in comparison to other schools. To deliver a curriculum based on essential, high-quality content standards, the system must monitor equitable learning opportunities and allow for flexibility in pace, learning style, and teachers' creativity.

Joyce, Wolf, and Calhoun (1993) highlighted embedded, ongoing accountability as one of five elements of a truly improving school. Other elements involve capitalizing on research about best practices to change curriculum, instruction, and supportive technology. In this model, everyone participates in the change process, which is fueled by effective staff development and general support systems. Self-renewing schools and districts are learning communities within three spheres of an organization—the teacher, the school, and the district. Navarro and Natalicio (1999) expanded the schema to include parents, community, business, and universities, each of whom have a role in and responsibility for a system of accountability to learn together how best to improve student learning.

Schmoker (1999) targeted three key elements for continuous school improvement: teamwork, measurable long-range and short-term goals, and frequent analysis and use of performance data. Short-term goals that produce rapid results fuel enthusiasm and commitment to continue striving toward the long-range goals.

Teamwork is essential and enhances individuals' learning. Reeves (2000a) outlined the responsibilities of all individuals at all levels (i.e. classroom, school, district, board of education, and state) working as a team to design and implement a system of accountability focused on improving teaching and learning.

Glickman (1990) believed "the movement to improve schools through empowerment may be the last chance in many of our lifetimes to make schools institutions that are worthy of public confidence and professional respect" (p.69). The indicator of a truly effective school should not be one-year gains, but patterns of improved learning across years.

Summary

Why not just wait for the state to tell the schools what to do, how much to improve, and whether student results improve? Why should a school or district take the initiative to develop its own system of accountability within a state accountability system? Can a local accountability system be the way to foster school improvement and achieve, at least, the results expected by the state accountability system?

A characteristic of truly improving schools and districts is the frequent analysis and use of student achievement results to inform school and district decisions. Feedback about results for the last unit of study must be readily available before teachers move on to the next topic. Feedback must be given frequently throughout the year so that teachers can refine practice while there is still time to improve learning for this year's students. When a school team uses student results to inform decisions about how to continually improve instructional practices, the team is working as a learning organization. When a school team continually focuses on the area of greatest need, it will likely achieve the improvement expected by its state.

Reasonable alignment between the local and state assessment and accountability systems provides coherence. If a state uses only multiple-choice tests, a school or district need not limit itself to this one type of assessment. A state's multiple-choice test is not a license to avoid teaching highly valued content standards not measured by the test. Schools can continue to use research reports, projects, presentations, and portfolios to assess students. When learning excites students and they can assess their own progress toward excellence in meaningful ways, they will tend to perform well on state tests, perhaps with minimal time spent on test prep.

Accountability is the process of collaboratively learning from past experiences and results to continually improve practices, it is seamlessly intertwined with professional development. Effective accountability involves teams of teachers frequently using results to reflect on classroom practices, district and state support for learning, and flexibility for innovation. Schools and districts that intend to improve must set a target—one, or a very few, quintessential content standards—and build instruction, assessment, and accountability around that target for as long as it takes to reach mastery and sustain gains.

The School BUS calls for a simple, bottom-up approach to school improvement that any school and district can use to begin, expand, and sustain change. A system of ongoing accountability at the school level can drive true and lasting improvement. Using standards-based assessment data is a key element. Teachers and their principal, the professionals who work directly with the students, should be empowered to make the decisions about how best to help all students succeed. An accountability system should respect these professionals and not just hold them accountable, it should also support them to make good decisions and show the impact of their actions. The School BUS approach calls for balance in the underlying system.

- Balance core practices used by all teachers with ample flexibility for addressing individual students' needs and interests
- Balance core decisions at one level of the management system with guidance and decisions at a higher level
- Find convergence between what is most important on the state test with what are the most valued concepts and skills in the local community
- Make immediate, meaningful step-by-step improvements in teacher and student

Teachers who strive for personal mastery describe themselves as learners, as do doctors and lawyers, continually upgrading skills and consulting each other on tough cases. They realize that the complete education of a child takes the combined effort of all teachers, families, and the community. They see school improvement and personal mastery as a never-ending process. They seek rather than avoid assessment and consider results as an opportunity to acknowledge successes; they learn from mistakes and keep on a steady course toward the ultimate goal of all students and all teachers becoming successful learners. As Checkley (2000, p. 5–6) said, "There is no failure, only feedback."

2 Content and Performance Standards

While there may be hundreds of standards, benchmarks, and learning objectives, only a handful need to be included in comprehensive accountability systems

—*Douglas Reeves*

Overview

Content standards define "what all students should know and be able to do." Federal IASA/Title I (Hansche, 1999) requires that a state's system of content standards, assessments, and performance standards challenge all students, including those with physical disabilities or limited English proficiency. However, many questions remain: How high should content standards be? Who should be expected to reach them? Should all students be expected to master standards at a very high or "world class" level? Should a lower level of functional literacy be set, as many states have done (Marzano and Kendall, 1996), or should there be some level in-between?

Once content standards are established, one must ask, "How well are students expected to perform to show acceptable understanding of the standards?" The answer requires developing *performance levels*: One level is designated as the *performance standard* that is, the expected level of understanding of the content standards. This chapter suggests that districts create one set of *General Performance Levels* (GPLs), which apply broadly across grade levels and subject areas, and then develop more specific *Mediating Performance*

Levels (MPLs) for a grade span, subject area, or quintessential content standard. *General Performance Levels* provide common terminology for all staff, students, and parents. *Mediating Performance Levels* help bridge the rigor of the general level descriptors to the rigor of the highly specific level descriptors of the scoring guides (rubrics) for each grade and content standard.

Academic content standards used for school accountability should be few and should be general to many or all grade levels. If not, the district should select the highest priority, or *quintessential* standards. In the School BUS model, schools should select only one or a few content standards for school accountability in any one year. To show students' understanding of content standards the School BUS model suggests using standards much higher than minimal competence, but lower than "world class." Examples throughout this book use five performance levels, but the School BUS allows for local school districts to use whatever number of performance levels they choose.

The *Basic School BUS Model* and *Advanced School BUS Model* use as examples the stories of two fictitious school districts. In the Basic model, a small rural district begins its first year of implementing the School BUS by selecting one quintessential content standard and adopting district performance levels. In the Advanced model, a mid-sized urban district begins its second year of the School BUS by establishing a complete set of quintessential standards and adding *Mediating Performance Levels* to existing levels for reading.

Additional Staff Development Activities encourage staff dialogue about beliefs and attitudes by asking the questions: Is there an expectation that all students can learn the quintessential standards? Why are content and performance standards important to teaching and learning? How many performance levels are appropriate for a local district and what should Mediating Performance Levels look like?

Academic Content Standards

How Many and by What Name

Academic content standards are the statements created by the state or school district to define what students should know and be able to do in academic subject areas. The School BUS can accommodate differences in local labels and types of statements, but school accountability should focus on quintessential standards or a few general standards that cross a grade span.

Across the United States, disagreements exist about what students should know and be able to do; there are no statements specific or numerous enough to guide teachers at each grade level. Should statements target high school graduation, grade spans, certain key grades, or every grade level? Some states or school districts have created a few broad statements that span many or all grades. Some rely on other guidebooks (e.g., frameworks and curriculum guides) to indicate key content within grade levels. Other states and school districts have created over a hundred statements that are very specific to each grade just for language arts. Should the statements provide general guidance to teachers or define exact concepts and skills to be taught at each grade level?

Some states have content standards that address only academic subject areas, while others include standards about general learning, reasoning, or life skills. Marzano and Kendall (1996) separated content standards into two categories: declarative (knowledge) and process (skills). Figure 2.1 presents a sampling of Marzano and Kendall's terminology for content standards and classifications. Level 1, *holistic content standards*, covers most or all grades from K–12. These standards are "umbrella" statements, general in nature and few in number.

FIGURE 2.1

Sample Taxonomy & Learning

Academic Content Standards (Knowledge and Skills)		
Level 1: K-12 Holistic	**Level 2: Grade Spans**	**Level 3: Grade Level/Course**
• Content Standards (might be organized upward by frameworks, strands, goals, and/or expanded downward into objectives)	• Benchmarks • Standards (Performance Standards for skills) • Expectations • Learning Outcomes • Curriculum Guides	• Benchmarks • Standards • Curriculum Requirements • Goals and Objectives • Frameworks • Basic Understandings organize Essential Knowledge & Skills

Adapted from Marzano and Kendall (1996)

Level 2, *grade span standards*, may cover all grades in the span or may point to the highest grade in the span as "culminating expectations." In other words, either all grades are taught the standards, or lower grade levels provide instruction that prepares students for mastering the standards at the highest grade in the span. In Level 3, *grade level standards* are specific to each grade or to certain "benchmark" grades (e.g., third, eighth, and tenth grades).

There is also no nationwide agreement on labels for statements or on headings for clusters of statements. Reeves (2000b) surveyed states and found that grade level expectations "of what students know and can do" are called "benchmarks" in Colorado, "performance standards" in Alaska, "curriculum requirements" in Georgia, and simply "[learning] standards" in New York. Visitors to a state or school district must seek clarification of the local labels; some local educators are unaware that everyone does not use the same terms.

To present a standard vocabulary and taxonomy, Reeves (1998a) used a pyramid with three layers. The top layer, *academic content standards,* represents the few broadly stated standards that cover all (or almost all) grade levels. The second layer, *benchmarks,* concepts and skills at certain grade levels and are greater in number and more specific in scope than academic content standards. (e.g., "By Grade 4, students will . . .") Clusters of benchmarks are organized within academic content standards. At the bottom layer of the pyramid are *scoring guides* (rubrics,) which are numerous, specific in scope, and describe proficient performance (and other performance levels) for a particular assessment.

In this book, the term *academic content standards* refers to statements about what students should know and be able to do in academic subject areas. The School BUS is flexible enough to satisfy local desires that standards be broad and few (Reeves' [1998a] and Marzano and Kendall's [1996] "standards") or narrow and many (Reeves' and Marzano and Kendall's "benchmarks"). We suggest that schools and districts target the more global statements of standards for schoolwide accountability and instructional program decisions for groups of students.

A school staff may decide to use the School BUS to evaluate how well they are helping students improve reading comprehension. Individual teachers or grade teams will want to focus instruction on subparts such as prediction, retelling, and drawing inferences and conclusions (perhaps locally called benchmarks). Teachers assess students on the subparts to make instructional decisions about which students in their classrooms need more help on retelling and which students need more help on drawing inferences. When teachers periodically come together as a school team to evaluate how well the school's reading program is working (their common core instructional strategies), they use the School BUS to make general decisions about the global target of reading comprehension. In the School BUS approach, the school team "sees the forest without getting lost among the trees."

We agree with Reeves that it is better to focus teachers on the most important facts and skills across most or all grades than to specify everything to be taught at each grade level. Benchmarks might be subsumed under the standards or contained in another teacher resource. Educators or politicians who champion many highly specific standards or benchmarks will say that their schema leaves little room for confusion about what should be taught. Opponents say that such schema limits flexibility in pacing or mastery attainment and leaves little room for teachers and students to explore their own intellectual interests. For example, one intermediate grade teacher has a passion for teaching plate tectonics as a science unit but first makes sure that students learn the grade-level standards.

When one of this book's authors, Carr, conducts workshops on standards and the School BUS, he is often asked how many standards a district or grade level should have. Before "how many" can be discussed, "what standards are we talking about" must be clarified. Is the local educator talking about Reeves' "standards" or "benchmarks?" Reeves (2000a) gives as an example seven seventh-grade standards covering language arts, mathematics, science, and social science. Reeves' examples of standards are global enough to pertain to many grade levels. Carr suggests using between five and ten standards. About five standards might be right for some districts, especially those just beginning to focus staff development and student assessment on common core standards, while up to ten standards might be appropriate for other districts with more experience and capacity, for teaching and assessing standards. The next section addresses the question "how many," taking a deeper and somewhat different perspective.

Quintessential Content Standards

Identify the few quintessential academic content standards in the school district for core classroom instruction, ongoing staff development, and student assessment at critical periods in the year. In the first year using the School BUS, focus on one quintessential standard schoolwide.

Beginning with one or a few standards ensures that all teachers teach certain core standards well. Many teachers are quick to agree that being expected to teach a hundred or so content standards and teach them well to all students within the normal day and working year is an overwhelming expectation. These teachers breathe a sigh of relief when they can begin with one or a very few content standards, concentrate on learning to teach them using a variety of instructional strategies so that most, if not all, students reach proficiency, and then add additional standards as they build capacity.

In the first year using the School BUS, a school or district might select just one academic content standard as the focus of learning and accountability. This one standard will be the focus of staff development, student assessment, and results analysis throughout the year to see if teacher learning is having a greater impact on student learning.

Because all standards are important even when there are a hundred or more, some districts with many standards set two or three priority levels in order to resolve the "capacity to teach well" issue. In the School BUS, *quintessential content standards* are those few standards that all students are expected to master throughout their years in the school system and hold important throughout their lives. *Quintessential standards* are the target of multiple, varied instructional opportunities to reach mastery. Assessment results are used at critical times during the school year to evaluate the program and make improvements. All academic content standards are taught, but only those few standards that are the major target for school improvement in a given year are included in the accountability process.

Teachers learn a variety of strategies to reach all students, and the school focuses intervention strategies for students who need extra support on these *quintessential standards*. Teachers also apply these classroom strategies to the second level of priority, called the *essential content standards*, and ensure adequate instructional coverage in the classroom. The school offers interventions to support classroom instruction for the *essential standards* as resources permit. The third level of priority—the *important content standards*—refers to the remaining standards that are taught within the remaining time. Effective teaching of the more important standards is preferred to "exposure" to many standards.

One school district may concentrate on their few general standards and the highly specific benchmarks within each standard. Another school district may devote efforts to their quintessential, essential, and important standards. In either case, the School BUS is focused on the few general, or quintessential, standards. This tactic prevents differences in terminology among states or local districts. The content standards should convey clarity and sufficient description for teachers to forge common, coherent expectations of what students should know and be able to do.

Marzano and Kendall (1996) caution against mixing "curriculum standards" (e.g., activities, projects, techniques) with "content standards." Teachers should be allowed the freedom to select the "means to the ends" (p.22). Content standards should not become so prescriptive that they constrain creative instruction or sufficient opportunity for deep learning and reteaching. There are good reasons for limiting the scope and number of quintessential standards.

> It is time to admit that at the ground level, where teachers teach and students learn, there is not coherence, but chaos. The chief problem is that there is simply too much to teach . . . This state of chaos was the rationale for the standards movement—and the most visible and influential manifestations are the state and professional standards documents. Yet these documents themselves have contributed to the very problems they were intended to solve. (Schmoker & Marzano, 1999)

As a practical example, American mathematics textbooks attempt to cover 175 percent more topics than do German textbooks and 350 percent more topics than do Japanese textbooks. American science textbooks attempt to cover 930 percent more topics than do German textbooks and 433 percent more topics than do Japanese textbooks. Yet both German and Japanese students outperform American students in mathematics and science on the international TIMMS assessment (Schmidt, McKnight, & Raizen, 1996). Critics may take exception with TIMMS and the student populations tested in different countries, but the fact that many American schools attempt to lightly teach many topics stirs little, if any, debate.

Some states have so many standards that it would take a 10-hour day to cover them, and even that does not allow for teaching the standards well (Wolk, 1998). Some districts have thick curriculum guides that are gathering dust because no one has the time or fortitude to wade through them. Teachers are unaware of the guides, do not understand the content standards, or find the guide's size and detail overwhelming. Standards were intended to help teachers in schools, districts, and states identify the *most important* concepts and skills that all students should learn and eventually master. However, when standard guides contain a plethora of detailed specifications about every imaginable fact and skill that "ought to be taught in a grade level," they can become a destructive force or have no impact at all.

Schmoker & Marzano (1999) state, "Clearly, U.S. schools would benefit from decreasing the amount of content they try to cover.

And teacher morale and self-efficacy improve when we confidently lay out a more manageable number of essential topics to be taught and assessed in greater depth." When a district cannot or will not limit the number of standards or benchmarks, it can at least prioritize them and identify those that can be taught well to assure student mastery within a reasonable amount of time.

In his book *Accountability in Action*, Reeves (2000a) narrows the scope from every conceivable concept and skill that might be taught and tested to a small set of state standards and actual classroom curriculum. Out of all that might be taught at fifth or sixth grade level, what are the most important skills that students must possess for secondary school? What do secondary school teachers say are "absolute musts," the skills that all students should have sufficiently mastered in order to enter secondary school and be able to tackle that curriculum? Reeves proposes seven requirements for sixth grade mathematics:

1. Perform number operations, with and without calculators
2. Draw in two-dimensional scale
3. Create and draw inferences from tables, charts, and graphs
4. Measure in different units (English and metric)
5. Given a story problem, draw a picture to illustrate it, and solve it accurately
6. Perform fraction and decimal operations
7. Apply the properties of a triangle and rectangle

Reeves (2000b) calls for "power standards," the enduring standards that are most important for future success and that provide focus and clarity to teachers. He gives an example of nine power standards, complete with descriptive statements for middle school students to enter high school "with confidence and success":

- three standards that cover narrative, analytical, and persuasive writing in response to reading material (language arts and social studies)
- four standards covering some of the skills mentioned above for sixth grade along with designing an experiment with hypothesis-testing and a report of findings (mathematics and science)
- a standard covering teamwork, organization and service
- a standard covering performance and self-confidence in other courses of study that require personal performances (e.g., music, speech, athletics)

Ten quintessential standards are offered as an example of their global nature. The labels of the quintessential standards are presented below. Descriptors might be added to provide greater understanding. For example, reading comprehension comprises main ideas, details, summarization, and sequence of events in literature and content areas. Key specific standards linked to the quintessential standard might be highlighted for each grade level. The ten quintessential standards are:

- reading comprehension
- interpretation and critical analysis
- written and oral focus, organization, and communication
- teamwork skills
- number sense
- algebra
- geometry and measurement
- data analysis and probability
- investigation and experimentation skills
- patterns and interactions

The first four are multidisciplinary. The fourth quintessential standard, Teamwork Skills, may not be found in state standards, but is a skill highly valued by corporations. The second four are germane to mathematics, but not all may be deemed quintessential at each grade level. The last two could be multidisciplinary or just pertain to science. Each quintessential standard could be matched to a state's specific standards in each discipline to assist teachers in making connections and pinpointing specific concepts and skills that are most important at each grade level.

Summarizing quintessential content standards, a district is encouraged to identify quintessential standards, secondary or essential standards, and perhaps tertiary or important standards. In the first year using the School BUS, a school should select one quintessential standard for improving how students learn and then look at student results on that standard during the year to determine if staff efforts have been successful. Each school in the district selects the quintessential standard most in need of improvement in that school. Coordination and mutual support by the district office is enhanced when the standard for improvement is common to all schools in the district.

In successive years, schools might include more quintessential standards until all are taught well, assessed well, and included in the accountability process. "Do not add more topics than can be taught and assessed reasonably and effectively," caution Schmoker and Marzano (1999). In the School BUS approach, teachers determine when they are ready and willing to add more—the process becomes more comprehensive and sophisticated from the bottom up, with guidance and support from the top down. Leadership builds the capacity to do more while it protects staff from burnout caused by taking on too much. Leadership has a long-range plan, ready to give the next step when teachers are ready to take it.

Standards as Year-end Targets

School staff use the School BUS at critical periods during the year to compare student progress toward reaching the proficiency level set by year-end grade level standards. Watching student results progress each reporting period toward the year-end target creates joy among staff, teachers, and administrators.

Grade level content standards usually describe what a student is expected to master by the end of the school year—no state sets incremental standards for each quarter of the school year. In the School BUS, the academic content standards are expectations of what students will learn by the end of the school year. Some standards endure throughout the year, such as reading comprehension. Some standards are "units of study" and are taught for a discrete time period (e.g., semester or quarter)—an example might be measurement in mathematics. Content standards are not defined for each grading period (e.g., semester, trimester, or quarter) in the School BUS approach. This book emphasizes year-end expectations because this breaks from the popular, traditional way of scoring student work in relation to grading periods during the year.

One set of content standards per grade level should be enough for any school district or teacher to create, understand, and teach to mastery. If a district wants standards for every grading period, then it must develop two to four times as many standards as year-end only standards—quite a quantity to generate, communicate, and truly teach and assess. Some districts attempt to split continuous yearlong standards such as reading comprehension into "quarter benchmarks or standards" for traditional report card grading. However, according to expert learning theorists and many experienced teachers, learning is rarely a linear event.

Learning theorists offer the S-curve, a frequent phenomenon in which the learner starts slowly, accelerates learning, and gradually tapers off at some ceiling in learning. Kindergarten teachers remark that young children's brain development leads to individual bursts, which teachers use to extend the student's learning vertically, and plateau periods, which the teacher can use to expand the student's learning horizontally. In everyone's life there are those "aha" moments when we finally "get it" after a long period of consternation. In short, personal experience seems to provide more instances when learning is nonlinear, occurring in uneven, incremental steps or chunks.

Some districts have no quarterly standards at all, but act as if they do. In these districts, there are no standards for each period during the year, but teachers continue to use the traditional practice of formulating grades idiosyncratically. Teachers may use personal judgments to decide whether students are making "adequate progress" toward year-end standards. Parents want to see As and Bs every reporting period, and because the district feels pressure to maintain that tradition, it merely switches As and Bs for 4s and 3s. Many schools are reluctant to change from the illusion of "period-based standards" and are slow to acknowledge that students start the school without full understanding of grade level standards and progress in a nonlinear fashion toward proficiency. Designing a reporting system that reflects reality means comparing where students are each period in relation to year-end standards.

Issues in developing standards-based grading systems (e.g., report cards) can be the single topic of a book (e.g., Trunbull and Farr, 2000; Marzano, 2000). In a truly standards-based system, all teachers understand the standards students are expected to learn and know how well students are expected to learn them. In a truly standards-based school district, a student will receive the same transparent score or grade regardless of which teacher assesses her.

The following chapters explain how the School BUS can be used to make instructional program decisions based on the results of one assessment of one standard a few times a year. The School BUS is not about summarizing a variety of assessment scores into a report card grade for an individual student. However, a discussion of setting content and performance standards for using the School BUS invariably leads teachers to see the connection, or often the disconnection, to their grading practices. It is suggested that a district concentrate on developing and using one good standards-based assessment within the School BUS model before attempting to reach agreement among all teachers about how to combine numerous assessments into composite scores for student grading systems. The grading system can become an issue "further down the road." To begin, schools must focus on the first steps towards a truly standards-based system.

Standards for Special Education and English Learners

All students should be expected to learn the content standards they are taught. All students should be taught grade level-appropriate standards with two exceptions—special education students and English language learners. Special education students are expected to master the content standards identified on their Individual Education Plans (IEPs). For the severely handicapped special education student who is not on a high school graduation track, this means mastering certain life management skills as the content standards. For the less severely handicapped special education students who receive instruction on academic standards, this means mastering the content standards appropriate for their grade level curriculum specified in the IEP.

Students who are beginning to learn English as a second language are (or should be) receiving intensive instruction in English language development. These students should be progressing through a set of defined developmental standards or levels of English acquisition until they reach sufficient proficiency to successfully learn the "regular" grade level language arts content standards.

Performance Levels and The Standard

Performance levels indicate the quality of student performance or degree to which the student has mastered the content standard. The performance standard is the expected level of mastery and often is labeled "Proficient" or "Meets Standard."

While academic content standards define "what students should know and be able to do," a performance standard defines "how good is good enough." But what does that really mean? Unfortunately, there is no agreement about what "performance standard" really means in education (Hansche, 1998; Marzano & Kendall, 1996). A standards-based assessment measures one or a cluster of standards and yields a performance level that is absolute or criterion-referenced. A student is compared to the levels, rather than compared to other students, as in norm-referenced standards.

The National Assessment of Educational Progress (NAEP) converts test scores into the performance levels of Advanced, Proficient, and Basic. Many states convert state test scores into three to six performance levels. Direct writing and other performance assessments use rubrics, or scoring guides, to rate student work according to performance levels. Some call all levels "performance standards," while others designate the level labeled "Proficient" as the "performance standard." There is no nationwide uniformity concerning the number of levels, labels, or terminology for what is a performance standard.

A U.S. Department of Education publication broadly defines a *performance standard* as "a system that includes performance levels, descriptions of student performance, examples of student work, and cut scores on assessments" (Hansche, 1998. p.4). A cut score is the lowest number correct score on a particular assessment; it identifies the cut, or boundary, for each performance level. Reeves (1998a) used the term *performance level* and identified the performance level that "meets or exceeds the academic content standard" as the *performance standard* (1998a, 2000a, 2000b). Similarly, Marzano and Kendall (1996) defined a *performance standard* as the one performance level that students are expected to reach to show mastery of a content standard.

> This criterion, or acceptable, level of performance is the performance standard. For example, a district or school might decide that the proficient level . . . is the performance standard or it might decide that the basic level is the performance standard. A performance standard, then, can be operationally defined as an acceptable level of performance embedded within a description of various levels (a rubric). (p. 66)

The School BUS also uses *performance standard* to mean the level of expected proficiency within a set of possible *performance levels* Content standards and performance levels are determined at the national, state, and school district levels, not by individual schools within a school district. A school with mostly economically poor students does not set a relatively low performance level, and a school with mostly economically affluent students does not set a relatively high performance level within the same district (or anywhere). The performance standard is not set to the district's current "average student" or to some politically motivated level, but to a high expectation for any and all students, a level that any parent or teacher would be proud to see students reach. It becomes the school's responsibility to find ways to help all students reach the performance standard. It may be that no student now performs at the performance standard, and it may be that in the future all students will be able to meet or exceed the performance standard.

Setting performance levels in a district should not be considered a perfunctory task. In the School BUS, the levels are set carefully and meaningfully because instructional program decisions are based directly on student achievement results at each performance level. In later chapters, the reader will be shown two simple ways to report and use student data: (a) the percentage of students meeting and exceeding the performance standard, and (b) the percentage of students at each performance level.

General Performance Levels

General Performance Levels (GPLs) are general descriptors with labels of levels of student performance that apply broadly to most or all grade levels and subject areas.

Districts that are "standards-based" tend to develop GPLs to create a unified vision about student performance. The GPLs are often communicated in brochures for parents and in standards-based report cards. GPLs are general descriptors of student performance that apply to most or all grade levels and academic subject areas. GPLs have labels (e.g., Advanced, Proficient, Approaching, Partial, Minimal) and descriptors. The descriptors use wording that is either qualitative (e.g., superior, solid, partial, or minimal understanding of standards) or quantitative (e.g., mastery of all, most, some, or few concepts/skills).

The National Assessment of Educational Progress (NAEP) has three general performance levels, called *achievement levels*, but also reports on students below *Basic* (in effect, there are four performance levels). The NAEP uses this set of GPLs to align scoring guides with the same set of labels and to include specific descriptors for each assessment of reading, writing, and mathematics at fourth, eighth, and tenth grades. Figure 2.2 presents the NAEP's general performance levels, and Figure 2.3 shows an excerpt from the Proficient level of the scoring guide for NAEP Grade 4 Reading.

FIGURE 2.2

NAEP Achievement Levels

Labels	Descriptors
Advanced	Superior performance
Proficient	Solid academic performance for each grade assessed. Students reaching this level have demonstrated competency over challenging subject matter, including subject-matter knowledge, application of such knowledge to real world situations, and analytical skills appropriate to the subject matter.
Basic	Partial mastery of prerequisite knowledge and skills that are fundamental for proficient work at each grade

States differ in the number of performance levels and labels they apply to their state tests of student achievement, as shown in Figure 2.4. Figure 2.4's sampling of states shows Virginia with three performance levels (the low), both Vermont and Florida with five levels (the high), and the remaining states with the most popular number of performance levels, four.

FIGURE 2.3

Part of NAEP Scoring Guide for Grade 4 Reading

Proficient	Fourth-grade students performing at the proficient level should be able to demonstrate an overall understanding of the text, providing inferential as well as literal information. When reading text appropriate to 4th grade, they should be able to extend the ideas in the text by making inferences, drawing conclusions, and making connections to their own experiences. The connections between the text and what the student infers should be clear.

FIGURE 2.4

Sample of State Performance Levels

State	#	Labels
Virginia	3	Advanced, Proficient, Does Not Meet the Standards
California	4	Advanced, Proficient, Basic, Below Basic
Colorado	4	Advanced, Proficient, Partially Proficient, Unsatisfactory
Kentucky	4	Distinguished, Proficient, Apprentice, Novice
Massachusetts	4	Advanced, Proficient, Needs Improvement, Failing
Florida	5	5, 4, 3, 2, 1
Vermont	5	Achieving Standard with Honors, Achieving Standard, Nearly Achieving Standard, Below Standard, Little Evidence

Figures 2.5 and 2.6 present models of four and five GPLs, respectively. Carr (1999) adapted these models from the four performance levels used in the San Juan Unified School District

(California). Some participants in School BUS workshops have adopted or slightly modified the five-level model for use in their school districts.

GPLs might be created by a district assessment panel that has broad grade-level and subject-area representation. The district panel should develop one set of GPLs that apply to as many grade levels and subject areas as possible. The scoring guides (rubrics) for all assessments in all subject areas at all grade levels will be aligned with these GPLs. If a district bypasses setting GPLs and moves directly to developing assessment scoring guides, the scoring guides may not align across grade levels and subject areas. In other words, if there are no unifying GPLs, the rigor of performance levels on one scoring guide may not match the rigor on another scoring guide.

FIGURE 2.5

Example of Four General Performance Levels

Labels	Descriptors
Advanced	These students demonstrate superior performance, above the breadth and depth of the key concepts and skills identified as the major grade level expectancies.
Proficient	This level represents solid academic performance. Students reaching this level have demonstrated competency of the key concepts and skills appropriate to the content standard, including application of such knowledge and skills to real-world situations.
Basic	These students demonstrate competency of some but not all, or almost all, of the key concepts and skills.
Below	These students demonstrate competency of few, or none, of the key concepts and skills. These students are working on key concepts and skills that are one or more years below grade level.

FIGURE 2.6

Example of Five General Performance Levels

Labels	Descriptors
Advanced	These students demonstrate superior performance, above the breadth and depth of the key concepts and skills appropriate to the content standard.
Proficient	This level represents solid academic performance. Students reaching this level have demonstrated competency, or complete understanding, of the key concepts and skills appropriate to the content standard, including application to real-world situations.
Approaching	These students demonstrate competency of most of the key concepts and skills but lack complete understanding of a few important concepts and/or skills.
Partial	These students demonstrate competency of some, but not most, of the key concepts and skills.
Minimal	These students demonstrate competency of few, or none, of the key concepts and skills. These students are working on key concepts and skills that are one or more years below grade level.

The *descriptors* are indicators or criteria of acceptable and unacceptable performance at each level, but we suggest creating descriptors about what a student knows and can do rather than what he does not know and cannot do. The criteria should target mid-level performance for a performance level. In other words, describe what the typical or "middle range" student knows and can do rather than what the student who meets the bare minimum of the level knows and can do.

Set Meaningful Performance Levels

Student results at the performance levels indicate the effectiveness of the school's comprehensive instructional program. Results at the Advanced and Proficient levels inform decisions about the effectiveness of the school's comprehensive instructional program. Results at the lower performance levels (e.g., Approaching, Partial, and Minimal) inform decisions about improving classroom instruction and school interventions (as well as family and community partnerships).

Setting the number of performance levels should be taken seriously, and should not be considered a perfunctory task. In the School BUS approach, instructional program decisions are made for fairly homogenous groups of students at each performance level. A school district should carefully craft their GPLs for "results-driven decision-making" (a term popularized by Schmoker, 1999). The School BUS can accommodate any number of performance levels, but we suggest using five levels similar to those of Vermont (see Figure 2.4) and the district model in Figure 2.6. Five levels seem to correspond well with fairly homogenous groups of students and with making instructional program decisions for each group. This relationship between performance levels and program decisions will be clarified below, beginning with alignment between district and state performance levels.

A district would be prudent to align local GPLs to their state's performance levels. Alignment between local and state performance levels makes it easier to compare local and state test results. While the school district might choose to have more levels than the state, the level of rigor at certain levels should be aligned. When a district desires more levels, it might split a state level into two local levels.

Figure 2.5 shows how a California school district has aligned its four-level model with California's four performance levels. Figure 2.6 shows an example of a California school district that chose to split the state's Basic level into two levels, Approaching and Partial.

The district panel starts by defining the Proficient level. Panel members discuss what they think a proficient student should know and be able to do in broad terms that can apply to many or all grade levels and subject areas. Panel members might use specific grade or subject area examples to clarify for others the level of rigor they envision. As stated earlier, this proficient student is a hypothetical student—currently there may be many students or no students in the district who meet the criteria. The Proficient level is set at a level of rigor high enough for a student to become a productive, contributing, knowledgeable citizen in America— it is not set at minimal competence nor at a level unreasonably high. Panel members reach agreement on a common vision of the Proficient student and descriptors that broadly apply to most or all grades and subjects.

Next, the district panel develops descriptors for the Advanced level. A district may want to create two or more levels above Proficient (we suggest creating only one level when beginning the School BUS). Then the panel decides how many levels below Proficient are appropriate and develop descriptors for those levels. Staff are trained to understand the purpose and use of the district's GPLs. The GPLs and the (quintessential) content standards are communicated to parents in brochures and to students in "kid-friendly" language on all classroom walls.

The following examples show what a school district's performance level might look like and the kind of instructional program questions and decisions that might be linked to each level. That linked relationship is illustrated in Figure 2.7. The term *comprehensive instructional program* is used below and will be discussed in more detail in chapter 5. The term is defined here as having three simple parts:

- core classroom instructional strategies that are schoolwide
- school interventions to support good first classroom instruction for students who need extra support
- family and community partnerships to support school staff

The Advanced Level. The student at the Advanced level shows solid understanding of content standards above grade level or shows advanced understanding of grade level standards with much greater depth and complexity than is expected for this grade level.

FIGURE 2.7

Performance Levels Linked to Program Decisions

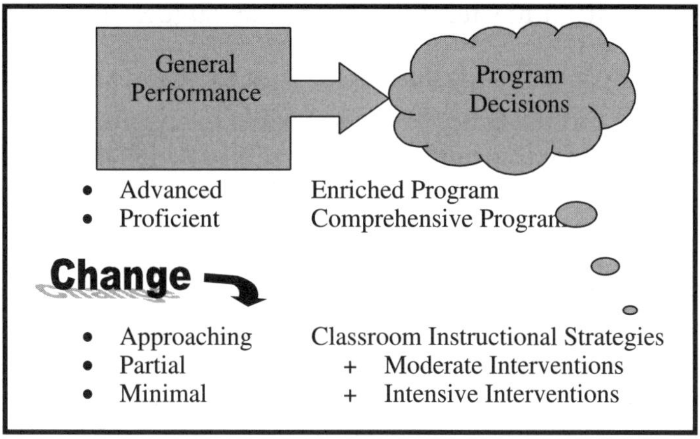

General Performance → Program Decisions

• Advanced	Enriched Program
• Proficient	Comprehensive Program

Change

• Approaching	Classroom Instructional Strategies
• Partial	+ Moderate Interventions
• Minimal	+ Intensive Interventions

The percentage of students at the Advanced level indicates the effectiveness of the school's enrichment program. The following are examples of questions for program decision-making:

- To what degree are AP (advanced placement) courses at the high school level and GATE (gifted and talented education) programs at the elementary and middle school levels having an impact on the number of students who reach the Advanced level?
- To what degree are all teachers using enriched curriculum and challenging students to exceed grade level standards?

The Proficient Level. The student at the Proficient level shows solid understanding of the quintessential content standards and all or almost all of the lower priority standards.

The percentage of students at the Proficient level indicates the effectiveness of the school's comprehensive instructional program. Example questions for program decision making are:

- To what degree is the comprehensive instructional program having an impact on students reaching the Proficient level?
- To what degree are school interventions helping students who need extra support to maintain progress or accelerate to the Proficient level? (For simplicity, the role of family/community partnerships is not addressed in this or lower levels.)

Now we discuss the performance levels below Proficient. As mentioned earlier, California followed the NAEP in adopting the term *Basic* for the next lower level; we believe this label can be misleading. Webster's dictionary defines basic as "fundamental," and some educators have historically defined "basic mastery" as sufficient competence. California and the NAEP describe the Basic level as having partial mastery; we, therefore, suggest using the term *Partial*.

Although many states and local districts have adopted a four-level model and the School BUS is flexible to any number of levels, we propose using five performance levels in which the Partial level is split into Approaching and Partial. Many educators familiar with using four-level scoring guides (rubrics) to assign performance levels to student work agree that the Partial level usually consists of a wide range of students, from those who master many concepts and skills and are almost Proficient to those who master little more than a few concepts/skills and are just above the lowest level (i.e., Minimal). Educators participating in School BUS workshops agree that students in the group labeled *Partial* are not homogenous and do not need the same kind of program changes or interventions. We suggest splitting this level into Approaching and Partial to form two fairly homogenous groups of students. The same appropriate program decision can then be made for each group or level—the Approaching level's range of achievement mastery tends to be narrower than that of the Partial level.

The Approaching Level. The student at the Approaching level shows solid understanding of many of the quintessential content standards. The percentage of students at the Approaching level indicates the effectiveness of the school's comprehensive instructional program. The primary focus is on classroom instructional strategies. Classroom teachers effectively taught many of the standards but should explore ways to improve instruction for the other standards. Example questions for program decision making are:

- Which content standards did students at this level tend to master? Which standards did they tend to not master? Were the same or different instructional strategies used for mastered and nonmastered standards?
- How can classroom instruction be changed to improve learning of all of the quintessential standards for these students? What strategies appear relatively ineffective and should be discarded? What strategies appear somewhat effective and should be improved? What strategies (e.g., in exemplary classrooms, schools, districts, or in professional literature) look more promising and should be added (to replace more ineffective strategies)?

The Partial Level. The student at the Partial level shows solid understanding of some of the quintessential content standards, or mostly partial understanding of the standards. The percentage of students at the Partial level indicates the effectiveness of the school's comprehensive instructional program. The primary focus is on the school's moderate interventions. Moderate interventions are exemplified by small group tutorial sessions held at least a few days per week using strategies that are coordinated with the classroom teacher's lessons and strategies. Support can be found in professional literature and from experienced educators that typical students at this level need moderate interventions in addition to improved classroom instruction.

Classroom teachers effectively taught many of the standards but should explore ways to improve instruction and improve supportive interventions for the other standards. Example questions for program decision making are:

- How can classroom instruction be changed to improve learning of all of the quintessential standards for these students?
- How can the school's moderate interventions be changed to help these students accelerate their learning to proficiency?

The Minimal Level. The student at the Minimal level shows solid understanding of few or none of the quintessential content standards, or mostly minimal understanding of the standards.

The percentage of students at the Minimal level indicates the effectiveness of the school's comprehensive instructional program. The primary focus is on the school's intensive interventions. Intensive interventions tend to be one-on-one daily tutorial sessions by a trained professional who uses strategies that are coordinated with the classroom teacher's lessons and strategies. Again, support can be found in professional literature and from experienced educators that the typical student at the Minimal level needs this level of support. For districts with a promotion/retention policy, students at the Minimal level are candidates for action (retention or intensive interventions).

Example questions for program decision making are:

- How can classroom instruction be changed to improve learning of all of the quintessential standards for these students?
- How can the school's intensive interventions be changed to help these students accelerate their learning to proficiency?

At the William Land Elementary School in Sacramento, California, teachers use the label "intensive kids" to describe students who need interventions. This proactive label implies that teachers take responsibility in and out of their classrooms to help each student to succeed. Although the school is located in an extremely impoverished area, the staff believes that every student who walks through the doorway can succeed and that the teachers are collectively responsible for ensuring student success.

We suggest two possible labels: Students at the Partial level who need moderate interventions might be called "MI students," and students at the Minimal level who need intensive interventions might be called "II students." These labels underscore two passionate beliefs of all teachers in a School BUS school: These students are "MI" (my) students and "II" (I), as part of the school team, am responsible for their education.

Year-End vs. Periodic Performance Levels

Some districts set performance levels for each reporting period (i.e., quarter or trimester) during the school year. Using several sets of performance levels can lead to confusion and a feeling of being overwhelmed by the assessment and accountability system. Reasons for not setting levels every period were explained in a previous section. In the School BUS approach, teachers focus on *year-end* content and performance standards and plan how to help students progress toward reaching proficiency by the end of the year.

Consider a school system using continuous content standards (those taught throughout the school year, for example, reading comprehension) quarterly grading periods. Using the School BUS approach, performance levels are often designed so that a student who finishes one grade at the Proficient level will be at the Partial level when assessed near the end of the first quarter (or trimester) at the next grade level. This is because the student is beginning the next grade and progression toward proficiency of standards of that next grade level. With good classroom instruction, a student at the Partial level in the first quarter is expected to reach the Proficient level by the end of the year. A student at the Minimal level in the first quarter likely will need at least moderate interventions to accelerate to the Proficient level by the end of the year. A student at the Minimal level near the end of the second quarter will likely need intensive interventions to accelerate to the Proficient level by the end of the year. One set of year-end performance levels serves decision-making each quarter. In the next section, *Mediating Performance Levels* further clarifies this topic by using a concrete example. For a more detailed discussion, see chapter 6, Using Student Results to Make Decisions.

Mediating Performance Levels

Mediating Performance Levels (MPLs) provide a deeper level of specificity, are perhaps tied to a grade span and/or subject area, and act as a bridge from GPLs to each scoring guide that defines specific performance on a particular assessment. MPLs help to ensure that the scoring guides for all assessments at all grade levels and subject areas are aligned with the one set of GPLs.

General Performance Levels (GPLs) are the focal point of reference for all assessment scoring guides for all grade levels and subject areas. However, GPLs may be too general for the district panel to adequately align them with all scoring guides. To minimize the chance of misalignment, a district is encouraged to develop *Mediating Performance Levels* (MPLs), which describe performance in more specific terms for a certain subject area, general standard or cluster of standards, grade span or level, or combination. MPLs bridge the "meaning gap" between GPLs and assessment scoring guides. These MPLs are not as specific as a scoring guide, but they are more precise than GPLs. Figure 2.8 illustrates the flow from one set of GPLs to several sets of MPLs to specific scoring guides for assessments at specific grades and subjects/standards.

Figure 2.8

Mediating Performance Levels as a Bridge from GPLs to Scoring Guides

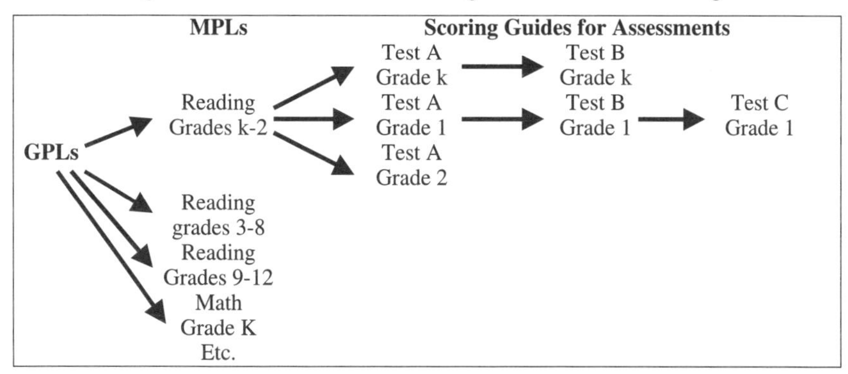

In step one, the assessment panel establishes GPLs. In step two, the panel creates MPLs aligned in rigor to the GPLs, for example, for subject areas within grade spans. In step three, the panel selects assessments and aligns scoring guides to the appropriate set of MPLs.

Figure 2.9 presents an example of MPLs for grade spans in reading, in particular general or quintessential standard of reading comprehension. Short descriptors are shown rather than longer descriptors that might better clarify the levels. The short descriptors in this example identify the difficulty level of reading material that the student independently reads with sufficient comprehension.

FIGURE 2.9

Alignment of General and Mediating Performance Levels for Reading

General Performance Levels	Mediating Performance Levels		
	Grades K-2	Grades 3-8	Grades 9-12
Advanced	Above	Above	Above
Proficient	At Grade	At Grade	At Grade
Approaching	Almost	1/2 Yr. Below	1 Yr. Below
Partial	1/2 Yr. Below	1 Yr. Below	2 Yr. Below
Minimal	1+ Yr. Below	2+ Yr. Below	3+ Yr. Below

Consider the short descriptors in Figure 2.9 for the grade span 9–12. The Minimal level might have a longer descriptor that says this student can read independently with solid comprehension text materials that are three grade levels (or more) below the student's grade level. This student is frustrated when trying to read grade level material without extensive help. Moving to the grade span 3–8, a student reading two or more grade levels below the current grade level is identified as performing at the Minimal level. For the grade span K-2, the gap narrows appropriately to reading one grade level or more below as defining the Minimal level.

We said in earlier sections on year-end standards that a clarifying example would be given later. The grade span 3–8 considered in more depth provides a good, concrete example of expectations about starting and ending levels for a district with year-end content and performance standards. Students who finish third grade at the Proficient level in reading are expected to be at the Partial level in the first quarter of fourth grade and progress to the Proficient level by the end of the year.

In Figure 2.9, the short descriptors used for MPLs (e.g., 1 Yr. Below) are criterion-referenced, and reference text materials by grade level difficulty. Do not confuse these criterion-referenced descriptors with Grade Equivalent scores that are reported for norm-referenced tests (e.g., SAT-9, Terra Nova, and ITBS). We discourage school staff from using Grade Equivalents in the School BUS because they are norm-referenced, not criterion-referenced or standards-referenced, and for other reasons not to be discussed here.

MPLs for mathematics might describe the Minimal level in terms of the student who does not have an adequate academic foundation to successfully begin the next grade level. By academic foundation, we mean the prerequisite or crucial concepts and skills for a student to function at the next grade level, not all that the teacher at the next grade level would like entering students to know. When a group of teachers is asked what a student *must* know, they narrow down the list of what they would *like* students to know to a brief list of essential concepts and skills. Mathematics tends to be taught as discrete standards within units/periods, not as a continuous standard throughout the year. For this reason, mathematics may have more critical concepts and skills identified than reading where certain skills are taught and practiced throughout the year.

Writing may be somewhere in between a continuous standard, such as reading comprehension, and a discrete math standard, such as measurement. In general, writing is continually taught and should continually improve with practice throughout the year. However, teaching and practicing certain genres of writing (e.g., poetry) tends to be more discrete in nature.

All content standards and performance levels target year-end expectations. Continuous standards truly ought to take all year to reach grade level mastery. Discrete standards might be taught within a quarter with the expectation that students reach grade level mastery by the end of the unit of study. Some districts such as Pleasant Grove (California) report only the standards actually taught during a grading period. They also indicate which standards are continuous and which are discrete so that parents understand their child's achievement in relation to year-end grade level expectations.

Scoring Guides

A *scoring guide* defines GPLs or MPLs in specific terms for an assessment intended for a certain grade level or high school course of study. Figure 2.8 illustrates the relationship of GPLs, MPLs, and scoring guides. Although some educators use the term *rubric*, Reeves

(1998a) preferred the transparent term *scoring guide*. *Rubric* comes from a Latin word for red clay, referring to the medium upon which important ideas or rules were written in ancient Roman times. A *scoring guide* is defined here as the descriptive criteria for judging student work according to the quality of each performance level.

There are two general types of scoring guides. The first is more common to teachers than is the second.

- Descriptors used by raters to judge overall student performance on task along some dimension of quality, often bolstered by models of student work at each performance level (This type can be further categorized as *holistic* or *analytic*.)
- Ranges of scores, often for traditional multi-item tests (e.g., multiple choice, short answer with many items), are converted to performance levels (e.g., 48–50 items correct = Advanced, 41–47 = Proficient, etc.). This will be fully explained in the next chapter.

Basic School BUS Model

Consider the Countryside Unified School District, a fictitious rural district in a small town with three schools—an elementary, middle, and high school. Human resources and time are scarce, requiring administrators to "wear different hats." Four years ago, the district adopted the state content standards, but after staff were trained to understand and teach the standards, teachers felt overwhelmed by their sheer number. Many teachers use scoring guides (rubrics) to rate student writing samples, but no common district performance levels or standards exist.

State test scores for the three schools have been relatively low and have not changed much during the three years mandated tests have been administered. The state is threatening dire consequences, called *sanctions*, if test scores do not rise and is offering rewards if scores do rise significantly. Regardless of the state rewards and sanctions, teachers agreed during a staff development day late last year that they really do want to find ways to improve student learning. The district's Assistant Superintendent of Everything Educational attended a conference last year and heard about the School BUS, an accountability model for school improvement just right for small districts without student computer databases or special expertise in assessment development or data analysis.

The state test is given only once a year. The district agrees with professional literature which states, that a truly improving school uses student results frequently during the year to keep refining its instructional program and to continuously identify students who need extra support. The assistant superintendent recalls that the School BUS uses a simple method for collecting, reporting, and analyzing local student assessment data a few times a year for program decision-making.

After discussing the potential of the School BUS with the superintendent and principals, a district accountability committee is formed. The committee includes representatives from the district office, the three schools, and the teachers' union (the union representative is included for her perspective and to ensure that any changes agreed upon by the committee would have union support). In August, only a few weeks before the start of school, the committee attended a two-day workshop to build a common understanding and to consider how the model of the School BUS method could be adapted to their local context. The School BUS's simplicity and quick-start features gave the committee confidence that they could begin using it in September.

After some discussion, the committee agreed that they did not have enough time or experience to carefully identify quintessential standards from the many state-adopted standards. They reviewed past state test results. Because they saw that test scores at the three schools were lowest in reading comprehension, they decided to first concentrate on using the School BUS to improve this one standard in all three schools.

The committee decided to adopt the five-level model of General Performance Levels (GPLs) they reviewed in the School BUS workshop (see Figure 2.6) and to refine statements later when they had gained experience using them. Because the Mediating Performance Levels (MPLs) for reading by grade spans (see Figure 2.9) also seemed sensible, the committee decided to try using them before considering any modifications. Activity 3 at the end of this chapter presents guidelines for establishing meaningful GPLs.

Using a standard rating system would be a big change from the traditional ways each teacher personally judged student progress. The committee planned how and when to present its work plan so that all teachers could accept using ongoing assessment and rating students in relation to year-end standards. But a big "selling point" was the idea that teachers could start with a focus on teaching and assessing one standard well, reducing the feeling of being overwhelmed by all the standards. Activities 1 and 2 at the end of this chapter were included in school staff development plans. These activities encourage dialogue about common standards and high expectations. This ended Day One of getting ready to implement the School BUS.

Advanced School BUS Model

The fictitious Cityscape Unified School District has 30,000 students and 30 elementary, 4 middle, and 4 high schools. Located in an urban area, 50 percent of the districts students are enrolled in the Free/Reduced Lunch Program. Cityscape USD, which is located in the same state as Countryside USD, also adopted the state content standards four years ago. Cityscape USD has a student computer database and for several years it has offered staff development on standards and, more recently, standards-based lesson planning (see chapter 5).

Cityscape USD teachers strongly believe in the integration of learning to read and learning to write—each informs and supports the other. Students regularly write essays in response to literature they have read. Students write in the genre they are reading and are encouraged to use words, phrases, and styles from their favorite authors or from the literature pieces they are reading. Students read their own and peers' writing for enjoyment and to practice the editing process. In this integrated approach, teachers believe the deeper understanding of language arts and skill application that students acquire is transferable to other subjects, such as science and social studies.

Cityscape has been implementing districtwide reading assessments three times a year at each trimester, and teachers may voluntarily assess more often. Kindergarten has a five-level developmental scoring guide (or continuum) in many areas, including reading, writing, and math. The fourth level was identified as the year-end grade level expectation—the performance standard. Kindergarten had been using the five-level instrument for several years; it was only a coincidence that it matched the five-level GPLs the district adopted last year for all grade levels. The assessment is an observation tool for watching and interacting with individual children as they show their understanding at learning centers. The reading comprehension assessment consisted of oral retelling of a story read aloud to each student. The assessments at other grade levels yield a variety of scores that were converted to performance level scores last year (a topic in chapter 3):

- "book levels" (e.g., 0-34) using running records in primary grades 1-3,
- grade-level scores (independent, instructional, frustration at a grade level difficulty text) using reading inventories in intermediate grades,
- grade-level scores (e.g., 6.0-8.0) using Accelerated Reading assessment computer program in the middle grades, and
- total correct scores from textbook assessments in high schools.

Writing is assessed once a year using district-developed prompts and scoring guides (rubrics) for Application (called Expression or Rhetoric by other districts or tests) with four performance levels in grades 1-3 and six levels in grades 4-12. (Writing Conventions is rated separately with a three-level scoring guide in grades 1-12.) Chapter 3 will describe options for double-scoring writing samples to verify consistency of raters for performance assessments such as this one.

Districtwide math assessments were established in 1998–99. The assessment system includes a 20-item test in grades 1-2, a performance task with a scoring guide in grades 3-5, and 50-item tests in grades 6-8 and in high school algebra 1 and 2 and geometry courses. All math tests are derived from the curriculum textbooks and materials. Each test measures one math strand (cluster of content standards) and is administered at a common time after teachers have had ample opportunity to teach the strand or unit. Number sense, geometry, and data analysis were selected as the three strands, with the expectation that future assessment would be expanded to all strands.

A few years ago, Cityscape's assessment committee believed it was off to a good start: It had established uniform assessments in key areas but it was concerned that district and school staff were "drowning in data" with no way to easily summarize student results across grade levels for school and district accountability. At that point, assessment was happening, but there was little utilization of results for making decisions about the effectiveness of a school's instructional program. Cityscape did not have district performance levels and, frankly, it did not see the need or usefulness. Then, in the spring of 1999, the district's assessment committee attended a series of workshops on the School BUS. During the summer months, the district prepared to fully implement the School BUS during the upcoming school year (1999–2000).

After attending the School BUS workshops, the assessment committee renamed itself the "district accountability committee" to reflect the broadening of its scope of work from assessing students to supporting schools in using results for program improvement. Committee members saw that reporting student results using one set of performance levels would make summarizing and reporting results much easier, and all teachers could then communicate using the "same language" about student proficiency. A school staff could quickly review school results and discuss whether classroom strategies or moderate interventions or intensive interventions needed improvement as schoolwide initiatives.

In reaction to the state results, the district had already initiated sustained staff development with a focus on integrated reading and writing instruction. Schools across the district tended to score equally low in reading comprehension and writing application on the state test, showing little change from previous years. Cityscape decided to adopt the model of five GPLs and MPLs for reading comprehension to begin the School BUS. Cityscape thought it best to concentrate on the one standard of reading comprehension in its initial year using the School BUS and standards-based assessments.

The district started full implementation of the School BUS the following school year (1999-2000). During the spring of that year, the district accountability committee held a series of meetings to develop a full set of quintessential standards spanning grades K–12. These quintessential standards focused on general concepts and skills that all students would be taught well and expected to master, that is, concepts or skills that would be essential for students to know and be able to do throughout their lives as global citizens in a new millennium. Reading comprehension, clear and expressive writing, and data analysis in mathematics (applied in many subject areas) were three of the quintessential standards.

The accountability committee developed Mediating Performance Levels for writing and mathematics during the same school year (1999-2000). Because staff development embedded within school improvement initiatives focused on integrated reading and writing, the committee decided that they had the increased capacity to examine both reading and writing assessments in their second year of implementing the School BUS. The committee agreed to align math assessments to the district MPLs; however, only the math departments at the secondary level schools would include results for the School BUS accountability process during this second year.

Staff Development Activities

Activity 1: What Do We Mean by "All Students"?

The purpose of this activity is to bring to the surface any deep-rooted individual beliefs about which students are expected to master the district's content standards. "Dialogue"—clarifying one's own ideas and listening deeply to others—is practiced, as opposed to "discussion," where people defend their ideas and debate in an effort to "win over" supporters to one side. Dialogue is when teachers ask students to "brainstorm" ideas, allowing respect for all ideas and "putting them on the board" for consideration.

Different beliefs about which students can learn, or what or how much they can learn, tends to have ramifications for how students are taught. One belief system may underly an education system in which students are taught using essentially one strategy and must follow a rigid pacing. Some students are expected to fail, some to achieve adequately, and a few to excel. Another belief system may underlie an education system that offers multiple and varied learning opportunities until each student reaches mastery.

Before school staff has a dialogue about what instructional strategies are best or what to change, attention must be given to the staff's beliefs about what students are capable of learning and what the role or responsibility of the teacher is in helping students learn.

Facilitator presents the activity:

Following are three beliefs that underly content standards. Content standards apply to all students in the school district. Participants in small groups are asked to read the three statements, then have a dialogue. Participants in each group either choose the belief closest to their own or role-play each of the beliefs as long as all three are covered. Explain what is meant by each belief for complete understanding by each member. Second, dialogue about the implications of each belief for teaching and learning.

There should be:

A. one set of standards and significant changes made in the system to assure that all students reach those standards.
B. higher standards set for all students, but the standards should be differentiated in recognition of students' different interests and abilities.

C. standards set at a level that would be ideal for all students, but recognition that all students won't be able to reach those standards.

Activity adapted from *Standards from Document to Dialogue* (Jamentz, 1998).

Activity 2: Standards Support Good Practice

The purpose of this activity is to build understanding of the reason for establishing content and performance standards in a district and then ensuring sufficient staff development in teaching to the standards so that all students have equal access to core content and skills at each grade level. The facilitator might mention statements by Schmoker and Marzano (1999) in the main body of this chapter about how many math and science standards are covered in the United States compared to other countries, such as Germany and Japan.

If the district has established or will establish quintessential standards in a district that has many specific content standards, this should be mentioned by the facilitator and added to the discussion.

Facilitator presents the activity:

Each small group reads the following page and then dialogues about the purpose of content and performance standards, how this is different from past practice, and where the change may lead. Small groups highlight key ideas in the passage and report on the questions below to the whole group as "quick-around" (where successive groups add new ideas without repeated statements made by previous groups).

If the staff is already aware of the School BUS, ask the whole group to connect the discussion to using the School BUS for a team approach to teaching, assessing, accountability, and school improvement.

1. What statement in the passage was a "key idea" for your group?
2. Why are content and performance standards important as part of a school and district initiative to improve teaching and learning?
3. How are districtwide content and performance standards different from past practice?
4. Where might the change to teaching and assessing standards lead us?

Content and Performance Standards

The emphasis on challenging content and student performance standards for all children provides a clear goal for the new Title I law: to enable children served by Title I to meet the challenging standards established by the State for all its children. States, districts, and schools are called on to break with past practice by replacing minimum standards for some children with challenging standards for all. Challenging content standards defining what knowledge and skills should be learned and student performance standards that set the levels of student achievement, therefore, are the centerpiece of Title I.

Standards are intended to provide a focus for coherent improvement in all the components affecting teaching and learning: curriculum, instruction, professional development, school leadership, student assessment, and parent involvement.

Standards, Assessment, and Accountability
Title I statute and regulations, US Department of Education, 1997

Standards aren't change in themselves—it's their effect that's important: nothing less than reversing the model of schooling as we know it. To this point, education has mirrored the stratification of society; 20% excelled and took professional positions expected by their socioeconomic status; 80% sat out their years in school and moved into blue color or service jobs . . . The system inputs remained the same and the outcomes varied . . . students were sorted and selected and the results could be predicted fairly accurately from race, income level and family background.

In a standards model, the outcomes are held steady and the input varies. The system is responsible for seeing that all students meet the standards, no matter how different their needs may be. "All children can learn" has become a shibboleth of educational moral rectitude, but in a standards system, we have the incentive to deliver on it. The consequences for the educational system are profound. At every level, from the district's central office to the classroom, one vital question determines policy and practice: "Does this help all students meet the standard?"

Ruth Mitchell, *Focusing on Learning: Change Driven by Standards.*
Center X Quarterly 7, no. 1 (Fall 1994)

Activity 3: How Many Levels for You?

The purpose of this activity is to develop *General Performance Levels* for the district or review and possibly modify existing performance levels. A district accountability committee participates in this activity, not individual school staff, although facilitators might adapt it for school staff to gain a deeper understanding why the district committee selected and defined its General Performance Levels as it did.

Before developing standards-based assessments, a school district must first decide how many performance levels to set and then align all assessments to those levels. The number of levels should correspond to fairly homogenous groupings of students by achievement levels. In this way, types of instructional programs can be directly matched to groups of students to support all students at least reach the proficient level. Assessment results, reported as the percentage of students at each performance level, inform instructional program decisions matched to those performance levels.

After deciding how many performance levels is right for your district, the next step is to reach consensus on a common vision of the "proficient student" (proficient reader, writer, mathematician). This is the *performance standard*. Next, create one, or perhaps two, levels above the performance standard to signify achievement that exceeds grade level expectations. Third, decide how many performance levels below the performance standard are appropriate for your school district and develop labels and descriptors for each performance level.

The committee might begin with a general discussion about the advantages and disadvantages of four or five performance levels (or three or six).

A. How many performance levels are right for your district?

B. What labels for the levels does the committee agree on?

C. What descriptors define the level yet are broad enough to apply to most or all grade levels and subject areas?

D. What types of instructional program decisions are matched to those levels, so you can use the student results directly to inform decisions for the group of students at that performance level?

Activity 4: Developing Mediating Performance Levels

The purpose of this activity is to develop *Mediating Performance Levels* for the district or review and possibly modify existing mediating levels. A district accountability committee participates in this activity, not individual school staff, although facilitators might adapt it for school staff to gain a deeper understanding why the district committee selected and defined its Mediating Performance Levels as it did. This activity is easier to conduct when the committee reflects on some real assessments that are being used or might be used in the district assessment system. Committee members who are teachers with valued experience and high expectations of students are crucial to this activity.

After creating General Performance Levels (GPLs) for the district, the next step is to create Mediating Performance levels (MPLs) that are more specific in terms of performance in reading, writing, or mathematics at certain grade spans. The labels for MPLs are the same ones used for the GPLs. The descriptors, however, are more specific statements about what students are expected to know and be able to do.

The committee begins by selecting one subject area (reading, writing, mathematics) or standard that will be the focus of the School BUS accountability system and staff development throughout the year. Decide on appropriate grade spans and then create the MPLs for each grade span. Repeat the process for other standards/subjects if desired or expand to these remaining areas in the future when time, capacity, and interest permit.

A. What is the primary subject/standard for accountability this year?
B. What grade spans cluster together for creating sets of descriptors?
C. What descriptors define each performance level for the first grade span? Repeat for successive grade spans.
D. What types of instructional program decisions are matched to those levels, so you can use the student results directly to inform decisions for the group of students at that performance level?

3 Standards-Based Assessment

The widely accepted maxim that "more is less" applies without question to the field of educational statistics.Statisticians who always opt for the most sophisticated and exotic statistical approach may impress others with their statistical wizardry, but they do not impress others with their good sense.

—W. James Popham and Kenneth Sirotnik

Overview

Developing district standards-based assessments is the first wheel of the School BUS. When we say "develop," we do not mean necessarily to create a new assessment, but perhaps identify existing assessments and modify administration or items on the instrument or simply keep the intact instrument and set score ranges aligned to performance levels. A standards-based assessment measures one or more content standards and yields a score as a performance level.

In the School BUS, one or more standards-based assessments are selected to measure the quintessential standard that is the target for school improvement. The assessment results are reported as the percentage of students at each performance level, and instructional program decisions are linked directly to these results. So before the BUS can "get rolling" at each school site, the district must establish at least one standards-based assessment for schools to use.

An educational system that is continually improving will continually improve its assessment system. Standards-based assessment is like a wheel—it helps move the vehicle, that is, the accountability process, towards continual improvement, and it goes through its own cycles of improvement.

Different types of tests can serve different purposes and vary in their accuracy to yield "true" achievement scores for different students. *Multi-item tests* (e.g., multiple-choice) are suited best to quickly and efficiently measure broad curriculum coverage. *Performance assessments* (e.g., one complex task requiring an extensive response) are best suited to measure the quintessential content standards; they have sufficient depth and enough critical, constructive thinking to mirror the depth of classroom instruction on these quintessential standards. Multiple, diverse measures can add the accuracy that one measure alone may not be able to provide for all students. A school or district can be confident that true program improvement was accomplished when test results increase over years on the district's internal assessment system and on an external assessment, such as a state or national measure.

An *internal assessment system* is necessary for the School BUS because external assessments are typically administered just once a year. Professional literature on truly improving schools indicates that school staff frequently uses assessment results during the year to continually refine and improve the school's instructional program. An assessment is administered three or four times a year in the School BUS process—at each grading period.

Formative assessment, known to many teachers as "checking for understanding," serves a different purpose than summative assessment, which is given at the end of a unit of study. When used to target appropriate instruction for particular subgroups of students, formative assessment can support very powerful teaching and learning. Summative assessment is used in the School BUS approach to make school-level decisions about overall instructional effectiveness.

A *standards-based assessment* measures one or more content standards and yields performance levels aligned to the district's General and Mediating Performance Levels. Chapter 6 will explain how the percentage of students at performance levels is used in the School BUS to make program decisions. The link between performance level results and types of program decisions, core classroom instructional strategies and school moderate and intensive interventions, was covered in chapter 2.

Criteria are defined to judge whether assessments meet high standards for quality. No assessment has yet been acclaimed as the "perfect" test for all purposes. A *good assessment* has at least an adequate degree of validity, consistency, accuracy, and fairness. It measures the content standards in a way that is aligned to how students are taught so that students can practice and perform to their true achievement level. Scoring is consistent—a student will achieve the same score regardless of who rates the responses. It accurately indicates true achievement levels for all students.

A *good assessment* provides information at critical times during the school year, which helps teachers modify learning and students adjust learning while there is ample time to take corrective action. The focus of the School BUS uses assessment data to inform school and district instructional program decisions. We suggest beginning the search for good assessment from the bottom up. First, "mine the gold" within the district by exploring assessments that are already being used in exemplary classrooms or are embedded in curriculum materials and build agreement that all teachers at a grade level will use the same test. Then, look outside to other districts, educational companies and agencies, and other resources, such as the Internet, where good assessments and pools of good items can be found. Development of a good assessment can take an enormous amount of resources and expertise.

The *Flag Tag method*, a fairly quick and easy method for converting raw scores (e.g., number correct score) to performance levels, can be used by any district panel to reach agreement on cut scores, the lowest score at each performance level. Some district assessments may already be standards-based—they measure specific content standards and yield performance levels aligned to district General and Mediating Performance Levels. Other assessments produce a variety of scores, all of which can be converted to performance levels using the Flag Tag method. The School BUS uses performance level results to summarize data quickly and easily and to make timely decisions. Team use of data is fostered when all teachers speak "the same assessment language."

Finally, the Basic School BUS Model continues the story of the small-sized Countryside USD as its district panel uses the Flag Tag method to establish standards-based assessments of reading comprehension. The mid-sized Cityscape USD in the Advanced School BUS Model expands the Flag Tag method to writing and math assessments. Writing performance assessments with different numbers of performance levels are converted to the district's five levels.

Multi-item math tests with two types of total scores (one point per item correct versus mixed points per item) are converted to district performance levels.

The last section on Staff Development Activities covers the importance of using multiple measures and mapping existing and potential district assessments for all as well as special education and English language learner students. Activity 3 gives "hands-on" practice setting a cut score using the Flag Tag method for a simple eight-item math test.

Types of Assessment

In the School BUS, a district or school selects an internal assessment that can be given three or four times a year (at grading periods). Multi-item tests, such as multiple-choice, are appropriate for quickly measuring a broad curriculum, while performance assessments with one or a few complex tasks are appropriate for deeply measuring quintessential content standards. A *standards-based assessment* measures one or more content standards and yields performance levels aligned to district GPLs and MPLs.

Some educators and educational testing experts refer to a "test" as the traditional multiple choice, true or false, fill-in-the-blank type of instrument that is scored by people or computer and yields a score, such as number correct or percent correct. They refer to an "assessment" as a real or direct performance of knowledge and skills that is evaluated by people according to some criteria contained in a scoring guide (rubric) and that yields performance level ratings. Others use the terms interchangeably. (Computer-based assessment programs are beginning to emerge but have not yet replaced human raters.) A dictionary does define a "test" as an exam and an "assessment" as an appraisal. The School BUS is equivocal on this point—"test" and "assessment" will be considered synonymous.

External vs. Internal

External assessments are developed and administered directly or with oversight provided by some external agency that dictates to the local school or district which assessment is to be used and to whom and when it is to be given. The NAEP test is an example of a national test given in states to samples of students on a fairly voluntary basis. Many states have state-adopted or state-developed assessments that local schools are mandated to administer. State tests tend to be administered once a year at particular grade levels. Some states wholly develop their own tests, while others adopt or adapt a test publisher's instrument.

Among the widely used "off the shelf" norm-referenced tests (NRTs) are Terra Nova, the Stanford Achievement Test Version 9 (SAT-9) and the Iowa Test of Basic Skills (ITBS). Some states have modified the "off the shelf" NRT by adding and deleting items to better measure the state content standards. Several states have created their own standards-based tests, either completely multiple-choice or mixed with open-response items, or writing assessments that are students' writing samples rated with rubrics, or scoring guides.

One benefit of national and state external assessments is that they give schools the ability to compare their performance with that of others in the nation or state. Some drawbacks are that external assessments are usually given only once near the end of a school year, tend to be fairly rigid in testing conditions, and delay feedback on test results for a month or more.

Internal assessments are developed or selected and administered by the local agency, that is, the school or district. An assessment might be selected from a test publisher, curriculum textbooks or materials, or other sources, such as Internet sites or other districts that maintain and provide access to test instruments or a pool of items. Development of a sound assessment can require a high level of human and fiscal resources. Developing a truly good multiple-choice test takes much more expertise than it may seem.

We suggest that a district explore existing assessments that can be used internally before attempting to create assessments (direct writing sample prompts are the exception) because of the enormous time and expertise necessary for sound test development. Before bringing an assessment "top down" into classrooms from the district level, explore assessments being used by expert teachers and high-performing schools in the districts. Bring these assessments from the "bottom up" to district-wide implementation, perhaps with modifications for large-scale use. Either way, it is important to have a district committee with broad school representation make the decisions to help garner from the teachers the support necessary to faithfully implement the assessment system.

The advantage to using internal assessments is local control over the instrument's format, testing conditions, frequency of administration, and length of time for feedback of results. Some disadvantages are inadequate resources for test development revisions, and inability to compare local student performance to the state or national norms.

When a school or district publicly reports a meaningful rise in local test results and implies that it is due to meaningful improvements in teaching and learning, it can bolster public confidence by showing a comparable rise in one or more external assessments. The school or district must assure the public that results did not rise because of "noninstructional factors," such as greater familiarity with the test items or selectively testing students (e.g., those likely to score high). Changes in internal test results do not always coincide with changes in external test results, but one expects that both types of tests will reflect meaningful improvement in the school's instructional program.

Because of local control over test development, an internal assessment likely measures more of the local curriculum and the way in which students are taught than does an external assessment. The internal results should also be more sensitive to change in the instructional program than are the external results.

A school with a good internal assessment system can anticipate the results of the external (state) test. A school that has made meaningful improvements in its instructional program and sees the impact on the internal (district) assessment will most likely see comparable improvement on the external (state) test. External test results can be used to corroborate internal test results. When both the internal and external results rise, the school can be quite confident that program improvements indeed had an impact on student learning, and the school should receive public recognition and rewards for its success.

Our advice to districts that criticize and largely ignore external (state) tests but have no internal testing system is to accept wholly what does exist until the district develops a better local testing system. After the district develops a valid, reliable, useful local system, it can include the best features of the external system to complement and enhance the local system. These districts must be aware that they are accountable to the public and that criticizing external test results without producing more reliable and accurate internal test data has the appearance of indifference to public accountability and refusal to examine where local teaching and learning can be improved. State testing plays an important role in the public education system, and the results can be informative and useful to schools and districts.

Our second piece of advice is for districts to concentrate resources on developing a sound internal assessment and accountability system. Professional literature indicates that a common characteristic of many truly improving schools is that staff uses (local) assessment results frequently during the year to make instructional program improvements (e.g., Joyce, Wolf, and Calhoun, 1994). Districts have control over an internal assessment system, which can be administered at key periods during the year. Results can be reported rapidly and simply to provide feedback for decisions about program improvement, which can then be implemented quickly. Because districts have control over internal assessments, and can include a variety of assessment methods, they can accommodate the special needs of certain students, ensuring that all student results are as reliable and accurate as possible. Districts can build confidence that local instructional improvements are having a positive impact on student learning by looking for comparable increases in both internal and external test results. If results are widely discrepant, the districts must analyze what concepts and skills each test measured, whether the test format and administration differed, and how well instruction aligned with the assessments.

NRT vs. CRT vs. Standards-Based Assessments

A *norm-referenced test* (NRT) compares student performance to that of other students. National test publishers create standardized tests by sampling curriculum across the nation. These tests, most of which are multiple-choice, reflect the publisher's perception of a "national curriculum," and items are tried out on a nationwide sample of students. In 1995, the SAT-9 was administered to a "norm group," a national sample of about 2,000 students per grade level in volunteer schools. Number correct scores, called *raw scores*, were converted to percentiles (technically called national percentile ranks), which indicate the percentage of students in the norm group who had a lower raw score. Any student taking the SAT-9 in any year after 1995 is compared to the 1995 norm group in terms of reporting percentiles.

A student with a 100 percent correct score is likely at the 99th percentile; one percent of the norm group likely scored 100 percent correct, and 99 percent of the norm group had lower (percent correct) scores. When a student has a 100 percent correct score and the percentile is, say, 97, it is because three percent of the norm group scored 100 percent correct. The 50th percentile is considered to be right "at grade level," but a little reflection shows that the 50th percentile is merely whatever percent correct score was achieved by the middle student in the norm group. Test publishers have technical manuals that show conversions charts for converting raw scores to percentiles; roughly 70 percent correct in any grade and on any test for the SAT-9 converts to the 50th percentile.

Consider Andrea, who correctly answered 58 items of the 84 items on the SAT-9 grade 11 Total Reading test in the spring of 1999. Andrea had a raw score of 69 percent correct. Her score was at the 49th percentile—Andrea scored higher than 49 percent of the 1995 norm group of eleventh graders. Some people might say that Andrea scored higher than 49 percent of students in the nation. However, this statement is not really true because not all students nationally take the SAT-9—only those districts and states that buy the test. This example highlights that a percent correct score is not the same as a percentile score and that a student's score is referenced to a norm group of students.

This example also highlights that results are compared to the year the test was normed—1995 for SAT-9—not each current year. Educators who state that their school's NRT scores cannot possibly rise because the results are compared to a current national group each year are misinformed. Because results every year are compared to the 1995 norm group (until the test publisher creates a new test and a new set of norms), it is possible for a school to improve teaching and learning and see the impact as a rise in NRT scores.

A *criterion-referenced test* (CRT) measures a specific curriculum and references student performance to some criterion of mastery, such as pass/fail or above/at/below grade level expectation. A CRT does not compare a student's performance to other students or some norm group. A curriculum or test publisher, a school district, or an individual teacher might create CRTs. Libraries of tests and pools of test items can be found on Internet web sites.

A *standards-based assessment* is a special type of CRT. A standards-based assessment measures one or more specific content standards and yields a score or rating that references established performance levels and a performance standard of grade level expectancy. Many states have created an assessment to measure its content standards and yield performance levels. A state might attempt to modify an existing NRT (e.g., add items to measure more content standards) and specify ranges of scores that convert to performance levels. In a school district, all (regular education) teachers at a grade level administer the same standards-based assessment. (Classroom "standards-based" assessments that each teacher might design individually are not discussed in this book.)

Traditional assessments can yield a variety of scores, such as number correct, percent correct, percentile, level on a developmental continuum, book difficulty level, pass/fail, or performance level particular to the assessment. A school or district with many types of assessments can have many types of scores being reported and might find it difficult to summarize school results or talk about what the results mean in terms of classroom instruction and school interventions. A district with standards-based assessments may have a variety of instruments that yield a score tied to one set of district-established performance levels. For some assessments, a score (e.g., number correct) will be converted to a performance level, but for other assessments (e.g., writing samples) scores will directly indicate performance level.

School districts should explore existing assessments that, perhaps with some modification, measure district content standards and provide performance level "scores." As stated in an earlier section, first try to "mine the gold" that exists in some of the district's classrooms and schools as a "bottom up" approach before looking for instruments outside. If, for example, running records are being used in some elementary schools with successful impact on teaching and learning, try to reach agreement with other elementary schools to make running records a district-wide assessment. Methods for converting raw scores (e.g., number correct) to performance levels will be addressed in a later section of this chapter.

The School BUS capitalizes on a standards-based assessment to quickly and easily summarize results for a school so that staff can make decisions about classroom instructional strategies and school interventions at crucial intervals throughout the year. A school cannot use the School BUS until the district has established a standards-based assessment to measure the content standard(s) that will be the focus of school improvement and accountability. A small district can "go districtwide right away," while a larger district may want to pilot the standards-based assessment and School BUS process in only a few schools during the first year.

A good standards-based assessment provides two tiers of information.

> TIER 1: The individual teacher can analyze student responses to specific items, or miscues in reading, or particular forms of writing conventions or expression, or steps in using problem-

solving strategies in math. This detailed information informs the teacher about specific areas and methods for corrective instruction targeted to his or her students' needs.

TIER 2: A team of teachers can analyze a summary of results for a classroom, grade level, course, or whole school in terms of the percentage of students at or above the Proficient level or, to provide more specificity, the percentage of students at each performance level. Results at the Approaching performance level inform decisions about classroom instruction. Results at the Partial and Minimal levels inform decisions about the school's interventions as well as classroom instruction.

Some schools and districts are using all sorts of assessments at different grade levels and different subject areas. Each assessment yields a different type of score. Because there are so many types of data, teachers and principals can feel as if they are "drowning in an ocean of data" and cannot "see the forest for the trees." Tier 2 addresses this dilemma by using a common set of performance levels for reporting student achievement. All teachers can communicate in a common assessment language. Teams of teachers can easily rise above the Tier 1 data and see what the overall school results look like when using performance levels aligned to district GPLs and MPLs.

From Multi-Item to Single Task Assessments

A *multi-item test* has many items that require a "selected response" (e.g., multiple-choice, true/false, matching, or Cloze with word bank) or "open response" (e.g., fill-in-the-blanks with one word, a few words, or a number). NRTs are often multiple-choice, but may also include open-ended response items. This type of test yields a number or percent correct score that can be converted to a percentile on an NRT or performance level on a CRT or standards-based assessment. Students might fill in bubbles on a scan sheet for a multiple-choice test or they might type, write, or verbalize their answers on any multi-item test.

A test with a few items usually requires a student to construct a more complex and lengthy response. This type of instrument might be called a *performance assessment*. Items might be questions or directions with or without background context. Usually this type of item asks students to show the steps or strategies in their thinking or problem-solving or to explain their reasoning as part of their response. Items might be scored as correct or incorrect but are often rated by some criteria of "levels of correctness." Either a simple sum of item scores or criteria for combining item scores yields a total score or overall performance level.

An assessment with one task that requires the student to construct a complex and lengthy response involving critical thinking and integration of several concepts and skills is called a *performance assessment*. The overall task might be split into subparts. A student might give an oral presentation or written performance (e.g., research report, essay, poem, or letter to a newspaper editor) or construct a project with or without oral or written explanation. One or more persons judge the performance task using a scoring guide (rubric) that has criteria or descriptors of quality performance to assign a performance level "score." The scoring guide might show associated models of student work or lists of acceptable and unacceptable example responses to help raters consistently apply the scoring guide. The scoring guide might be *holistic*, providing one overall rating, or *analytic*, providing a rating for each dimension of the task.

An advantage to using multi-item tests such as multiple-choice is that they can efficiently and broadly measure a curriculum, with relatively quick administration and scoring; a disadvantage is that a teacher cannot be sure whether a student really knew or guessed the correct answer. An advantage to using performance assessments is that they effectively measure specific content standards in depth and require students to perform in a way that simulates real world application of concepts and skills. We suggest that districts use a variety of types of tests and concentrate their use of performance assessments on the quintessential content standards.

Shavelson and others extensively examined science tasks and determined that a single performance assessment was not a good indicator of the overall content area. Anywhere from 10 to 36 performance tasks are needed to accurately measure a general content area (Linn, 1994; Shavelson, Gao, & Baxter, 1993). Haertel (1999) agrees and warns that "high-stakes testing programs have led to the creation of a kind of performance task that bears little resemblance to the high-quality performance assessments that teachers are able to use in their day-to-day instruction." We suggest that a district design a system of assessment that:

- matches the type of assessment to what and how the curriculum content is taught
- considers the relative importance of the content taught to the time and effort needed to assess, score, and report results

- acknowledges that some students prefer and perform better on multi-item tests, while other students prefer and perform better on performance assessments with one or a few items

A portfolio is a collection of student work assembled to show cumulative learning over time or the highest level of achievement. Some portfolios are treated as an assessment instrument and are assigned a performance score, while others are meant to showcase student work. Performance samples are chosen carefully, and often the students write a "reflection piece" about what they have learned and what direction they want to go. Self-reflection and planning fosters personal responsibility for and metacognition (knowing what they do and do not know) of the learning process. The teacher holds conferences intermittently with each student to discuss the portfolio and build its contents. During parent conferences at grading periods, the teacher might supervise students in each corner of the classroom as they discuss their portfolios with their parents.

Summative and Formative Assessment

Teams of teachers use *summative assessment* results used in the School BUS model for "results-driven" decisions about the school's instructional program at critical periods during the year. Individual teachers use *formative assessments* to guide corrective instruction and adjust lesson plans.

Summative assessment is administered at the culmination of a unit of study or after good first teaching of one or more content standards is complete and students are expected to have mastered the content. Ideally, students not performing at mastery are offered opportunities for further instruction and re-assessment, especially for quintessential standards.

Professional literature states that students should be assessed before, during, and after instruction. Identifying students' prior beliefs helps a teacher design lessons that challenge students to explicitly compare and contrast facts or opinions and construct new understandings. For example, before a science lesson about optics, students might be asked how they are able to see objects. Many students believe that an object is seen when light "comes out of the eye and hits an object." The teacher might set up an experiment to test their hypothesis and explore alternative hypotheses. If students cannot see in a dark room, then an alternative must be true—light bounces off an object and enters the eye.

Assessment before instruction can pinpoint crucial prerequisites that a group of students have not mastered and can offer interventions so that students can quickly gain enough of a foundation to learn the proposed lesson. Assessing lesson content before instruction can identify students who have already mastered the content and can help teachers design a more advanced lesson.

Formative assessments are given during instruction to provide students with feedback that guide their learning and to provide teachers with feedback to guide their lesson planning and delivery to meet students' specific needs. While formative assessment is the technical term, many teachers call this set of techniques "checking for understanding." Teachers report a variety of techniques. Some are formal, such as the types of testing discussed earlier in which every student is assessed. Others are informal, such as calling on a few students to sample class understanding, having students write answers on personal writing boards, or requesting that students signal their answers with their hands.

Math Matters is a set of instructional strategies that engages students in thinking about and using mathematics. In Math Matters, students use a "thumbs up" to signify agreement with another student's answer, politely wave a hand low and horizontally to signify disagreement, and make a hand gesture over the top of the head to signify confusion or lack of an answer. Requiring all students to signify a response quickly gives the teacher visual feedback and requires all students to attend to each other's answers to the teacher's question.

Research supports the notion that formative assessment can be quite powerful when it is used to pinpoint what certain students need to master. The teacher can select appropriate strategies for these students while designing other learning activities for students at mastery. Black and William (1998) reviewed a number of research studies linking formative assessment to impressive learning gains when the feedback to teachers was detailed and used to guide instruction.

Benjamin Bloom (1984) explored teaching strategies that were feasible in a regular classroom of about 30 students. He reported on studies that compared *conventional instruction* to *mastery learning*. In *conventional instruction*, teachers taught a complete lesson or unit, then tested students, assigned grades, and retaught or moved on to the next unit. In *mastery learning*, teachers assessed as they were teaching and used the feedback to adjust teaching strategies for specific groups of students. This ongoing assessment feedback alerts a teacher to when certain students need more practice or presentation in a different form.

Mastery learning was found to dramatically increase student learning and narrow the range of achievement, as shown in Figure 3.1 (slightly adapted from Bloom, 1984). The average student in the *mastery learning* group outperformed 84% of the students in the *conventional instruction* group. One-on-one *tutoring* was more effective than *mastery learning*, but that is just not a feasible option for all students in a school.

FIGURE 3.1

Impact of Conventional Instruction vs. Mastery Learning

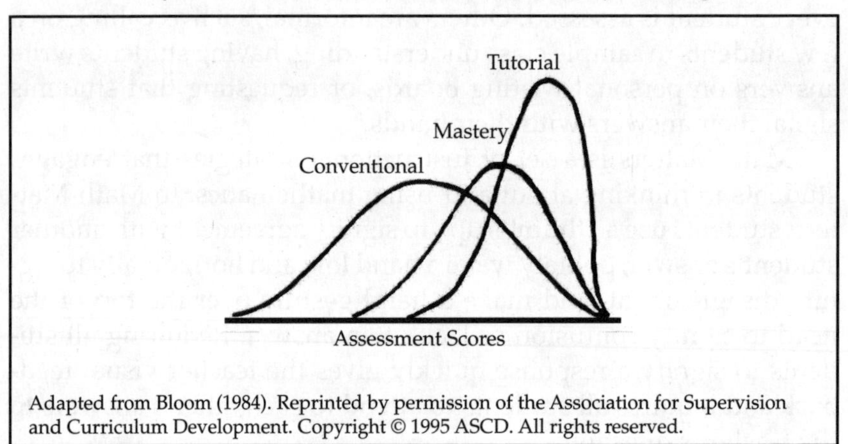

Adapted from Bloom (1984). Reprinted by permission of the Association for Supervision and Curriculum Development.

Characteristics of Good Assessment

A good assessment measures content standards that all students had equal opportunity to learn, yields accurate results for all students, and is credible and meaningful to adults and students. It can be administered and results quickly summarized to inform instructional program decisions several times a year.

Characteristics of good assessment of student achievement of content standards are related to high standards for the assessment instrument and the scoring of student responses. How well students are prepared for the assessment has an impact on the quality of the assessment because the assessment should measure what students had the opportunity to learn. A further extension of a judgment about the "goodness" of an assessment is the degree to which teachers regard the assessment as worthwhile and have the time and skills to use the results to improve instruction. For example, a teacher who relies on information from running records to plan corrective instruction is more likely to judge running records as "good" than is a teacher who is directed to administer running records but does nothing with the results.

Criteria of a High Quality Instrument

Traditionally, there have been two major criteria for judging the quality of an assessment—validity and reliability. *Content validity* is the degree to which an assessment measures the content curriculum that it purports to measure. Typically, a panel of "content experts" compares the content of the test items to the curriculum that the test designer says it measures to determine the degree of alignment. Sometimes alignment between performance in instruction (e.g., learning activities to practice performance) and performance in assessment are considered. School districts can and should review locally developed tests for content validity.

Reliability is concerned with how consistent a student's score is in the hypothetical situation of retaking the test under the same conditions. The *reliability of multi-item tests* (e.g., multiple-choice) is investigated using complex statistical methods. A school district should have a qualified measurement expert determine the reliability statistic for a locally developed multi-item test.

NRTs and any state's multiple-choice test are not perfect—any student's score can be expected to vary within a certain range of points due to "measurement error." Rogosa (1999) chose the SAT-9 to show the error of measurement in a test developed by a national test publisher. As an example of one test and grade level, there is about a 50-50 chance that two students with "identical real achievement" at the 45th percentile obtain scores more than 10 percentile points apart (one below the 40th percentile and the other above the 50th percentile). As proven during the 2000 presidential election, a machine's ability to count vote markings can be flawed and unreliable.

Reliability for a performance assessment is examined differently than it is for multi-item tests—the quality or level of correctness of students' responses on performance assessment tasks is judged by people (computer programs are being developed). For "high stakes" performance assessments, two highly-trained persons might rate each student's response, and a third person (the "chief reader") might resolve any discrepancy between the two "primary" judges. Consistency across raters is the measure of reliability for performance assessments. *Interrater agreement* is the percentage of agreement ratings between raters. Agreement might be set at "giving the exact same rating" or "being within one point or performance level of discrepancy." Usually, a minimum of 75 or 80 percent agreement is considered sufficient reliability for a performance assessment.

With the advent of performance assessments, Herman, Aschbacher, and Winters (1992, p. 10-11) proposed an expansion of the criteria for judging tests "to hold assessments to high standards." Their book, *A Practical Guide to Alternative Assessment*, is an excellent resource to guide districts in developing high quality performance assessments. Figure 3.2 is a summary of their eight criteria. Figure 3.3 presents five criteria proposed by Carr (1999) as a modification to the Herman et al model for a local school district to judge the quality of its assessments, with a special emphasis on equity for all students. A high quality assessment is valid, consistent, equitable, credible, and meaningful.

A high quality standards-based assessment is *valid*—it clearly measures one or more content standards. It is *consistent*—a student receives the same performance level rating by any rater with the help of a clear, specific scoring guide and models of student work. It is *credible*—teachers and students believe it is a fair assessment of the standards. It is *meaningful*—assessment results give teachers and students valuable feedback. Teachers' efforts to prepare students for and administer the assessment and students' motivation to try their best are influenced by participant's perceptions of the assessment's credibility and meaningfulness. The time and money invested in assessment should at least equal the usefulness of the results. On a high quality local assessment, teachers receive results quickly and can then make adjustments and reteach in a different way for those students having difficulties before moving on to the next topic.

A high quality standards-based assessment provides Tier 1 information, not just a raw score such as number of items correct. It should also provide rich, detailed information about each response that teachers can use to plan specific strategies to correct misunderstandings or give more practice to increase fluency. The same assessment yields Tier 2 results, more global performance level data that can be used to make global instructional program decisions.

FIGURE 3.2

Eight Criteria for a High Quality Assessment

Consequences	Does it foster good instruction or narrowly constrict the curriculum or adversely affect disadvantaged students?
Fairness	Have all students had equal opportunity to learn what is assessed and does it avoid favoring certain groups of students?
Transfer and Generalizability	Are results reliable across raters and support inferences about general capability in the content area?
Cognitive Complexity	Does it really require the student to use complex thinking and problem solving, or does it only appear "on the surface" to do so?
Content Quality	Does it measure concepts and skills important enough to be worth the time to assess and analyze the results?
Content Coverage	Does it measure the curriculum appropriately?
Meaningfulness	Do students find the assessment tasks worthwhile so they try their best and feedback contributes to their learning?
Cost and Efficiency	Is the information about students worth the cost in time and money?

(Herman, Aschbacher, and Winters, 1992)

FIGURE 3.3

Five Criteria for a High Quality Assessment

Validity	The content the assessment measures and how it is measured is aligned with what and how students were taught.
Consistency	A student's score accurately reflects the student's true achievement level. The score remains the same regardless of who rates the performance or if the assessment was repeated (same conditions).
Equity	All students' scores accurately reflect their true achievement levels. The assessment is fair for all students and allows each student equal opportunity to show what he or she has learned. Flexible accommodations in test administration and alternative instruments are intended to yield fair and accurate test scores for all students. Equity in assessment assumes there is concomitant equity in instruction.
Credibility	The degree to which a teacher believes that the test is accurate may influence the teacher's efforts to prepare students and administer the test in a way that elicits students' efforts to try their best. The degree to which a student believes the test is accurate influences the student's effort.
Meaningfulness	The degree to which a teacher perceives the assessment as worthwhile influences the teacher's effort to prepare students and administer the test in a way that elicits students' best effort. The degree to which a student perceives the assessment as worthwhile influences the student's effort. Meaningfulness of an assessment also is related to its cost to administer, score, and report as well as its impact on decisions about students or an educational system.

(Carr, 1992)

Equity in Instruction and Assessment

Equity in instruction and assessment is an interrelated concept. All students must have equal opportunity to learn if the assessment is to be considered fair and accurate in reporting student learning. Equity in learning does not mean all students learn the same one way. Students have diverse strengths, weaknesses, and interests in their learning, and teachers must continually explore more ways to reach and teach a diverse population of students. Students who need extra support to learn core content standards have equity in instruction when they receive extra instructional services to meet their needs.

If it holds true that equity in instruction means diversity of opportunity for equal access to the curriculum, then it also is true that equity in assessment means diversity of opportunity for students to show what they know and can do. Many practitioners learn in "Assessment 101" that standardization of an assessment, that is, administering and scoring a test under the same conditions for all students, is important. But what if as a test is standardized for a diverse population of students, the more unfair and inaccurate the test scores become for many students?

The primary purpose of assessment is to accurately measure what a student knows and can do. To this end, educators should seek and use whatever accommodations for administering the test or alternative ways of measuring the student lead to the greatest accuracy for all students. Equity in instruction and assessment means all students are expected to learn the same content standards to the same level of proficient performance, but the means to learning and assessment are designed to vary to meet diverse needs.

Time to Assess and Use Results

To allow sufficient time to assess students frequently and in different ways, teachers must balance time to instruct, with time to reflect on results, both of which are needed by individual teachers in order to carefully plan lessons and by the team of teachers in order to plan program improvement.

> It doesn't make a lot of sense to continue to assess students when we are not given the time to modify our methodology. Without ample time to reflect and change, aren't we simply assessing either old practices or underfunded, undervalued, half-hearted attempts at educational change? . . . Some studies indicate that teachers need 40 or

> more hours of retraining to change the way they teach in one subject. (Angaran, 1999)

The School BUS approach starts with one or a few assessments to measure the quintessential academic content standard that is the target of school improvement and accountability. Using the results of one good assessment administered several times a year can lead to improvement in teaching and learning, whereas not having time to use the results from many assessments leads nowhere.

Running records and similar individually administered assessments can take a great deal of time, especially in the beginning as teachers increase efficiency and establish students' performance levels. Often teachers have a good sense of "about where a student is performing." A suggestion for the first assessment is to start a little lower and work up to the student's highest achievement level. A common practice with running records is to start at the beginning of the school year and frequently reassess at least the lower achieving students. The assessment results for all students from the end of the (quarter) grading period are used in the School BUS for team decisions about the school's instructional program.

An advantage of running records and reading inventories is that information can be gained from decoding miscues as well as from responses to comprehension questions. Practice giving, scoring, and using an individually administered assessment gradually decrease the time factor. Classroom management is also an important factor. The teacher who regularly has students engage in learning activities for 20-minute intervals without the need for direct supervision finds that running records and similarly individually administered assessments are "manageable."

An oral reading fluency assessment is an alternative that can be administered more quickly than a running record, is correlated to reading comprehension, and is a good predictor of achievement on standardized tests (Davidson and Myhre, 2000). This test measures the number of words a student correctly reads in one minute from a passage with content and difficulty levels comparable to that used in class. The advantage of speed is offset by the disadvantage that the assessment does not provide direct information about a student's decoding and comprehension skills.

Assessment in Time

Assessments given only at the end of the year produce data ill-timed to refine instruction and accelerate learning. As mentioned in an earlier section, a characteristic of improving schools is frequent use of student assessment results to make program improvement decisions (Joyce, Wolf, and Calhoun, 1994). Schools should select assessments that can be administered at critical times during the school year. Frequent assessments provide teachers with feedback to inform decisions about corrective instruction and provide school teams with periodic schoolwide results to inform decisions about program improvement. The end of each report card grading period might be the best time to administer assessments, which can then serve the dual purpose of student grading and school program accountability.

The time between test administration, scoring, and feedback should be short. When there is a long delay, instruction usually moves on to other topics, and the test results are not used for corrective instruction for students below proficiency. Assessment time can be reduced later in the year by not reassessing students once they reach the Advanced performance level.

Who Administers the Assessment

The classroom teacher is expected to administer the assessment to ensure the person responsible for instruction directly observes and judges student responses and uses this assessment knowledge to plan instruction. For individually administered assessments, we suggest that the classroom teacher always assess at least the lower-achieving students who will need that teacher's professional corrective instruction. Other trained adults might aid the classroom teacher by assisting the high achieving students. An exception might be a school in which a specialist administers the individualized assessment and teachers review the results to plan instruction, provided that classroom teachers are trained in the assessment analysis process.

To use assessment results for lesson planning, a teacher must possess a range of instructional strategies from which to select what will be best for groups of students. For the best staff development, methods of instruction, the use of assessment to analyze students' learning needs, and material selection are integrated with the appropriate instructional strategies. Training teachers to score and use the information from district standards-based assessments sharpens their ability to score and use information from their own classroom assessments.

Scoring Consistency

Consistency among teachers in rating student performance on performance assessments can be achieved in several ways. Formal staff development and ongoing informal discussions among teachers can build a common vision of expected student achievement. A variety of scoring methods for performance assessments maintains and verifies scoring consistency.

Assessment Training

Formal professional development in assessment administration strengthens consistency during scoring sessions. Building consensus about student work during informal conversations about instruction prior to actual scoring sessions reduces the need for multiple ratings to resolve discrepancies. Ongoing professional development that integrates instruction with assessment is the best way to build consistency among teachers. When districts sponsor opportunities for teachers from different schools to discuss student work in relation to instruction and assessment, they can help build consistency across schools, especially when schools have different student populations.

Teachers are more likely to score student work consistently if they have equivalent expectations about student competency levels and use the same scoring guides and models of student work. Opportunities to review student work and agree on performance judgments should precede or be a part of formal training during a scoring session.

Consistency of a Single Teacher

Fatigue can affect a rater during a long scoring session. Consider a continuous content standard, that is, one taught throughout the school year. The expectation that students should improve over time may influence a teacher to rate student work higher at the end of the year than at the beginning. The reverse—being too lenient in rating student work at the beginning of the year—might occur. Measurement experts describe conditions where ratings tend to gradually increase or decrease as "drift" from "true achievement ratings" to "biased ratings." Figure 3.4 presents some ways a teacher can check for or avoid drift when rating her students' performance assessments.

An added advantage to involving students in using scoring guides and judging their own performance is that their understanding of expectations deepens and leads to powerful, accelerated learning. Instead of simply wondering what grade they received, students learn what they need to do to improve (McTighe, 1996/97). More often than not, students' ratings are accurate.

FIGURE 3.4

Avoiding Biased Rating for an Individual Teacher

Method	Description
Student Anonymity	Students write their names on the back of the test paper to minimize the chance that knowing the student might bias the rating.
Check at the End	After the last student paper is rated, the teacher rescores the first few to check for consistency. If an inconsistency is noted, the teacher rescores where drift was likely to have occurred.
Check During	The teacher writes the score on the back of the first ten or so papers and randomly intersperses them within the rest of the batch. Rescoring these pre-scored papers provides a check for drift.
Check by Other Teacher	A teacher score all papers and then ask a colleague to score the first five and last five papers (without seeing the initial scores). If there is more disagreements in the first or last five papers, it might be a case of drift and papers in that area need rescoring.
Check with Student Ratings	Students rate their own or peers' responses. Then the teacher rates their work and compares to those of the students.

Consistency Across Teachers and Schools

Some means of maintaining and verifying consistency across raters (i.e., teachers) needs to be in place when student results are grouped and compared across teachers and schools. If teachers received the same training in how to rate student work on performance assessments, it cannot be assumed that they will actually rate student work consistently either as an individual (see the previous section) or when compared to other teachers. Consistency is crucial for high stakes assessment and accountability. To increase confidence that scoring is consistent and accurate across teachers, some form of cross-group analysis and report is necessary.

Cross-group scoring increases scoring time and requires formal scoring sessions. Deploying a small panel of highly trained raters to score all students in a school yields high consistency, but removes involvement of all classroom teachers. When all teachers are not involved in the scoring process, ownership of the results can weaken, and teachers lose an opportunity to learn from the process of judging student work. Double scoring with resolution for all students, though more costly and time-consuming, provides the best verification of consistency across readers. When the cost of such double scoring of every student's paper is prohibitive, there are options.

Eleven of these options for cross-group scoring are presented below, ranging from most (1) to least (11) intensive. Advantages and disadvantages are inherent in each method. A district might begin an assessment program at a relatively intensive level and then relax to a less intensive option as teacher experience and consistency is established. The scoring option should fit the consequences of the findings—the higher the stakes in making decisions about students or schools, the more intensive the method of selected scoring should be.

1. *Double Scoring with Third Judge*. Random pairs of teachers in a group rate papers. No reader sees scores from any previous rater. A third reader rates papers with discrepant ratings. In formal, high stakes scoring situations, the third readers have particular expertise and specialized duties as "chief reader."
2. *Double Scoring, Immediate Resolution*. Random pairs of teachers separately rate each paper. After the second reader assigns a score, he or she sees the first reader's score. Any discrepancies are resolved by the two readers or, if necessary, by a third person.
3. *Double Scoring, Average Score*. Random pairs of teachers in a group rate each paper with no reader seeing any previous scores. The two scores are averaged to compute a final score.
4. *Double Scoring by Students' Teacher and Other Teachers*. Each teacher rates her own students' papers, which are then given to a second teacher for rating. Discrepant scores are averaged, or rescored by a third reader.
5. *Sample Double Scoring*. Papers are single scored, and every nth paper (e.g., 5th, 10th) is double scored.
6. *Single Scoring, Interspersed Calibration Papers*. Percent agreement is based on calibration papers (a special set of papers with known scores), which are interspersed in the batch and scored by all readers.
7. *Single Scoring, Sample Double Scoring*. Random papers are selected prior to scoring for double scoring and interspersed in the pile. Percent agreement is based on the set of commonly read papers.

8. *Single Scoring, Followed by Central Group Sample Double Scoring*. Each group single scores papers. A central group double scores a random sample of papers (at least 10 percent) and a third "chief reader" resolves discrepancies. The context might be a central school group for a school assessment, or a central district group for a district assessment.
9. *Single Scoring Own Students with Sample Double Scoring*. Teachers rate papers for their own students. Other teachers score a sample of papers from other teachers.
10. *Single Scoring by Other Teacher*. Teachers do not rate their own students' papers. Consistency is assumed but unknown; bias of "overrating" one's own students is reduced.
11. *Single Scoring*. All teachers in a group score some of the papers from all classes so each teacher only scores some of her own students' papers. Consistency is assumed but unknown; bias of "overrating" one's own students is reduced.

Marzano (2000) investigated ways to increase teacher's scoring consistency while keeping the methodology simple. He found that the simpler the method, the greater the agreement. When teachers were asked to simply give a holistic rating on a four-point scale, there was far greater agreement than when they used some elaborate scheme for scoring each item's response and formulating a total score. Marzano also advocates allowing raters to give midrange scores (e.g., 2.5) when they cannot decide between two performance levels.

Wilson (1992) proposed a *moderation process* that involves statistically adjusting local results when they are significantly different (beyond chance difference). A school district might use the moderation process when a district performance assessment is scored at local school sites and school results are publicly reported. The district trains school staff to use the scoring guide and one method of cross-scoring. A random sample of 10 or, if feasible, 20 percent of the papers are scored by a district panel of "expert readers." A simple statistics procedure, such as chi-square, can be computed to determine if there is a significant difference between ratings for the school and central panel. The easiest, most straightforward adjustment would be to substitute the central panel's results for the school's results when a significant difference is found. (More sophisticated statistical techniques exist, but they are beyond the scope of this book.)

Unwritten Performance Tasks

The eleven options for checking consistency across readers (see previous section) pertain to students' *written responses* to a performance task. But what about constructed projects, orations, and oral reading? There are no definitive answers for assessing consistency across teachers in the case of oral performances, such as oral reading of leveled passages, but some suggestions can be offered.

One suggestion is to randomly videotape some teacher-student interactions and ask each teacher to explain his or her rating at the conclusion. An "expert" person or panel reviews the videotape, rates the student, and provides feedback to the teacher about scoring agreement. Disadvantages to taping assessment observations are that the camera might intimidate students, the microphone must be good quality and close to both teacher and student, and background noise level can interfere. Another option is to have an "expert" visit the classroom to observe a random sample of oral assessments and compare ratings to those of the classroom teacher. Expert visits can be a natural activity in schools with a history of peer coaching, frequent supportive visits by administrators, and collegial conversations about teaching and learning.

The Flag Tag Method

The *Flag Tag method* is a simple, fairly quick procedure used to convert raw scores (e.g., total number correct score) to performance levels. The district panel's professional judgment is used to identify meaningful *cut scores*, the lowest raw score at each performance level. Performance level results are used in the School BUS to make instructional program decisions.

As explained in a previous section of this chapter, a standards-based assessment yields performance level scores. Any type of raw score (e.g., number correct, running record book level, or developmental scale level) can be aligned to or converted to a district's General and Mediating Performance Levels to make the instrument a standards-based assessment. The Flag Tag procedure helps schools to develop cut scores on scoring guides for the specific standards-based assessments of specific standards at specific grade levels.

The School BUS model's purpose is to report results across all grades and subject areas in a school and district using one common set of performance level labels. Mediating Performance Levels (MPLs) bridge meaning and alignment from the district's General Performance Levels (GPLs) to each assessment's scoring guide that pertains to one grade and one subject area or content standard. The scoring guide for a multi-item test might be simply a statement of the raw score ranges assigned to each performance level.

This section describes the Flag Tag method for converting various types of raw assessment scores to district performance levels. Any school district can apply this simple method to its local assessments. The School BUS uses five performance levels but is flexible enough for a district to use any number of levels it chooses.

The name *Flag Tag* comes from the colored film tabs (a type of *Post-It*™ note) that are used to flag important lines or pages in a text. Color coding can be used to mark or comment on certain types of ideas to note the editorial corrections or queries, or to bring action to someone's attention (e.g., read carefully or sign here). The name Flag Tag is meant to signify a simple method derived by Carr from the Bookmark method created by educational researchers at CTB/ McGraw-Hill and used by the NAEP, many states (e.g., The Colorado, Florida, Hawaii, Maryland, and Wisconsin), and local school districts (e.g., Sacramento City Unified School District in California). (Colorado Department of Education's website, www.cde.state.co.us/cdedepcon/asperf, has a thorough explanation.)

While the formal Bookmark method can take one or two days to complete, the Flag Tag procedure for assessments at many grade levels can often be finished in a half-day, which may be all the time a small district can afford to spend on this task. While the Bookmark method requires some sophisticated measurement expertise, the Flag Tag method is simple yet solid enough for school district use and is especially appropriate for small to mid-size districts that do not have assessment experts.

Ready Step A: Establish District Assessment Panel and Parameters

In addition to key district office administrators, panel members should include principals, specialists, and teachers from all or a sample of schools, with representation from each grade level. In short, panel members must know their grade levels and subject areas and have high expectations for student learning, regardless of local student characteristics. Panel members should be aware of what advanced and proficient students "look like" at each grade level and within each subject area in the highest performing schools in the district and state. This vision of the hypothetical advanced and proficient students was created when the district created the GPLs.

Not every assessment will yield an Advanced performance level. If an assessment only measures up to grade level expectations, there can be no Advanced level. An assessment must include items that measure content standards above grade level or allow extended responses that indicate advanced understanding, such as giving a more complex answer than is typically expected (e.g., more in-depth, insightful, comprehensive, or sophisticated). The session facilitator must highlight this point.

Panel members participate in the Flag Tag procedure according to their knowledge of and experience with the actual assessments and grade levels. When it is time to review an assessment's items and set performance levels, the facilitator of a grades K–12 panel, for example, divides the panel into grade span subgroups. The facilitator then leads the whole group in Ready Step A.

The facilitator states the purpose and parameters of the Flag Tag panel session, which is to identify ranges of raw scores on grade level assessments to define performance levels that are aligned with district GPLs and MPLs. School staff will use assessment results from the School BUS process, a system of ongoing, local accountability used for making school improvement decisions. Performance levels should represent year-end grade level expectations, regardless of which period during the year the assessment is given. The panel will also be identifying the scores on scoring guides for actual assessments that maintain alignment with the GPLs and MPLs. If the panel members were not part of the group that set the GPLs and MPLs they must not review and discuss the GPLs and MPLs.

Ready Step B: Rank Order Test Items

Items on a multi-item test can appear in order of difficulty, in random order, or by topic. Items on a performance assessment may or may not have a difficulty order. Some assessments, such as running record book levels, already have a logical, preset order. For tests without a preset difficulty order, items are rank-ordered from easiest to hardest. Items are physically (cut and pasted) arranged in rank order from easiest to hardest. Items of equal difficulty could be indicated by placing them side-by-side or clustering them in a box, for example.

If possible, districts should use test information, either from prior administrations or from the test's publisher, that provides an empirical rank ordering. Empirical data has been found to be much more accurate than "guestimates," even by experienced teachers. When empirical data is unavailable, a small group with expertise in the subject area might rank the items prior to the Flag Tag session. The small group should be composed of people highly experienced with the grade level or grade span being assessed. If item ordering cannot be done prior to the Flag Tag session itself, this should be the panel's first task.

To give items a rank order, the district group should take the following steps. First, individuals draft their own rank orders and place them in a column on a wall chart, one column per individual. The group next compares the columns and discusses differences until they have reached agreement on one common rank ordering.

The Flag Tag panel is then given a booklet that shows the items rank-ordered but gives no additional information about the items, such as empirical statistics about item difficulty. Finally, the items should be numbered by rank order for easy use by the panel.

Step 1: Individual Flag Tagging

Assign each panel member a symbol (a letter or other symbol but not a number, which could be confused with item numbers). Using symbols instead of names provides some level of anonymity when the group reviews and compares individual judgments and makes it easier for panel members to locate themselves on a wall chart. Each person writes his or her assigned symbol on flag tags, and each has a booklet showing items that he or she will rank order of difficulty. Items also appear on a large wall chart (just item numbers or perhaps also the item content).

A panel may choose to start at the Advanced performance level and work downward or start at the Minimal level and work upward. Alternatively, a panel might move from the Proficient to the Advanced level, and then continue downward to work on the Approaching and Partial levels. Because Carr has found this to be a matter of personal preference, he asks the group members which working order they prefer before he leads them through the procedure. In this book, we will work from the bottom up in order to stay true to the School Bottom-Up Simple approach.

The facilitator asks each panel member to examine items of increasing difficulty, starting with the easiest (item #1) and ending with the most difficult item that a typical student at the Minimal level should answer correctly. The facilitator tells members to place a red Flag Tag at the next most difficult item, which will be considered the lowest difficulty item that a typical student at the Partial level should answer correctly. The Flag Tag thus sets the boundary between the Minimal and Partial levels. After all panel members have finished placing their red Flag Tag beside an item in their booklets and indicate that they understand the task, the facilitator asks them to continue the process of placing Flag Tags beside the items that start the levels of Approaching (yellow), Proficient (blue), and Advanced (green).

When all panel members finish placing Flag Tags at the lowest difficulty item at each performance level in their booklets, the facilitator asks them to place Flag Tags (on which their personal symbols are written) next to the corresponding items on the large wall chart. This allows everyone to see initial agreements and disagreements without identifying members by name.

Step 2: Seeking Group Agreement

The facilitator leads a group discussion in which members volunteer to explain their Flag Tag selections without criticizing the choices of others. The facilitator explains how a final set of Flag Tag items will be selected, and makes sure that members are aware of the "Flag Tag rules" (see Step 3 below). At the end of this discussion, which might take about 20 minutes, the facilitator asks members to change the placement of their Flag Tags on the wall chart, if they wish, based on information from the discussion.

Step 3: Setting the Final Flag Tag Items

One of three situations exists at this point: The first is the ideal situation in which all panel members adjust their Flag Tags so that all are in perfect agreement at each performance level. In the second situation, only a few members are in slight disagreement with the majority. The facilitator asks if these discordant members "can live with" the majority's opinion (one way of seeking group agreement or consensus) and reminds members that the final selections are only the "best guess." "Live administration" of the real assessment in the district and experience using the results will either justify the choices or suggest adjustments.

In the third situation, total agreement cannot be reached, significant disagreements remain about which item should be the Flag Tag item at one or more performance levels. In this case, the facilitator selects the middle item in the "disagreement range" of flagged items. If two items share the middle the item closest to the most flags is selected.

Measurement error exists in any assessment, as mentioned in an earlier section. Acknowledging "to err is human" reminds teachers that it is preferable to err in favor of the students by adjusting the Flag Tags down one or two items. For a test with roughly 50 items, adjust downward by one item. For a test with roughly 100 items, adjust by two items. For a test with roughly ten or fewer performance items, the panel might have enough confidence in their selections to make no adjustment downward, since any adjustment would be quite significant.

Suppose a test has 50 items and the panel flags the ninth item as being the one a student at the Partial level should answer correctly and a student at the Minimal level should miss. To "correct for measurement error," an adjustment is made by moving the tag to the next easier item, the eighth item. Now a student can reach the Partial level by getting eight items correct rather than nine.

The cut score, that is, the critical total scores at each performance level, equals the difficulty rank number of the Flag Tag item minus one or two points for measurement error when each item is scored "0" for wrong or missing and "1" for correct. The cut scores do not equal the item ranks when different items have different numbers of points possible. For example, five items on a math test might require more extensive answers, such as showing steps to or giving a rationale for the solution, and be scored "2" for completely correct, "1" for partially correct, and "0" for completely wrong or missing.

Step 4: Repeat for Each Assessment in the Grade Span

At this point, the panel or panel subgroup has completed the Flag Tags for one assessment at one grade level. The group repeats the process for the next grade level in the grade span.

The Flag Tags may form a pattern across grades for assessments that cover several grade levels (e.g., running records that cover book difficulty levels from grade 1–3 or developmental scales with levels spanning the primary grades). This pattern is illustrated in Figure 3.5 and explained further in an example given in the Advanced School Model below.

Step 5: Application to the Real Assessment

One reason the rank-ordered items were assigned item numbers (e.g., 1 = easiest item, 50 = most difficult item on a 50-item test) is that the nth item selected at each performance level is also the number of items a student must answer correctly to be assigned to that level. On the real assessment, the student need not get the specific items from easiest upward all correct—it is the total number of items answered correctly that matters.

Students are expected to answer all items correctly up to a difficulty level above their achievement and then answer all higher items incorrectly. But in reality, people just do not perform as expected. They tend to get most easy items correct and to miss items above their difficulty level, but sometimes they miss some easier items and correctly answer some harder items. One student may get the easiest eight items correct and all higher difficulty items wrong and achieve at the Partial level, using the 50-item example above. Another student may answer only six of the easiest items correctly, but answer two of the more difficult items correctly. That student would also receive a total score of eight and achieve just at the Partial level.

Measurement experts use the term *cut scores* to refer to the minimum number of items a student must answer correctly at each of the performance levels. After gaining experience using the assessment and its results for about a year, the district panel can take the school's advice and decide to maintain the Flag Tags (cut scores) placement or make adjustments.

Figure 3.5 shows several examples of score ranges and cut scores (lowest score in a score range) for a variety of reading assessments at several grade levels. All assessments are linked to district Mediating Performance Levels (MPLs) to maintain alignment across assessments. The MPLs are aligned with the district General Performance Levels (GPLs). At the Minimal level, a student cannot function in grade level textbooks and literature or at grade level expectations without intensive support by the teacher. The student at the Partial level may be able to function in grade level texts, albeit with a struggle and some moderate assistance by the teacher or peer group.

Notice how the score ranges for running records for grades 1–3 form a pattern. It is not necessary to force a pattern, but it may happen and is a plus when it does. In some examples, notation such as "1.1, 1.2" is used to represent first semester (beginning) first grade and second semester (ending) first grade. Many reading inventory instruments place students at the Independent, Instructional, or Frustration reading level. Notice that the Proficient level at first grade is set at the "Independent grade 1.2 assessment level." The wording of district content standards implies that the student can read grade level material independently (without teacher assistance); therefore, a student who is performing at the Independent reading level on year-end grade level material is also performing at the Proficient level.

FIGURE 3.5

Examples of Scoring Guides Aligned to MPLs for Reading Assessments

Performance Levels	Running Record			Accelerated Reader
	Grade 1	Grade 2	Grade 3	Grade 6
Advanced	17+	22+	27+	8.0+
Proficient	12-16	19-21	24-26	7.0-7.9
Approaching	10-11	17-18	22-23	6.0-6.9
Partial	5-9	12-16	17-21	5.0-5.9
Minimal	0-4	0-11	0-16	1.0-4.9

General Performance Levels	Grades K-2	Grades 3-8	Grades 9-12
	Mediating Performance Levels (MPLs)		
Advanced	Above	Above	Above
Proficient	At Grade	At Grade	At Grade
Approaching	Almost	1/2 Yr. Below	1 Yr. Below
Partial	1/2 Yr. Below	1 Yr. Below	2 Yrs. Below
Minimal	1+ Yr. Below	2+ Yrs. Below	3+Yrs. Below

Performance Levels	Kindergarten	Grade 1	Grades 2
	Concepts About Print	Reading Inventory	
Advanced	18-24	Independent Grade 2	Independent Grade 3
Proficient	15-17	Independent Grade 1.2	Independent Grade 2.2
Approaching	9-14	Instructional Grade 1.2	Instructional Grade 2.2
Partial	5-8	Instructional Primer	Instructional Grade 2.1
Minimal	0-4	Preprimer/Below	Instructional Grade 1/Below

Basic School BUS Model

Countryside USD, a small rural district with three schools, decided to use the School BUS and concentrate on improving teaching and learning for one quintessential standard of reading comprehension (see chapter 2). The district identified that area for improvement based on state test results. The district accountability committee adopted the GPLs and MPLs given in examples at the School BUS workshop they attended (Figures 2.6 and 2.9, respectively). At that time, the district had not established any districtwide assessments, but some or all teachers at a grade level were already using the same assessment.

Session to Select Assessments

The committee planned to devote one hour of its August staff development day (prior to the start of the school year) for school staff to meet in grade level teams. Teams working at tables in the same room were arranged by grade spans (K–3, 4–5, English 6–8 and 9–12). Each grade level team's task was to identify an assessment of reading comprehension and to later regroup as a grade span team to examine selections to see if they could agree to the same assessment, where appropriate.

The kindergarten team selected Marie Clay's *Concepts About Print* (CAP) which all teachers had been using for a few years. CAP does not actually measure reading comprehension but promotes the awareness about print materials that is a precursor to reading. The teachers know that, for kindergarten students, the ability to orally retell and answer simple factual and prediction questions about a story they have been reading is a direct measure of reading comprehension, however, they wanted extended time to explore other possible assessment instruments. Teachers thought they would be able to select an instrument for trial use within a few months, that they could fully implement later that year or starting the next year.

Many teachers in grades 1–3 were already using running records, and all teachers were using "trade books" leveled by difficulty in accordance with a national reading organization's standards. To keep a running record, a teacher listens to a student read a short book at a specific difficulty level and uses special symbols to record miscues. After finding the highest level book the student can read with at least 90 percent accuracy, the teacher asks comprehension questions that the student must answer adequately. All teachers agreed to use a simplified running record in which miscues would be recorded as tick marks because some teachers had not yet had miscue analysis training. Trained teachers were free to use miscue recording and analysis. Most leveled books already included comprehension questions (e.g., facts, event order, main idea, and inferences) and the teachers agreed to create sets of questions for the remaining books that did not.

All teachers at grades 4–5 were using some form of reading inventory. They agreed to use a common instrument that contained short text passages leveled by grades and was followed by four types of comprehension questions (i.e., word meaning, facts, inferences and conclusions, and main idea and generalization).

English teachers at the middle school (grades 6–8) were already using the computer-based Accelerated Reader test program, but realized its comprehension questions did not require highly critical thinking. The teachers agreed to create one question per grade level assessment that required higher level thinking and an extended student response. Later, they will consider adding results from the curriculum textbook that asked tough, open-ended comprehension questions.

High school English teachers (grades 9–12) were using language arts textbook assessments that contained a good mix of types of comprehension questions. They identified particular assessments for each quarter of the year (grading period). Students earned credits and progressed to the next course based on achievement; otherwise, they repeated the course the next semester or year or elected to attend summer school to complete the coursework at the expected level of achievement. (In reality, some students may be accelerated to AP or other higher courses, but this fact is ignored here to keep the example simple and to focus on the majority of students.)

Flag Tag Session to Set Cut Scores

The accountability committee added teachers and reading specialists so that all grade levels at elementary and all grade spans at secondary were represented by at least a few persons. They convened later in August as the "Flag Tag panel." Their task was to set cut scores on each assessment and all scoring guides linked to the district's MPLs for reading. Figure 3.6 presents each assessments' cut scores, that is, the lowest score at each performance level.

FIGURE 3.6

Reading Assessments for the Basic School Model

Assessment	CAP	Running Record			Reading Inventory
Grade	K	1	2	3	4-5
Advanced	18+	17+	22+	27+	Independent Above Grade
Proficient	15	12	19	24	Independent at Grade
Approaching	9	10	17	22	Instructional at Grade
Partial	5	5	12	17	Instructional 1 Yr Below
Minimal	0	0	0	0	Instructional 2+ Yr Below

Assessment	Accelerated Reader			Textbook Instruments (10 Items)
Grade	6	7	8	9-12
Advanced	8.0	9.0	10.0	10/10 At Grade + Advanced Responses
Proficient	7.0	8.0	9.0	90% at Grade
Approaching	6.0	7.0	8.0	9/10 1 Yr. Below or 7/10 at Grade
Partial	5.0	6.0	7.0	9/10 2 Yr. Below or 5/10 at Grade
Minimal	1.0	1.0	1.0	9/10 3+ Yr. Below or < 5/10 at Grade

The total score for CAP in kindergarten was the simple sum of items answered correctly out of a possible 24 items of increasing difficulty that measure book awareness (e.g., front/back), letters, words, sentences, and punctuation. CAP provides instructions for administration and a guide for scoring.

The grades 1–3 subgroup set cut scores for running records by starting with the book levels suggested as year-end grade level expectations by the national organization of Reading Recovery. These grade level expectations became the cut scores at the Proficient level in grades 1–3. One subgroup member suggested that students at the Advanced level should be able to give "fairly in-depth" answers to at least three of the four comprehension questions, and the other members quickly agreed. The subgroup used the Flag Tag method to individually identify cut scores at the Approaching and Partial levels, posted their Flag Tags on the wall chart, and reached agreement on one set of cut scores. They did not subtract one level for measurement error because of the narrow range of scores at a grade level and because they had confidence that their cut scores were in accordance with research by the national organization as well as with their own past practice with the assessment. Cut scores are shown in Figure 3.6.

The grades 1–3 subgroup created scoring guides for teachers that gave the cut scores and defined parameters for acceptable and unacceptable answers. For example, the in-depth answers for the Advanced level were illustrated with a few examples and guidelines were set that required students at other levels to correctly answer at least 3 ½ items (i.e., partially miss one question or need assistance/ prompting but correctly answer the others without assistance).

The grades 4–5 subgroup used the Flag Tag process to examine the types of "final scores" derived from the reading inventory, that is, independent, instructional, and frustration levels for each grade level. They agreed that the MPLs looked realistic and needed no adjustments at that time. Because the reading inventory could not easily be rank ordered by difficulty, the subgroup decided to individually identify a "final score" to be the cut at each performance level, place their selections on the large wall chart, and then reach agreement. There were no disagreements, largely because the type of scores from the reading inventory so closely resembled the MPLs. Finally, the subgroup created a scoring guide for teachers to use as a guideline for judging about acceptable and unacceptable responses and knowing how much prompting is permissible.

The grades 6–8 subgroup started by discussing the types and

meaning of scores yielded by the Accelerated Reader test program. Grade equivalent scores were discarded as an option because group members had experienced problems with this type of score and knew it was more norm-referenced. They agreed on a criterion-referenced score that referred to a student's instructional grade level and reflected the text difficulty typical for that level of instruction. They also agreed that a score one level higher appeared to represent a student's independent reading level. A score of 7.0 for a sixth grader would classify that student as Proficient, an independent reader of sixth grade material.

This discussion about Accelerated Reader scores enabled the group to use a short version of the Flag Tag process to quickly agree on the cut scores for two reasons. First, the scores for the Accelerated Reader instrument were straightforward. Second, because they had already agreed on the cut scores for Advanced and Proficient as a whole group, the Flag Tag process was used to set the levels below Proficient individually and then as a whole group. After setting cut scores for sixth grade, seventh and eighth grade scores became automatic (see Figure 3.6). No correction for measurement error was applied since the score range was narrow and appeared to have adequate reliability. They created a scoring guide along with an additional critical thinking question with guidelines for an acceptable extended answer to "beef up the assessment" for each grade level.

High school English teachers used the Flag Tag process in its entirety to set cut scores on the textbook assessments. Ten items per assessment required open-ended short responses. The teachers rank ordered the items in each assessment and found three layers of difficulty. Two items were difficult and required deep critical thinking, four items were moderately difficult, and four items were fairly easy (e.g., required one word or a few words about facts) for the typical Proficient student at that grade level.

The group individually set Flag Tags in their booklets for the first quarter assessment, entered the Flag Tags on the wall chart, and then discussed and resolved disagreements. They decided that it was more natural to first set the Flag Tag for the Proficient student, then the Advanced, and then to proceed to lower performance levels (the third option mentioned in the earlier section describing the Flag Tag method). They set the cut score for Proficient at correctly answering nine out of the ten items. While this could be shown as 90% correct, they wanted to avoid the appearance of setting arbitrary cut points that some teachers traditionally use in grading; instead, they defined cut scores as exact numbers of items.

The Advanced student must correctly answer all items and provide more extended, or more advanced, responses for the two items that involved longer responses and deep critical thinking. The cut scores for the lower levels depended on whether the student was enrolled in a grade level English course. If enrolled in a grade level course, the student must get seven items correct to be Approaching or five items to be Partial. If enrolled in a lower grade level course, then nine out of ten items correct for that course material became the cut score, as shown in Figure 3.6. These two scores covered the majority of students, but panel members recognized that other scoring possibilities existed for students enrolled in an English course below their grade level (e.g., seven out of ten items for lower grade level material). The group decided to keep the general "cut score chart" simple and include a full set of options in the scoring guide to make it easy for a teacher to reference the situation pertaining to a particular group of students. The group then proceeded to the assessments selected for the other quarters and found that the cut scores and scoring guides applied universally: The one set fit all assessments.

Countryside USD had successfully developed local standards-based assessments that measured (mainly) the quintessential content standard of reading comprehension and yielded performance levels aligned to district GPLs and MPLs. Since the district did not have a student database for assessment data yet, teachers were directed to reserve two columns each quarter in their grade books for the quarterly standards-based assessment data. The raw score (e.g., running record book level, number of items correct) was to be entered in one column, and the converted performance level entered in the other column. This record-keeping procedure would simplify the process of summarizing data and using the results (see chapter 6).

Advanced School BUS Model

In the Advanced School BUS Model presented in chapter 2, Cityscape USD had established a five-level developmental scale for kindergarten for a variety of subject areas or content standards, for example, reading comprehension was measured by retelling a story read aloud to the student. Cityscape used the same reading assessments that Countryside used at other grade levels. In addition, Cityscape used districtwide writing and mathematics assessments with a variety of types of raw scores.

The story of how the Cityscape accountability committee established cut scores and scoring guides for reading was very similar to that described above for Countryside. Because the kindergarten five-point developmental scale corresponded one-to-one with the five performance levels, the only additional task was to report scores using the district's performance level labels (e.g., Advanced, Proficient, etc.).

The district's writing and mathematics assessments were described in chapter 2 as having five levels. Cityscape used a four-point scale (scoring guide or rubric) on the writing assessment in grades 1–3 and a six-point scale in grades 4–12. The math tests used multi-item formats. Because dissimilar score formats needed to be transformed to align with the district's performance levels (GPLs and MPLs), these assessments had to become standards-based and uniform with reading assessments.

Modify Existing Performance Assessments to GPLs and MPLs

First, we consider how the district modified its existing four and six performance level scoring guides for writing samples to match the five levels in the district GPLs and MPLs. The following example shows how to convert various performance assessment scores into a standards-based assessment model in which one set of district performance levels fits all assessments in the district. Teachers can continue to use the "old" levels in their classrooms, but schools and districts must use the one set of district levels to report results and accountability in the School BUS model.

The accountability committee reviewed and discussed the results of the four and six performance levels on the writing assessments. They agreed that the assessment for grades 1–3 could be converted to five performance levels by splitting the second lowest level, Partial, into two levels, Approaching and Partial (see Figure 3.7). The committee reviewed the descriptors in the existing scoring guides in relation to the GPLs and writing MPLs and determined that the existing Partial level contained too wide a range of achievement. They agreed that teachers would use the five-level model for the School BUS accountability process, but found the model too complex for the students to use in self and peer assessment. The "classroom" three-level scoring guide was maintained for student use. The group reviewed the upper grade results and use of results, especially for program decisions in the School BUS model. The two levels above Proficient were not useful because teachers had difficulty reaching adequate consistency in these two ratings; therefore, the Superior and Exceptional levels were combined to form the Advanced level (see Figure 3.7).

Figure 3.7

Modify Existing Performance Assessments to GPLs and MPLs

4 Performance Levels	5 Level GPLs & MPLs	6 Performance Levels
Advanced	**Advanced** ←	Exceptional Superior
Proficient	**Proficient**	Proficient
Partial ←	**Approaching** **Partial**	Approaching Partial
Minimal	**Minimal**	Minimal

Convert Scores on Multi-Item Tests to Performance Levels

In this section, Cityscape's math tests will be used to model how to use the Flag Tag method to convert total test scores on a multi-item test into district performance levels so that the tests become standards-based assessments. Activity 3 in the staff development activities section gives very simple hands-on practice in setting one cut score for an eight-item math test. Cityscape schools will immediately use the reading and writing assessment results in the School BUS to measure their progress toward improving their reading and writing programs, with a special emphasis on the reading comprehension quintessential standard. In a year or two, the district might consider adding math results into the School BUS accountability process as schools shift the major focus for staff development from language arts to math.

The example in chapter 2 stated that the math assessments were administered across the district in the prior year. For a mid-sized district, this produced empirical (real) data about item difficulty for roughly 2,000 students per grade level. Item difficulties were reported at p-values, the proportion of students answering the item correctly (technically "the probability"). More sophisticated Item Response Theory (IRT) measures exist, but this statistic will suffice for districts with limited technical expertise. Remember that a proportion ranges from 0.0 to 1.0; a proportion equals a percent when it is multiplied by 100, for example, .5 x 100 = 50%. The district's assessment administrator arranged the math test items into a booklet in rank order of their item difficulty from easiest to most difficult, without showing the actual p-values. Thus, the district had empirical data on which to base ranking of items rather than depending on a panel's judgments, which tends to be less accurate.

Cityscape administers a 20-item test in grades 1–2 and 50-item tests at grades 6–8 and in high school algebra and geometry courses. Tests were selected from curriculum textbooks or materials. The Flag Tag panel split into three subgroups for grades 1–2, 6–8, and high school. Each subgroup used the Flag Tag method to individually place Flag Tags in their booklets by color (green = Advanced, blue = Proficient, yellow = Approaching, red = Partial, as described in Step 1 of the Flag Tag Method section). The Flag Tags were placed next to the easiest item in that level to form a border between that level and the next lower level. The group started from the bottom level, the easiest item, and worked upward to Advanced. After a fair amount of discussion, the group arrived at agreement on common Flag Tags.

All subgroups decided to subtract one point for possible measurement error, which yielded the final Flag Tag items. All items on the tests in first and second grades were scored "1" for correct and "0" for wrong or missing. In this simple case, the ranking of the final Flag Tag item equaled the cut score, that is, the total number of correct items a student needed to be classified at each performance level. The cut scores are shown as the lowest score in the score ranges in Figure 3.8 for a 20-item, 20-point test. For better readability and understanding in a scoring guide, a panel may choose to show score ranges rather than just cut scores.

FIGURE 3.8

Example of Cut Scores and Ranges for Two Multi-Item Tests

20 Items, 20 Points	Performance Levels	50 Items, 60 Points
20 + advanced responses	**Advanced**	60 + advanced responses
16-20	**Proficient**	52-60
13-15	**Approaching**	44-51
6-12	**Partial**	12-43
0-5	**Minimal**	0-11

On the 50-item math tests in grades 6–8 and high school, a scoring guide identified items for mixed scoring so that the highest possible score was more than 50 points. Some items with simple answers were scored as "1" correct and "0" wrong/missing, and a few others requiring more lengthy responses (e.g., steps to solution or rationale) were scored as "2" for completely correct, "1" for partially correct, and "0" for wrong or missing. The total number of points, from the easiest item up through the final Flag Tag item, became the cut score for that performance level. Figure 3.7 shows the results for a 50-item, 60-point test.

The panel created scoring guides stating that to reach the Advanced level, a student must provide in-depth, "advanced" explanations of solutions or rationales for the items worth two points and that prompted an extended answer. Because no items were of a difficulty above grade level difficulty, a perfect score without advanced explanations could not be considered performance at the Advanced level. As described at the beginning of the Flag Tag Method section, for a student to perform at the Advanced level, an assessment must be constructed to measure student achievement above grade level expectations. Either the assessment must have items measuring above grade level standards or it must at least require a depth of response greater than is typically expected for that grade level.

Staff Development Activities

Activity 1: Where is our district?

This activity is appropriate for the district assessment panel but can also be used at school sites to solidify understanding about the need for local assessments that support school instructional program improvement. The group might discuss each topic in turn, or topics might be assigned to "table groups" who then report to the whole group and entertain whole group comments.

Topic A: What Do We Have?

- What assessments exist in the district that are considered valid, reliable, equitable, credible, and meaningful?
- Does the district have a variety of types of assessment that meet the needs of a diverse student population?
- Do local assessments provide results when important decisions need to be made
    - for pupil promotion/retention early and final identi fication?
    - for instructional program improvement decisions at key points in the year?

Topic B: Who Decides What When?

- Do individual teachers and teams make decisions informed by student results?
- What types of "results-driven" decisions are made individually and by teams?
- When are decisions made? Are results available when decisions should be made?

Topic C: Do We See the Forest or Just Too Many Trees?

- Is there a common understanding of the proficient reader (or writer or mathematician)?
- Does staff know which students are proficient on grade level standards?
- Can teachers across grade levels and subject areas communicate about proficient students and schoolwide results regardless of the test?

Carr (1999)

Activity 2: Multiple Measures Are Good Practice

The purpose of this activity is to heighten understanding by staff of the need for multiple, diverse assessments to strengthen accuracy of results. The process of adding different types of summative assessments into a system of multiple measures may take several years. In the beginning, staff can concentrate on one good summative assessment used several times a year for school team decisions combined with formative assessments used by teachers during lessons to make decisions about their instructional strategies.

Multiple-choice tests can be appropriate for broadly measuring curriculum quickly. Performance assessments can be appropriate for deeply measuring the district's quintessential standards or the one standard the school selected for the School BUS accountability process. Test formats can influence how teachers teach; for example, 30-second recognition of one correct answer versus constructing a complex solution to a real world problem with no one correct answer. Good practice matches types of assessment to importance of the content and methods of teaching and learning.

Multiple measures in terms of internal and external assessments can benefit a school and district. Local, internal assessment might be more sensitive, more accurate, and more timely than state external assessments. Schools and districts want to corroborate increases in internal assessment results with increases in external assessment results to be very confident that the instructional program did improve meaningfully (both by how much and in what ways).

A facilitator asks participants to read the section on Multiple Measures and then discuss the question below for "reporting out" to the whole group. Successive groups add new ideas not mentioned by a previous group and entertain comments.

Why are multiple measures important as part of a school and district initiative to improve teaching and learning?

Multiple Measures

The SAT-9, a norm-referenced test (NRT), is a timed, multiple-choice test with rigid administration that measures a "national curriculum" and reports scores as percentiles, reflecting a student's performance to the norm group, not absolute criteria or performance standards. The SAT-9 may not be able to measure all content standards and may or may not be equitable for a diverse population of students, especially English language learners and certain special education students.

A traditional criterion-referenced test (CRT) contains many items yielding a number or percent correct score. This test may be better aligned with some of the district's content standards, but it may not be able to measure standards requiring deep thinking and real world application. The district may or may not allow accommodations in administration or alternative methods for students to show what they know and can do. These CRTs may not be able to measure all content standards and may or may not be equitable for all students.

A district might select a performance assessment, such as a writing task or science project, because it measures a benchmark requiring deep thinking, or it is more authentic and aligned with the curriculum and instruction. The district may or may not allow accommodations in administration or alternative methods for students to show what they know and can do. Generally speaking, a performance assessment may be too time-consuming to measure the broad curriculum. These performance assessments may be best for measuring high priority standards, with administration flexible and alternatives to provide equity to students.

cont.

> Clearly, no one assessment can measure all content standards equitably for all students. All students should be held to the same content standards, measured by the same performance standards, but, just as instruction must be delivered multiple times and ways to meet students' diverse needs, assessment must be done multiple times and ways to meet students' diverse needs and accurately measure true achievement.
>
> Imagine a painter who uses only one shade of green to paint a picture of a landscape. Does the picture accurately represent the true landscape? Obviously not. Using many diverse colors representing the diverse elements in the real landscape renders a truer picture. Likewise, we need diverse assessments to measure different content standards for a diverse population of students to obtain an accurate picture of what each student truly knows and can do. Different students have different interests and communication strengths; we need to allow each student to accurately show what he/she has learned.

Carr (1999)

Activity 3: Practice with Flag Tag Method

The purpose of this activity is to give participants a "hands-on" activity to apply the Flag Tag method of setting cut scores. A fourth grade math test with only eight items is presented to keep the task simple and the activity time short. Only one cut score is to be established to set the boundary between Proficient and Not Proficient.

The facilitator asks participants to quietly set their individual cut score, that is, to set a Flag Tag at the easiest item that a Proficient student should answer correctly. Then small groups discuss their judgments and seek group agreement on one marking, if possible. The facilitator allows about 15 minutes and then calls on groups to report their "agreed-upon" cut score.

The facilitator records the cut scores on a wall chart or transparency for all to see, and then the whole group is asked to comment on the task. The facilitator reinforces that it is NOT the specific items but the total number of items answered correctly on the real test that determines whether a student is scored as Proficient or Not Proficient.

To Be or Not To Be Proficient: Grade 4 Math Test (Activity 3)

- At the bottom of the page are eight math items, numbered 1–8.

- Rank the grade 4 math items in terms of level of difficulty by entering the item number next to the rank in the box below.
- Set the cut score for the Proficient level. A cut score is the lowest score for a performance level. This example has two levels: Proficient and Not Proficient.
- Flag Tag the item for the Proficient level—one item above the most difficult item a Not Proficient student is expected to answer correctly (i.e., the easiest item a Proficient student should answer correctly but a Not Proficient student would get wrong). Flag the item by writing "Proficient" in the rightmost column next to the item. Draw an arrow going up to the most difficult item to signify all the items a Proficient student should answer correctly (and a Not Proficient student get wrong).
- The rank of the Flag Tag item equals the total number of items, the *cut score*, a student must get correct to be classified as Proficient.

Difficulty Rank	Item #	Performance Level
8 (most)		
7		
6		
5		
4		
3		
2		
1 (least)		

Grade 4 Math Assessment

1. $\begin{array}{r} 654 \\ +\underline{451} \end{array}$

2. $\begin{array}{r} 407 \\ \underline{\times 4} \end{array}$

3. $^{1}/_{2} + {}^{1}/_{4} =$

4. What is the average of 23 32 11 18?

5. If you have a $1 bill and you buy food for 73 cents, how much change should you get?

6. ____________________
Measure this line to the nearest inch and write your answer.

7. Each side of a square measures 3 cm. If you make each side twice as long, what is the new perimeter?

8. What is a number between 20 and 50 that can be divided by 6 without a remainder?

Items adopted from NAEP sample items (Carr, 1999)

Activity 4: Chart of District Assessments

This activity is appropriate for the district assessment panel prior to a Flag Tag session and after reading the sections on types of assessments and characteristics of a good assessment. The purpose is to create a map of existing local, internal assessments to discuss what might need modification and any gaps that need additional assessments. The map might be created on a large wall chart for all participants to see.

In this activity, participants identify existing district assessments and any potential assessments that may be selected/developed soon. Two student populations, special education and English language learners, are considered by noting whether they will be administered the same assessments as the general population with or without accommodations or be given alternative assessments of some kind. The core subject areas of reading and writing in language arts and mathematics are the focus of the mapping process, and assessments are identified by name for a grade or grade span, as appropriate.

- On the lines for "All" students, write the name of the current district assessment. Indicate that it measures reading [R] or writing [W]. Write its name inside ( ) if it is a potential test that might be added. Write the grade span in the leftmost column.
- On the lines for English learners (EL) and Special Education students on a graduation track, write the test name if it is different. Use ditto marks (" ") if these groups will take the same test as the general population, or use an asterisk (*) if accommodations will be used.
- Use a yellow highlighter pen or draw a star if the assessment is already a standards-based assessment (measures content standard(s) and yields performance levels tied to district General/Mediating Performance Levels).

The structure of the map for language arts and mathematics on the following page allows for five grade spans. If more are needed, modify accordingly.

The activity is meant for mapping only internal district assessments. However, the group can include external state assessments if the state test is meant for all students (i.e., not a voluntary test such as for advanced placement or vocational education).

		Language Arts Assessments		
Grade Span	Students	NRT	CRT: Multi-Item	CRT: Performance Assessment
	All			
	EL			
	Special Ed			
	All			
	EL			
	Special Ed			
	All			
	EL			
	Special Ed			
	All			
	EL			
	Special Ed			

		Mathematics Assessments		
Grade Span	Students	NRT	CRT: Multi-Item	CRT: Performance Assessment
	All			
	EL			
	Special Ed			
	All			
	EL			
	Special Ed			
	All			
	EL			
	Special Ed			
	All			
	EL			
	Special Ed			

Carr (1999)

4 The School Culture

At the heart of a learning organization is a shift of mind—from seeing ourselves as separate from the world to connected to the world, from seeing problems as caused by someone or something "out there" to seeing how our own actions create the problems we experience. A learning organization is a place where people are continually discovering how they create their reality. And how they can change it.

—*Peter Senge*

Learning is what most adults will do for a living in the 21st century.

—*Sydney Joseph Perelman*

Overview

The second wheel of the School BUS—developing a culture of a learning organization—lays a foundation to create and sustain improvement in the school's instructional program. Culture is the defined as shared beliefs, attitudes, and actions of an organization. A learning organization is where adults as individuals and in collaborative teams learn to continually improve their personal and collective pedagogical skills. The school as a learning organization is like a wheel—it moves the school towards continual improvement as the culture itself goes through cycles of improvement.

A school staff must want to change, to continually improve their collective professional knowledge and skills. Staff then can discuss which changes to make in their classroom instructional strategies or school interventions. The culture of a learning organization fosters enthusiasm and supports a common vision and processes to search continually for ways to improve the instructional program. The school culture that emulates a learning organization has a causal relationship with program implementation. Staff engaging in team learning and personal mastery around a shared vision of all students reaching mastery fosters better teaching.

The district works in tandem with the school to build culture and internal capacity to sustain change. Leadership is balanced, but likely weighted a little more toward site-based decision-making. School and district management creates the structures, resources, and time necessary for teachers to meet, plan, reflect, and celebrate.

Principals and teachers in a learning organization define themselves as professionals continually learning about the science and art of teaching and learning. Peter Senge writes and speaks about the need for corporations to become learning organizations in a fast-changing global economy. The business of education is about learning, so educational institutions should exemplify a learning organization, a place of organized learning. Professional literature points to the school as the "unit of change." The School BUS focuses on continuous school change with continuous district guidance and support.

This chapter begins with lessons to be learned from the business world about embracing change and engaging all members of the organization in creating new ideas to reach a common vision of excellence in teaching and learning. As the discussion shifts from the business world to the business of teaching, teaching is defined as a profession. One characteristic of professionals is that they are life-long learners of a discipline. The chapter concludes with a description of the scoring guide, process, and reporting form that school staff will use to assess their school culture and design an action plan for improvement. Additional staff development activities engage a school staff in deeper understanding of shared leadership and the school as a learning organization and the unit of change.

The Business of Change

Change means survival in business today. Educators have much to learn from business as they prepare students to enter the business world. Schools are in the business of teaching youth what they need to know to work in the new millennium and in yet-to-be-imagined future careers. Do our schools teach students what they need to learn to be successful in business, and do schools and districts practice norms and skills that are valued in successful businesses?

According to a survey by the National Association of Colleges and Employers, *Job Outlook 2000*, the top three qualities that business employers seek in potential job applicants are adaptability, the ability to work as part of a team, and good interpersonal skills. Participants said that a highly intelligent and skilled employee does the business little good unless that person can work effectively with others on team solutions within deadlines.

Jet travel has had a powerful impact on business globalization, allowing cargo and businesspersons to reach other continents in hours. Phone and facsimile transmissions via satellites make global communication fairly inexpensive and instantaneous. Now the Internet is connecting the world and changing business practices at an ever-increasing speed. The corporate culture of today demands rapid team learning not just to respond to change but to initiate change. The ability and desire to learn constantly, search for new information, and share knowledge and skills as part of a team have become paramount values in the world of business. To what extent have schools changed to prepare students for the new world of work? To what extent do schools reflect the new business culture as a learning organization in a rapidly changing world?

It has been said that all successful businesses will soon be using the Internet. California's high school standards expect students to use multimedia and the Internet for research projects. How many schools are wired to the Internet? Are we preparing students for the job market of today and tomorrow? Do teachers have access to the Internet and have they embraced it?

Do students learn and practice the skills that businesses require just to survive? Do schools and districts model those skills for students? Schools and districts are in the business of educating youth, but do they practice the prized cultural behaviors of the business world? Educational institutions must nurture a culture among their employees that thrives on, not just reacts to, change—or worse yet, resists change.

A *USA Today* feature article on April 10, 2000, described the transformation of Corning and its meteoric rise in stock price as a result of resisting complacency and taking bold steps into the future. Founded before the Civil War, Corning sold its famous Corning Ware line in 1998 to concentrate on optical fiber. Now Corning is the world's largest maker of the pipelines used for Internet communication, causing its stock to skyrocket over 700% since 1998. Corning had a good business practice, but it changed its practices in anticipation of a changing world. Leadership recognized that what was fairly effective in the past may not be most effective now and may, in fact, lead to the demise of the company in the future. Some best practices have a short life span and then become inappropriate as the world changes.

In the article, the vice president of strategic planning and innovation referred to Corning's culture of "confident nervousness." This culture generates a burst of new ideas in an environment where a product may have a commercial life of one year. This short product life cycle in turn makes change vital to long-term survival. What lessons can those in the business of education learn from Corning? Is the school bursting with new ideas? Do instructional strategies and materials have a commercial life of perhaps one year, or are there teachers who proudly pull out five- and ten-year-old lesson plans from their file cabinets?

United Parcel Service has been quite successful delivering packages, but the company's "confident nervousness" has led it to seek new ventures and made it a leader in changing how business is done. UPS delivers products bought by customers on the Internet, and allows clients to track delivery status on the Internet, and it is also vying to sell the software customers need for accounting and inventory control. A UPS client can track a package's exact location through barcode information scanned into hand-held computers used by technologically literate truck drivers. All sorts of jobs that once required muscle "from the neck down" now demand critical, creative thinking, the ability to use computers, and constant learning and changing.

Corning and UPS provide examples of companies welcoming change. In contrast is a story about how resistance to change can lead to failure. Not too many years ago, people prized Swiss-made watches for their handcrafted mechanisms. When cheap, battery-operated, electronic watches were introduced, the Swiss scoffed at the new idea. The Swiss watchmakers' flawed "mental model" led them to believe people wouldn't buy mass-produced watches with electronic circuitry. According to their mental model, Swiss watches had always been what everyone wanted to buy, and, it followed, they always would. But we know what happened. Swiss watchmakers lost their market dominance by failing to adjust their mental models to correspond with advancing technology and a growing shift in consumer preferences.

Sometimes failure, even repeated failure, leads to abundant success. An article by Chris O'Brien in the *Contra Costa Times* newspaper on April 16, 2000, discussed the rapid changes in Silicon Valley, south of San Francisco.

> The commercialization of the Internet is only the latest in a long line of upheavals that have shaken the valley's power structure. There was the shift from vacuum tubes to semiconductors; semiconductors to microprocessors; mini-computers to PCs. Somehow, the valley always survives these seismic shifts and emerges stronger than ever. But each shift has also moved away from its silicon roots and the days when the most influential companies made components for computers. Instead, this is increasingly becoming a place where the pecking order is determined by a company's success selling the tools . . . needed to put other businesses on the Web. "The key to staying successful is constant innovation," [Doug] Henton [president of Collaborative Economics] said.

How many faculty rooms are bursting with excitement about new ideas and risk-taking? In how many classrooms do students learn in teams, excitedly engage in innovative projects, and take risks to solve meaningful problems? Are teachers preparing students for the work culture of the new millennium? Are teachers modeling these job skills for their students? Is continuous learning a valued norm of a school's culture?

At one elementary school, a teacher stood up during a staff development day, said that school was a "living hell" and that she feared of the destructive effect her attitude and complaining at home were having on her family. She said she was ready for change, and exhorted her colleagues to join her to improve their work environment and job satisfaction. She commented further that if they were at "rock bottom" now, any change was likely to be for the better. Another person stated that fear of "the unknown" could be no worse than the constant feeling of known frustration and failure. In that defining moment, staff made a commitment to change and work as a team toward improving their lives and the lives of their students.

Teaching as a Profession

Teaching is a profession and, as such, it requires lifelong learning. The professional teacher continually changes, updates, and refines his or her instructional practices to meet the needs of all students. In a professional organization, teachers collaborate, consult with one another, read and contribute to the professional literature, and attend and participate in professional conferences and workshops.

Change is a cultural norm in a professional organization. How do teachers define their role within the school, specifically, and in education, in general? Do they define teaching as a profession? Teachers expect their dentists to be professional, continually updating their skills and improving their practice. No teacher wants to go to a dentist who has pulled and drilled teeth the same way for the last 30 years, does not bother to read professional literature, attend professional conferences, or discuss new ideas with colleagues. Like medicine, law, and dentistry, teaching is a profession. It follows that the school needs to foster a professional culture that encourages continuous learning opportunities, such as consultations with colleagues, subscriptions to professional journals, and attendance at professional conferences.

Career professionals expect the culture of their profession to be one of continually seeking paths to better performance. Better performance does not mean discarding everything from yesterday to begin anew today. Rather, better performance for the professional means continually examining past performance to separate best practices that achieved stellar results from mediocre practices that fell short of high goals. The professional identifies and explores new practices that promise even better results, or reacts to a shift in clientele needs. Professional teachers introspect their own performance and explore the science and art of teaching, always striving toward personal mastery.

When one of the authors (Carr) worked in and visited classrooms in a school district, he noticed that expert teachers frequently asked him, " What advice can you give me to improve my teaching?" These teachers seized every opportunity to learn from others, even a visitor from the research office. Professional, expert teachers continually take advantage of every occasion to improve their art and science of teaching. They neither avoid conversations about their teaching nor blame the students for problems with learning. When professional teachers in a school embed their zeal for personal mastery within a system of team learning, they form a learning organization with synergistic impact on student achievement.

Do teachers see their role to be synonymous with assembly line workers doing a repetitive task and punching a time clock or with professional scientists using research-based strategies combined with artistry to create state-of-the-art lessons? Professional teachers model qualities such as love of lifelong learning, respect for the diverse ideas and opinions of others, and personal mastery heightened by collaboration. Teachers believing and acting as a team of professionals create a learning organization with a common vision of high expectations for themselves and their students.

It is counterproductive to write a school plan, buy new materials, or allocate additional time and money for staff development if the staff simply does not want to change. It is pointless to debate the merits of a different instructional program if staff simply does not want to revise past practice. When staff believe they know all there is to know about teaching and no change in the program is necessary, then looking at student results is futile. The belief that students need to change to fit the program leads staff to view poor results only as the failings of students and their parents, not the need to improve teaching practices. Yes, students do have a certain responsibility for their own learning. Yes, parents do have a responsibility for their children's education. Yet, too often teachers and administrators abdicate their responsibility as professional educators to find ways to address the challenges that make it difficult, but not impossible, to teach all children.

Change is a fact of life. Some people attempt to resist change or react to it grudgingly or complacently. Others seize the opportunity to shape the conditions whereby change flows in an intended direction. Granted, teachers and principals have been forced to protect themselves from the whims of federal and state policy makers and changes in local school leadership. But too many school cultures do not reflect the values of professional organizations—they do not seek to be innovative and exciting and strive to assist every student to be a successful learner. Persistent change concentrated on one initiative until mastery is achieved should be the cultural norm in every school, not change as a flip-flopping back and forth, a quick fix, or a different focus each year.

Learning is all about changing, growing, and expanding knowledge and repertoire of skills. It is what every teacher desires for every student and what all teachers and administrators should desire for themselves. Teachers must be engaged learners if they expect students to be engaged learners. We cannot change who the students are who enter the school's doorway, but we can change how well they learn once they are in the classrooms. As the school becomes more "learningful" about how to improve the instructional program, staff will find new and better ways to reach more students. When a district and its schools promote learning about the art and science of teaching, student learning improves.

A fundamental goal in the business of the district and school is to create a climate that fosters professionalism and a focus on the five disciplines of a learning organization: striving for personal mastery, reflecting on mental models, building a shared vision, engaging in team learning, and approaching problem-solving through systems thinking.

The Five Disciplines of a Learning Organization

Professionals in a learning organization practice five disciplines. Each teacher continually strives for *personal mastery* in subject matter knowledge and teaching skills, and reflects on his or her *mental models* about teaching and learning through thoughtful dialogue with others—changing beliefs when appropriate. The school team members have a *shared vision* of what their own and student mastery looks like, and they engage in *team learning* to advance toward their shared visions. Stakeholders in the educational system employ *systems thinking*—they think about how the actions of each person affects all others, so they design action plans for improvement that involve collaboration by all stakeholders.

Peter Senge, a professor at the Harvard School of Business, addresses the corporate world with his theory about a successful business being a learning organization, yet his words echo loudly for educators. Educators should study Senge's ideas about a learning organization for two reasons. First, educators are in the business of organized learning. Second, corporations are stepping in and taking over schools where educators have failed (e.g., the Edison Project).

In his book, *The Fifth Discipline: The Art and Practice of the Learning Organization* (1990), Senge predicted, "The most successful corporation of the 1990s will be something called a learning organization . . . As the world becomes more interconnected and business becomes more complex and dynamic, work must become more 'learningful' . . . The organizations that will truly excel in the future will be the organizations that discover how to tap people's commitment and capacity to learn at *all* levels in an organization" (p.4). Senge's prophetic statement about the 1990s became a reality within that decade and promises to apply even more urgently to this decade.

In an interview in *Educational Leadership* (O'Neil, 1995) Senge explained that many institutions, including those in education, have learning disabilities, marked by a culture resistant to change. Yet change is at the heart of learning. Senge said:

> A learning organization is an organization in which people at all levels are collectively, continually enhancing their capacity to create things they really want to create. Our fundamental challenges in education are no different than in business. They involve fundamental cultural changes, and that will require collective learning. They involve people at multiple levels thinking together about significant and enduring solutions we might create, and then helping those solutions come about.

When a school becomes a learning organization, all members of the school community participate as a team in long-range planning, implement best practices for the success of all students, and continually search for better strategies by looking back at results and forward to new ideas. A learning organization is proactive: it anticipates the need and plans for change.

Senge (1990) said, "Today's problems come from yesterday's solutions" (p.57). He explains the "vision of horizon," where we see but a short distance into the past or future. Moving past the "horizon" allows us to understand that the cause of this year's problem may not be rooted in events that occurred this year, but may be the result of a complex series of events that started many years ago. Patching over problems with "quick fixes" often creates bigger problems, which is why crisis management generates even more crises than it attempts to fix.

If, as the African saying goes, "it takes a village to raise a child," consider how many teachers it takes to educate a student. Suppose a second grade teacher with a vision horizon that is limited to inside her classroom walls considers herself effective because she taught the writing process and her students performed well on the writing assessment. Now suppose that teachers in successive grade levels do not teach the writing process at all. How proficient will those second grade students be as writers at the end of elementary school, middle school, or high school? Students' writing skills will likely atrophy, and whatever writing skills they mastered in second grade will not suffice in twelfth grade. In the broader K–12 vision of the student, was the teacher's instruction truly effective? For that second grade teacher to really have a profound, long-lasting effect, all teachers in grade levels before and after second grade must use a team approach to teaching an articulated writing process.

Senge's learning organization is founded on five disciplines—personal mastery, mental modeling, building a shared vision, team learning, and systems thinking, as illustrated in Figure 4.1. The learning organization practices all five of these interrelated disciplines. "To practice a discipline is to be a lifelong learner. You 'never arrive;' you spend your life mastering disciplines. You can never say, 'We are a learning organization,' any more than you can say you are an enlightened person" (Senge, 1990, p. 11).

FIGURE 4.1

Senge's Five Disciplines of a Learning Organization

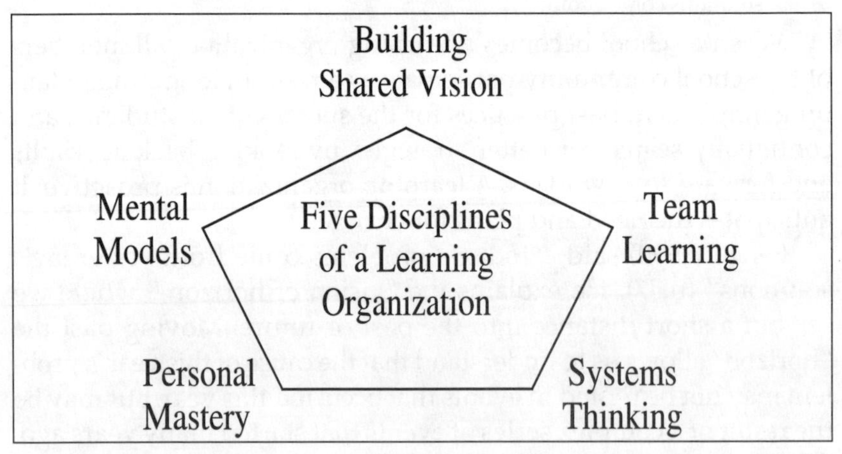

Senge's five disciplines facilitate the transition of a dysfunctional institution to a learning organization. It is vital that all five disciplines develop as a whole system, an ensemble. At the heart of the learning organization is a shift in orientation and thinking from seeing ourselves as separate from the rest of the world to seeing ourselves as interconnected in the world; from seeing how others'

actions create problems to seeing how our actions illuminate solutions. A learning organization is a place where people are continually discovering how they create their own individual reality and the collective reality of the organization.

Personal Mastery

Personal mastery refers to a special level of proficiency similar to that of the master craftsman who is committed to lifelong learning to perfect his craft. It requires a discipline of continually clarifying and deepening one's personal vision and energies. Personal mastery is a characteristic of the professional teacher with "confident nervousness" who self-reflects, exchanges ideas with colleagues, studies professional literature, and participates in workshops to continually improve the science and art of teaching.

The masterful teacher mentors beginning teachers while learning from them the latest ideas being taught in the universities. University professors go into public school classrooms to learn from expert teachers and experience "the children of today." A superintendent in one district puts himself on the substitute teacher list for 20 days each year (Reeves, 1998b). Senge sees personal mastery as an essential cornerstone of the learning organization, since an organization's commitment to and capacity for learning can be no greater than that of each individual member.

Mental Models

A mental model is a person's image or perspective of an event, situation, activity or concept. These are deep-seated assumptions that influence how we understand the world, make sense of events, and take action. Each teacher has a mental model of *school, administrator,* or *student* based on deep-rooted personal experiences and perceptions.

A teacher who has a mental model that some students can learn and others cannot may never question whether her one method of teaching has an impact on some students but not others, or how diverse methods may enable all students to learn. As one principal told her high school teachers, "I hope that you all believe all students can learn if you find the right ways to teach them. But if you do not believe as I do, then I expect that you will wholeheartedly *act* like all students can learn." A good teacher does not try one way to teach and then blame students who do not learn for failing. A good teacher sees student failure as a challenge to find the right method that will work with that particular student. One mental model blames outside forces for student failure, while the other looks internally for solutions.

A district superintendent who has a mental model that students from low socioeconomic backgrounds cannot achieve will be reluctant to "waste" placing the best teachers in schools in low-income neighborhoods. A district superintendent with the mental model that socioeconomic status does not in itself obstruct student achievement but presents special challenges that require the utmost teacher quality to overcome will instead work for policies that place the most effective teachers with the students most in need. Mental models of what can or cannot be done in different situations vary tremendously from person to person, are deeply entrenched, and are difficult to change. The best way to uproot and become aware of our mental models is through honest dialogue in which we freely express our beliefs and opinions and listen attentively to understand other perspectives. Activity 4 at the end of this chapter addresses mental models and their impact on teaching and learning.

Building Shared Vision

A shared vision is valuable for the learning organization because it provides a focus and energy for learning. "When there is a genuine vision (as opposed to the all-too-familiar 'vision statement'), people excel and learn, not because they are told to but because they want to. What has been lacking is a discipline for translating individual vision into shared vision" (p.9). Consider an elementary school principal who lamented that his personal visions rarely became school practice or soon fizzled out. Visions didn't start to become enduring practice until after he formed a teacher leadership team and "visioning" became a team and whole school process. Owning the vision leads to commitment to the practice.

Taylor Magnet (elementary) School is located in a high poverty neighborhood in Stockton, California. The school staff studied the five disciplines of a learning organization during the first of a series of workshops. They created a new school vision, "Taylor School is a learning organization that encourages and supports collaboration between staff, parents, and community and where all students are able and expected to reach their highest learning potential in an environment that is safe, secure, and positive."

Taylor School staff also created a second vision about powerful learning: ". . . Teachers model for and coach students to be lifelong learners. Technology and current educational research and practice are the springboards for our powerful learning community." A previously fragmented staff had a dialogue about their deep beliefs and hopes and began to coalesce around a common vision of what was best for students. They began to see that what was best for students was also best for themselves. To move from a vision as a written statement to living practice, they used the Culture Scoring Guide found in Activity 1 of this chapter to assess where they were and to design an action plan to strengthen their school culture as reflected in their vision statement.

First, teachers in the workshop read brief descriptions about a learning organization and the value of building a common vision. Then they used a rubric to assess their school culture and, drawing from descriptors in the next higher level of the rubric, planned action to improve. The rubric served as an assessment tool, another explanation of a learning organization, and a guide for selecting ways to improve. Last, they created a vision statement that naturally embodied much of what they had just read and discussed.

Team Learning

Team learning focuses on the process of aligning and developing the capacity of a team to create the learning and results its members seek. "When teams are truly learning, not only are they producing extraordinary results but the individual members are growing more rapidly than could have occurred otherwise" (Senge, 1990, p.10). The discipline of team learning starts with dialogue, akin to the brainstorming strategy that teachers use with their students. It is not a debate in which one tries to convince others or defends one's opinions. Dialogue involves dangling ideas in front of a team for full understanding. Like a mobile on strings hanging from the ceiling, the team views each idea from different perspectives, making connections that may not have been obvious otherwise, respecting diversity, and ultimately reaching the goal of consensus. When the team dialogues about their beliefs and visions, a common direction emerges, and individuals' energies harmonize.

Team learning involves the need to think insightfully about complex issues so that a team may learn how to best tap the potential of many minds. Outstanding teams in organizations develop an operational trust where each team member remains conscious of the other team members and can be counted on to act in ways that complement the actions of all members.

There are no limitations on who should participate in team learning. Think about instructional program decisions your school has made in the past. Consider how they indirectly affected the school secretary, custodian, librarian, parents, and, of course, students. What was the reaction of each person left out of the decision-making loop? Did any one person or group not in the decision loop bring the innovation to a screeching halt?

Consider including union representatives in district team learning processes. In one district, the president of the teachers union and a committee of diverse teachers were involved in developing a kindergarten assessment instrument and process that would fundamentally change how teachers approached instruction and classroom management. When the plan was explained to the 25 district schools, a kindergarten teacher at one of the schools rallied her colleagues to resist implementation. In an attempt at reconciliation, the union president accompanied the district's assessment administrator (Carr) to meet the teachers at the school. As soon as they sat down, the union president said, "Now, explain to me how you can make this assessment work in your school." Silence and dismay soon gave way to an agreeable plan offered by the resistant teacher. Inclusion of the union president assured that the union contract was not breached or viewed as a barrier and added another perspective to the development and planning process.

Systems Thinking

The discipline of systems thinking involves the awareness that all actions in a system are interrelated in an invisible fabric. Like a pebble thrown into a pond, the waves ripple outward to its edges. The failure of a noon duty supervisor to settle a dispute between two students on the playground ripples into the classroom after recess as the teacher starts a lesson but notices that those two students are not attentive and ready to learn. When teachers take a systems-thinking approach to problem solving, they realize that they cannot just go into their classrooms and shut their doors. They must come out of their rooms, meet with others as a team, and collectively solve the problems in the system. "At the heart of a learning organization is a shift in mind—from seeing ourselves as separate from the world to connected to the world, from seeing problems as caused by someone or something 'out there' to seeing how our own actions create the problems we experience" (Senge, 1990, pp.12–13).

Building a culture for change is the foundation to support any specific school program modification. Workshop activities at the end of this chapter present some ideas and questions for dialogue about understanding change, learning to change, and improving school culture. Sometimes these activities are enough to galvanize a staff to emulate a learning organization. More workshop ideas and exercises are presented in Senge's fieldbook (1994).

Change: Will and Ownership

Why is it that many instructional programs found to be very effective in the originating schools are failures in the adopting schools? The answer can be summed up in two words, *culture* and *ownership*. A school staff must have a culture in which change is a norm; they must have the desire to make changes, not resist them. Staff must own the decision to change and the decision about what innovation they will adopt or adapt at their school.

In this book, we consciously avoid the business term "buy into" because it depicts a nefarious pitchman "selling a staff on a program." Sometimes a new program is pitched to a school staff in hopes that they will "buy into it" after the fact. In reality, they will be forced to accept it without any choice. "Buying into" often connotes undue persuasion or coercion. Asking staff to *commit to* an idea or program conjures a process of back-and-forth dialogue, careful consideration, and final decision by the stakeholders to take ownership.

Reaching a unanimous decision to initiate a particular change can take a fair amount of time and is not always possible. Consensus does not require unanimous agreement. A notch below unanimous agreement is agreement among staff that they either enthusiastically support the idea or at least "can live with it (it won't kill me to try it)." A suggestion is to build into the decision sufficient time for trial and formal evaluation of impact to decide whether to continue, modify, or stop. The Accelerated Schools Project views this process as selecting a hypothesis and then testing it. When 100% agreement is not possible, staff might agree to accept a decision that receives a majority vote, perhaps 70% or greater. The levels or rules for decision-making are best defined prior to actually tackling problems and solutions. Reflection on diverse perspectives is balanced by expediency to improve student learning.

The seven levels of attitudes towards a vision in Figure 3.3 address a school's vision statement but could be modified to fit any decision about an action to be taken. Notice that apathy is a level below noncompliance. Participants could be polled by raising their hands or using anonymous ballots to indicate their level of commitment. This activity also brings with it a certain amount of humor (e.g.,"Is it time to go yet?").

FIGURE 4.2

Possible Attitudes Toward a Vision	
Commitment	Wants it. Will make it happen. Creates whatever "laws" (structures) are needed.
Enrollment	Wants it. Will do whatever can be done within the "spirit of the law."
Genuine compliance	Sees the benefit of the vision. Does everything expected and more. Follows the "letter of the law." "Good soldier."
Formal compliance	On the whole, sees the benefits of the vision. Does what's expected and no more. "Pretty good soldier."
Grudging compliance	Does not see the benefits of the vision. Does enough of what's expected because he has to, but also lets it be known that he is not really on board.
Noncompliance	Does not see the benefits of the vision and will not do what's expected. "I won't do it; you can't make me."
Apathy	Neither for nor against the vision. No interest. "Is it time to go yet?"

(Unknown source)

Managing and Sustaining Change

The second wheel of the School BUS is about improving the culture of the school as a learning organization. The cultural norm of desire and action to continually learn and improve in a school forms the foundation for making and sustaining schoolwide improvements in teaching and learning.

Comprehensive school reform programs can be classified into programs that have a primary focus on improving culture and organization as a foundation for making instruction improvements, and programs that have a primary focus on improving particular instructional practices. Examples of a few programs focused on organizational development to support changes in classroom practices are Comer's School Development Program (info.med.yale.edu/comer), Levin's Accelerated Schools Project (Hopfenberg et al, 1993; www.stanford.edu/group/ASP), NWREL's Onward to Excellence (Blum, 1999; www.nwrel.org/scpd/ote), and Sizer's Coalition of Essential Schools (www.essentialschools.org). The Accelerated Schools Project believes that remediation efforts have not effectively helped underperforming students catch up and supports methods to accelerate student learning, but does not directly prescribe any one teaching methodology. Rather, staff in an Accelerated School work in cadres to build unity of purpose, shared strengths, and a system of shared decision-making. They explore a variety of instructional programs and strategies to select what might work best for their particular school and then put the new idea to a test and see if it does indeed lead to higher student achievement.

The School BUS shares a common thread with these nationally recognized organizational models. The second wheel of the School BUS is devoted to continually improving a school's culture to support continuous improvement of instructional practices. In a school environment marked by trust, respect, collegiality, and patience, teachers have high expectations for students and for themselves, accepting both child and adult as interconnected learners in a learning organization.

Roland Barth (1990) states that "teacher growth is closely related to pupil growth" (p.49). He asserts that "schools have the capacity to change themselves [and a] major responsibility of those outside the schools is to help provide the conditions for those inside. What needs to be improved about schools is their culture, the quality of interpersonal relationships, and the nature and quality of learning experiences" (p. 45).

Moffett (2000) offers lessons about managing change:

> Develop a reform-support infrastructure where the district provides leadership and changes dysfunctional structures and practices that impede school change, with multiple channels of two-way communication among district offices, schools, and the communities they serve.
>
> Districts must remember that they are in the business of culture building and that research and practice have demonstrated that the right school culture is essential. Strong professional learning communities enable teachers to respond effectively to the needs of students and sustain change.
>
> Districts sustain school change by reducing principal and staff changes.

Moffett concludes, "Focus on culture, stick with it for the long haul, frontload support during implementation, build relationships, insert professional development at every opportunity, build reform support infrastructures, train and use change facilitators, strengthen communication, reduce overload and fragmentation, seek coherence, stabilize turnover, remember the implementation dip [when test results dip as a major change is being learned], restructure the use of teacher time, balance pressure and support."

Donahoe (1993) remarks how often overlooked yet crucial structure, time, and culture are to sustaining school improvement. Some schools had money available for staff development but no time. He advocates "the rearrangement of the use of time in schools to allow them to create and sustain the kind of interactive culture and supporting infrastructure they need to improve student learning." Teachers need the time, professional development, and structures to separate from their classrooms and take an active team leadership role in the school program to minimize the shortage or departure of effective principals.

Some districts have a policy of routinely transferring principals after four years, just when change might be starting to take hold. RAND found that after two years only half the schools that had started whole-school reform were implementing the core elements across the school. Schools that had the time to thoroughly research and freely choose a reform design had much higher levels of implementation than schools with too little time or where the design was forced (Berends, 1998).

"Perhaps the greatest challenge to reform is sustaining it. Sustaining schoolwide reform programs past the initial stage of enthusiasm is one of the biggest problems that schools face" (McChesney & Hertling, 2000). According to Hargreaves and Fink (2000), only three things matter about educational reform: (1) Does it have depth? Does it improve important rather than superficial aspects of student learning? (2) Does it have length? Is it sustainable over long periods of time? (3) Does it have breadth? Can it be extended beyond a few schools, networks, or showcase initiatives?

Leadership

Sustaining the culture of a learning organization depends on a competent principal who shares leadership responsibilities with school staff. The district provides stability, guidance, and support to school leadership teams.

A strong school leadership team with a competent principal at the helm—guiding toward the vision, fending off distractions, facilitating or making decisions, and providing resources and recognition for success—is key to implementing the School BUS. Everyone has a role in driving the School BUS, but it is primarily the principal and leadership team who hold the map and chart the course. A teacher on the leadership team, rather than the principal, may facilitate some staff meetings.

"Principal and staff turnover was one of the most significant factors associated with abandoning newly implemented changes" (Berman & McLaughlin, 1977). Staff turnover, from board members to teachers, jeopardizes sustained school reform, not to mention staff development, which never has a chance to move forward because those trained soon leave and new people enter without the knowledge or the same vision (Mizell, 1999). Developing school leadership teams composed of school administrators and teachers with certain qualifications and whom peers respect can not only mitigate departure of a strong principal-leader but can also build ownership of ideas, team learning, and decision-making at all levels.

The definition of leadership has shifted from bossing to managing to leading. The definition of bossing is "people at the top direct the people in the middle to tell the people at the bottom what to do." Managing is "coordinating people and resources to efficiently produce goods or services in an organization." Leading is "the process of influencing others to achieve mutually agreed upon purposes for the organization" Patterson (1993, pp. 2-3). Similarly, Leithwood (1992) discussed the shift from *transactional leadership*, in which employees are told how to implement a manager's goal, to *transformational leadership*, in which employees meaningfully participate in setting team goals and deciding strategies to achieve the goal. "Leadership is essentially building and maintaining a sense of vision, culture, and interpersonal relationships, whereas management is coordinating, supporting, and monitoring organizational activities. To perform both roles successfully requires a careful balancing act" (Day, 2000).

According to Lambert (1998a), "Leadership is about learning together, and constructing meaning and knowledge collectively and collaboratively. It involves opportunities to surface and mediate perceptions, values, beliefs, information, and assumptions through continuing conversations; to inquire about and generate ideas together; to seek to reflect upon and make sense of work in the light of shared beliefs and new information; and to create actions that grow out of these new understandings." To establish enduring leadership capacity, the school needs a sufficient number of skilled teachers with a shared vision, resources to strive toward that vision, and a staffwide commitment to school self-renewal. *Constructivist Leadership*—constructing meanings through reciprocal relationships of exchanging ideas and concerns—leads school teams toward a common purpose of effective schooling (Lambert, 1995, p. 29). Leadership is a shared endeavor and redistribution of power and authority that leads to constructive change in adult and student learning (Lambert, 1998b).

While much has been written about the role of the school principal as the leader of leaders and school improvement, these principals derive their authority and freedom to innovate from the central office and, in particular, the superintendent. The superintendent models the style of leadership expected of all administrators and leads the whole district to emulate a learning organization focused on improving student learning. The superintendent provides ongoing professional development and fiscal and human resources to build capacity of site principals. The superintendent designs district management structures that foster collaboration and local decision-making. Finally, the superintendent minimizes external and district paperwork or policies and mandates that distract principals from their chief role of observing classroom instruction, coaching teachers, collaborating with other principals, and leading school teams to frequently analyze student achievement data, plan improvements, monitor progress, and celebrate successes.

Superintendents, assistant superintendents of instructional services, and principals must rethink their use of time and how often they involve staff on meaningful discussions about teacher pedagogy and student learning that leads to observable improvement. Donahoe (1993) urges schools and districts to not only use resources wisely to have time to frequently collaborate on learning and problem-solving, but to be creative in their use of time and structures. Teachers in a school not involved in the leadership team might take the students of team teachers for an afternoon while the team meets. All PE, art, music and other programs can be offered on a Friday while regular classroom teachers meet all day each week.

When educational leaders actually record time spent on various topics in meetings over several weeks or months, they often find that only about 10 to 20 percent is spent on "value-added" work (Freeston and Costa, 1998). "Value-added work is work that leads directly to learning," such as exploring best instructional practices, observing classroom learning, and professional dialogue on learning. "Necessary work" involving management tasks can be completed as efficiently as possible and "waste work," such as correcting mistakes and holding meetings with no positive outcomes, can be eliminated to create more time for work that leads directly to learning. Assign a small task force to take charge of the problem of graffiti and vandalism in the restrooms instead of spending whole staff meetings talking around and around the problem. Staff meetings should not be used to read a bulletin because staff members do not read what has been placed in their mailboxes. This is unproductive and enabling behavior that avoids dialogue about improving pedagogy during staff meetings.

Experimentation with school-based decision making has had mixed results. "The issue is not *whether* you centralize or decentralize, but *what* should be decentralized and what should be centralized. Unless the schools can use their resources as needed, every time you turn around, they are focused on resource acquisition instead of on instruction," Strembitsky says in an interview by O'Neil (1995/96). He was gratified to find that after school-based management was implemented, "people were more committed to their work and enjoyed it more and that translated into how staff related to students. Students were the beneficiaries, registering significant gains in achievement."

There is no one definition of site-based management and decision making. Most authorities encourage some sort of balance between top-down and bottom-up decision processes, both between district and school and within a school between principal and teachers. Perhaps an example of an appropriate approach is a district office that expects schools to improve student results without dictating the methods to achieve the goal yet simultaneously provides guidance and support to school staff. The disciplines of *team learning*, *building a shared vision*, and *systems thinking* at both school and district levels support a balanced, professional management style and help avoid defective *mental models* that blind staff to new and better ideas.

Should leadership use the carrot, the stick, or both? The "stick-only" approach, the authoritarian style, has not proven effective in long-range, sustainable school self-renewal. Brandishing state test results and telling schools to improve or else is an approach that tends to breed resentment and fear rather than enthusiastic efforts to build on best practices.

The "carrot only" approach may remove accountability from some people who choose to opt out of participation in an improvement initiative. A state's rewards program becomes an incentive to only those schools that attempt to grab the carrot, but has no effect on a school staff that fold their arms and grab at nothing. Combining a demand for meaningful improvement in achievement results (a stick) with consequences for failure (a stick) or success (the carrot) often proves more successful than dictating how the improvement is to be accomplished. But neither the carrot nor stick will prove effective unless schools receive assistance necessary to change. It may not be that schools refuse to change, but that they do not know how. School leaders provide the necessary guidance, resources, and time for staff to learn new strategies.

The School BUS and Balanced Leadership

The School BUS approach to school program management within a balanced system of leadership in a school district empowers school teams to use results to make program decisions, starting at the bottom level of grades/departments and swiftly moving upward to the district level. The district engenders a unified vision, provides resources, and offers guidance to the schools under its supervision. Schools are accountable for improving student achievement, and districts are accountable for support and guidance. Schools remain free to decide what instructional strategies to use to help all students reach the districtwide standards.

Decisions made using the Bottom-Up Simple approach bubble up from a grade or department and then move through the whole school and out to the district. But the School BUS provides checkpoints along the way. The school leadership team can question whether, for instance, an action plan chosen by a grade team really is linked to the student results. When a difference of opinion occurs, both leaders and team members work together to resolve the issue. Likewise, the district team can question school decisions, but with the condition that they work with the school team to reach a resolution. Except for rare aberrations, team decisions will be sound or, at least, "sound enough" if staff systematically reflect on results and consider diverse perspectives and new ideas through professional dialogues. It will be up to the team to demonstrate that the decision was right by showing evidence of greatly improved student achievement. Lack of improvement requires the team to go back to the drawing board and try something else.

Assessing School Culture

As part of the School BUS process, teachers use a scoring guide to reach agreement on a common rating of the school culture as a learning organization at the beginning and end of the year. They create a brief action plan for improvement during the year and celebrate their success at the end.

At the beginning of the school year, school staff members use a scoring guide to rate the culture within the whole school based on where they believe the school is in its progress toward becoming a learning organization. Staff reaches agreement on one rating. After rating the culture at the beginning of the school year, staff then develops an action plan to work toward improvement in a specific area. At the end of the school year, the assessment is repeated to evaluate the school's change in culture.

All ratings can be submitted on an anonymous ballot, tabulated, and then openly discussed to find a point of consensus. Teachers might be asked to provide concrete examples to support their ratings on the ballot form or during the group discussion as a check for accuracy. If the school has an internal or external school improvement facilitator, that person might observe or interview staff prior to the assessment meeting in order to seek evidence relating to the scoring guide descriptors and provide that evidence during the discussion period.

Staff meeting time is used periodically during the school year to discuss progress implementing the action plan as part of ongoing staff development and accountability. Staff creates a bar chart and posts it on the wall in the teachers' meeting room. Figure 4.3 illustrates a bar chart with a rating of "2" at the beginning of the year in September and a "3" at year-end in June. Columns for each month between September and June are added to the bar chart. Staff members are encouraged to write anecdotes that are evidence of action plan implementation each month. These anecdotal records might be written on Post-It™ notes so they can be removed, entered into an accountability report, and then replaced on the wall.

FIGURE 4.3

Culure Ratings Bar Chart & Anecdotes

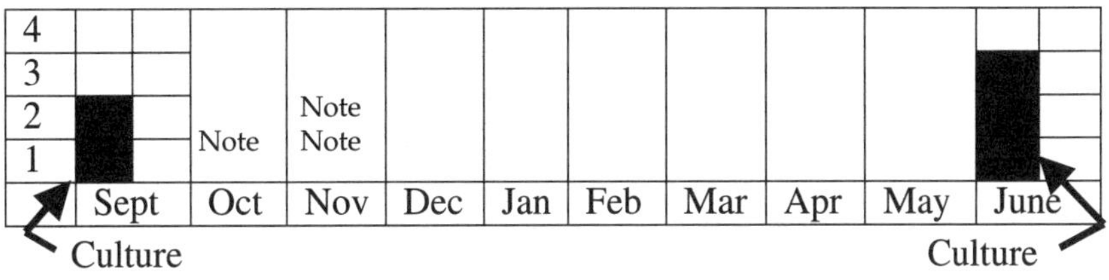

	Sept	Oct	Nov	Dec	Jan	Feb	Mar	Apr	May	June
4										
3										
2			Note							
1		Note	Note							

Culture Culture

Suppose math teachers in ninth grade saw that measurement and geometry were weakest for their school on the state math test. Math and physical education teachers collaborated on strategies to apply measurement and geometry in their classes in October. One of the teachers writes a Post-It™ note about the collaboration and, perhaps, its impact on student achievement in the column for the month of October. In November, a teacher writes about an instance when she collaborated with other sixth-grade teachers to solve a problem she experienced using reciprocal teaching for reading comprehension.

Scoring Guide, Process, and Report Form

The school staff formally rates the school culture, and results are recorded. One or more activities in the Additional Staff Development Activities section might precede this rating process if staff do not have a solid understanding of what it means to be a learning organization. The scoring guide, shown in Figure 4.4, is adapted from WASC (Western Accreditation of Schools and Colleges) scoring guides as part of secondary school program review and accreditation, but the adapted form applies to all school levels.

The Culture rating is an agreed upon rating, not the percentage of teachers who select each level. If all staff do not initially agree on a common rating, they discuss evidence and reasoning until agreement is reached. Beforehand, the criteria for reaching agreement is decided upon, such as an "I can live with it" attitude or at least a 70% vote. The reason a common rating is used rather than percentage of teachers at each rating or level is that school culture is about the school's being the unit of change and working toward a common vision. In keeping with the theme of culture as a school's unity of vision and purpose, a common rating is recorded.

The school or district decides beforehand whether a rating must be a whole number or whether a split rating, such as 2.5, will be allowed. A whole number indicates that a preponderance of descriptors apply to a particular level. A school truly split between descriptors in two adjacent levels either stays with the lower rating or level because there is not yet enough evidence of mastery, or it gives a split rating because the school is "halfway" to the next level. A suggestion is to use whole number ratings that reflect the lower level, the level most indicative of mastery.

Descriptors at the higher level in the scoring guide that are true become the Strength statements in the Culture Report. One or more descriptors not yet attained are selected as the Challenge for action.

Finally, the school and district prearrange whether the Culture report form stays at the school site, is made public to the school's community, or is submitted to the district office. Perhaps during the first year implementing the School BUS, the beginning report form can be kept at the school as a working document, and a year-end progress rating (year-end rating minus beginning rating) can appear in the year-end comprehensive report as a public document. Later, when comfort, trust, and respect are well established, the entire process might be a source of ongoing public communication and accountability. An alternative is for principals to share results with district supervisors at a meeting to collaborate on action plans for improvement.

Process

1. *Distribute copies of the scoring guide* and discuss the purpose of the assessment and School Culture Form. (The scoring guide is used as an assessment and learning tool—it provides descriptors of different levels of school culture, and the reporting form is part of the School BUS accountability process. The culture of a learning organization supports continual instructional program improvement efforts. Part of the School BUS program theory is that improvement in school culture leads to improvement in program implementation.)
2. *Give participants a small ballot* on which to write a score of 1, 2, 3, or 4 according to the levels in the scoring guide shown in Figure 4.4. Each participant uses his or her ballot to rate the culture of the whole school. Certain descriptors in different levels may be true of the school, but participants should select which level *best describes* the school. Encourage participants to rate the school using a whole number rather than a split score (e.g., rather than using 2.5 for meeting some descriptors at level 2 and some at level 3, settle on 2 until level 3 is fully met).
3. *Collect the ballots* and immediately tabulate the results for all to see (on easel paper, chalkboard, or transparency). Reach *agreement on a common rating* through a discussion of individuals' rationales and give concrete examples to support ratings.

4. *Create a large bar graph* on the wall to show the beginning rating. Months (September to June) are entered on the horizontal line. On the vertical line, write *1, 2, 3, 4* and create the bar for the beginning rating (e.g., September), as illustrated in Figure 4.3. (Leave space in September for another bar to be created beside the Culture bar. This other bar will be described in Chapter 5).
5. *Identify school strengths* aided by descriptors in the scoring guide and record consensus statements. (Sometimes staff can draw from their strengths to solve their problems.) Strengths can be desriptors in a high level on the scoring guide that staff agree are reflective of their school culture.
6. *Identify a challenge* to reaching the next higher level on the scoring guide. Pick one or a few related descriptors in a higher level (at least level 3) as the improvement target.
7. *Draft a mini action plan* briefly stating what the school staff will do to improve school culture, in relation to the target descriptors. One or a few sentences or "bullet points" are sufficient. If the school culture is now at the Partial level, what change will be implemented to reach the Proficient level?
8. Each month, staff members are asked to record on Post-It™ notes any *anecdotes* of actions that show an improvement. These *anecdotal records* are then placed on the bar graph above the appropriate month. (When a new action is repeated, it becomes a habit, that is, a cultural norm.) For example, grade level teams may begin meeting weekly to share ideas, review results, and plan instructional improvements.
9. After the meeting, enter the rating and statements on the *School BUS Culture Form*, as shown in Figure 4.5. Give a copy to each staff member or post it on the wall. An agreement between the district and schools determines whether the form stays at the school or is submitted to the district.
10. *At the end of the year,* staff again reach agreement on a common rating and *complete the bar graph* (create a bar for May or June). All the information can be entered into a school's annual comprehensive accountability report (this report is described fully in Chapter 7). The "multipurpose" graph shows *quantitative* data (the beginning and year-end ratings) and *qualitative* data (the implementation anecdotes) as evidence that the school has improved its culture as a learning organization.

11. *Celebrate meaningful progress.* Opportunities for celebrating successes are important in the School BUS.

Figure 4.4

School Culture Scoring Guide

Culture The culture of the school supporting the school's vision for students is characterized by trust, professionalism, high expectations for all students, and focuses on continual school improvement within a safe and nurturing environment.

	4 Advanced	3 Proficient
PRACTICES	Staff expertise is formally and routinely shared and built upon, and collegiality is valued and nurtured. Staff members regularly research and review current educational ideas and practices. Innovations and teamwork are celebrated and supported. Staff is encouraged to maintain what works best, try new approaches, and modify or discard ineffective methods.	Faculty and staff expertise is highly valued, and ideas, research, and innovations are shared regularly both formally and informally. Faculty and staff are provided opportunities to extend their knowledge and share new ideas.
COLLABORATION	Teachers collaborate with students, colleagues, administrators, and other members of the school community to solve problems hindering students' achieving the standards. Teachers cooperatively plan and implement improvements. Time and opportunities for these collaborative efforts are systematically provided.	Teachers and administrators collaborate in problem solving related to teaching, assessment, and student support. Staff members who increase their effectiveness receive both encouragement and support.
COMMUNITY	In the learning community, there is abundant evidence of energy, enthusiasm, and excitement; a commitment to excellence; and active, conscientious support of alternatives to achieve the school's vision.	The school is characterized by a common sense of purpose and enthusiasm. The school focuses on ongoing improvement of educational processes and staff development.
SAFETY	Adults provide an environment that actively promotes student learning. The climate in all classrooms is one of respect and concern for others. Student learning and active inquiry are paramount, and all students and adults are encouraged to ask for the help they need as lifelong learners.	All staff members see themselves as helping to promote a climate of caring and nurturing, and the school provides a safe, orderly environment to enhance student learning.

cont.

FIGURE 4.4 (CONT.)

School Culture Scoring Guide

Culture The culture of the school supporting the school's vision for students is characterized by trust, professionalism, high expectations for all students, and focuses on continual school improvement within a safe and nurturing environment.

	2 Partial	1 Minimal
PRACTICES	The school culture values both effective past practices and proven new methodologies. However, the primary focus is on the staff's effectiveness in terms of class management, curriculum coverage, and student performance as reflected by grades and test scores.	The school culture places primary value on past practices and meeting the educational expectations of colleges, parents, and faculty. Staff input and sharing of ideas and innovations occurs only on an informal basis. Staff development usually relies on outside expertise, ideas, and experience.
COLLABORATION	Although faculty and staff expertise is respected, ideas and innovations are generally shared only on an informal or cluster basis. Teachers work together on specific projects or tasks (e.g., discipline, attendance, and classroom management issues), meeting routinely in cluster groups to deal with logistical and budget issues. Generally, however, teachers work on curriculum and teaching strategies in the isolation of the classroom.	Although teachers have considerable autonomy within their own classrooms, they are expected to follow a chain of command and protocol, receiving official approval before initiating innovations or making any significant changes.
SAFETY	Students are occasionally concerned about their safety, and the school makes an effort to provide security and promptly address safety issues as they arise. Promoting a climate of caring and nurturing, however, is left up to individual teachers.	Discipline and school safety is seen as the exclusive responsibility of the administration. School environment issues are addressed informally and often in response to situations as they arise. Students and staff often fear for their own safety.

Adapted Accrediting Commission of Schools, Western Association of Schools and Colleges, Self-Study Documenmt

Basic School BUS Model

The School BUS was described briefly to all Countryside USD staff during the staff orientation day in August. Following the description, about 35 minutes was planned for small table groups to engage in Activity 4 from the Additional Staff Development Activities section below (five minutes for directions, 10 minutes for reading and small group dialogue on an assigned topic, and 20 minutes for whole group reporting and discussion). This activity underscored that the School BUS was a system of local accountability that focused on improvement at the school level nurtured by a culture of a learning organization. In the fall, activities 1–3 were conducted at individual school sites according to local need.

The School Culture Form was completed during the staff meeting at each school in September. The principal announced that im-

FIGURE 4.5

School Culture Form

School: ______________________________

Year	1 Minimal	2 Partial	3 Proficient	4 Advanced
Start				
End				

Description (major finding):

Analysis
School strengths:

School challenge:

Action plan:

proving instruction was an ongoing process best accomplished by team learning in a risk-free environment. It was not expected that staff would be "perfect" at the beginning of the year, just as students were not expected to be at grade level at the beginning of the year. But teachers were expected to learn and improve their professional skills and use common school strategies as they engaged in ongoing, sustained professional development and accountability dialogues. The purpose of self-assessment of the school's culture was to determine the current status and steadily improve over time until reaching, at least, the Proficient level. The School Culture Form would remain at the school site as an "in-house document" during this first year. However, the Assistant Superintendent of Everything Educational would have a conference with the school's leadership team to review the adequacy of the mini-action plan.

Countryside Elementary School was the first to conduct its staff meeting and assess its school culture. Tabulation of individual ballots showed agreement of 2, or Partial, an X was marked on the School Culture Form. Staff talked about descriptors in levels 2 and 3 and gave concrete examples as evidence; they finally selected a few descriptors to list on the form as particular strengths. Then they discussed which descriptors at level 3 would be targeted for school improvement during the upcoming year. The next step was to agree on a mini action plan for development and practice that would help staff make it a cultural norm.

The facilitator (a teacher on the school leadership team) distributed copies of Saphier and King's list of cultural norms (see Figure 4.6) and discussed them as examples of "what cultural norms looks like." The district periodically conducted workshops for school leadership teams, and professional literature "gems," such as this list of cultural norms, were a part of each session.

Figure 4.6

Saphier and King's List of Cultural Norms

Cultural Norms that Affect School Improvement	
1. Collegiality	7. Appreciation and recognition
2. Experimentation	8. Caring, celebration, and humor
3. High expectations	9. Involvement in decision making
4. Trust and confidence	10. Protection of what's important
5. Tangible support	11. Traditions
6. Reaching out to the knowledge bases	12. Honest, open communication

Chart in *Assessment in the Learning Organization* by A. Costa & B. Kallick, 1995, p. 9

Ideas for the mini action plan were written on a large chart paper in "rough draft" form. Another teacher on the leadership team good at writing clear summary statements volunteered to transform the draft statements into a formal statement after the staff meeting. A large font version was posted in the staff meeting room beside the bar graph on the wall, and a one-page School Cultural Form report was distributed to all staff. Figure 4.7 shows the completed form for Countryside Elementary School. Notice that statements in the Description, Strengths, and Challenge sections tend to come directly from descriptors in the scoring guide. The mini action plan mentions *who* will do *what when*, and *how they will know* if practices (cultural norms) have improved.

Advanced School BUS Model

Last year, many schools in Cityscape USD really "traveled far" with the School BUS and progressed at least one level on the School Culture scoring guide—many exemplified half to all of the Proficient level by the end of the year. Those schools who improved in some areas to the Proficient level's descriptors targeted the remaining descriptors for improvement this year and developed mini ac-

FIGURE 4.7

Example of Completed School Culture Form

School: Countryside Elementary School

Year 2000-01	1 Minimal	2 Partial	3 Proficient	4 Advanced
Start		X		
End				

Description (major finding):
The school is a "strong" 2, partially proficient as a learning organization. Grade level teams work together well, sometimes on common lesson units but it is rare for teachers to discuss and help each other with instructional strategies.

Analysis
School Strengths: (numbers in parentheses refer to scoring guide level)
Classroom management (2) is strong and experienced teachers help new teachers quickly learn the school's "core class management strategies." All teachers have high expectations for all students and reflect on student grades as an indication of what the teacher is doing that is effective or needs improvement (2). We have a common sense of purpose and enthusiasm (3), but we need to apply it more to best teaching strategies.

School Challenge:
Teachers and administrators collaborate in problem solving related to teaching, assessment, and student support (level 3).

Action Plan:
In the past, we did not have one common instructional focus as a team all year. We selected reading comprehension as our focus for school improvement this year. The school leadership team will plan staff development for the whole year on effective teamwork techniques and certain "research-based" instructional strategies. We have scheduled grade level and whole staff meetings at the end of each quarter to review student results as part of our staff development. Each quarter, we will examine the school interventions to see if they are supporting students at the Minimal level who need extra help to accelerate their learning. We will post notes on the wall chart each month that show how we are working better as a team on improving instruction and we will use the Culture scoring guide again at the end of the year to see if we have improved.

tion plans with the intention of reaching the fully Proficient level by the end of this year. These schools tended to pick clusters of descriptors or all the remaining descriptors in the higher level. Teachers in these schools believed they had capacity to initiate greater levels of improvement in their second year of using the School BUS.

Some schools started at the Minimal or Partial level on the scoring guide and for one reason or another, made little, if any, improvement. District administrators had held conferences with the leadership teams at these schools at the end of the previous year to pinpoint why they did not improve as much as expected and to collaborate on more elaborate action plans to implement during the current year. District administrators initiated a variety of "district interventions" to provide extra support and guidance to these schools and to accelerate improvement in their school cultures. For one intervention, principals at exemplary schools were selected to coach principals at "underperforming" schools if site administrators needed intensive intervention. Because a few of these schools had experienced considerable staff turnover, the district administrators explored reasons, including district policies and contracts.

Staff Development Activities

Activity 1: Lessons from the Geese

The story of the geese and the accompanying "lessons learned" have appeared in various forms in professional development workshop materials for the purpose of building awareness of the need for and value of shared leadership. We suggest arranging workshop participants in small groups if staff is large. Each group reads, discusses, and reports one section to the whole group. One option is to have groups sequentially read and discuss each section and then "report out" to the whole group. Allow about three minutes for small groups to discuss each section. Sample lesson responses are provided for the activity facilitator and are not meant to be shown to participants.

Lessons from the Geese

1. As a bird flaps its wings, it creates an "uplift" for the birds following. By flying in a V" formation, the flock's flying range is 71% longer than if each bird were to fly alone.
2. When a goose falls out of formation, it suddenly feels the drag and resistance of trying to fly alone and quickly gets back into formation to take advantage of the lifting power of the bird immediately in front.
3. When the lead goose tires, it rotates back into formation, and another goose takes over the point position.
4. People, like geese, are dependent upon each other. The geese in formation honk from behind to encourage those in front to keep up their speed.
5. When a goose becomes sick or is wounded or shot down, two geese drop out of the formation and follow her down to help and protect her. They stay with her until she is either able to fly again or dies. Then they start out again, either joining another formation or catching up with the original flock.

Sample Lesson Responses

1. People who share a common direction and sense of community can make progress quicker and easier by traveling on the uplift of one another.
2. If we have as much sense as a goose does, we will stay in formation with those who are headed where we want to go.
3. Taking turns doing the hard tasks and sharing leadership avoids burnout, builds commitment, and allows everyone to practice leading and following.
4. We need to make sure our honking from behind is encouraging, not discouraging.
5. If we have as much sense as the geese do, we'll combine our strengths and support each other, just as they do.

Activity 2: Lessons from Corning

Arrange the staff to sit in small "table groups." Read excerpts from the following article about Corning. Then answer the discussion questions in one of two ways. Option One: small groups discuss the first question, follow with whole group reporting and comments, and then move onto the next question. Option Two: assign one question for each table group to discuss and report on to the whole group, allowing for whole group comments.

Not many companies founded before the Civil War are on the cutting edge of the technological revolution. But Corning, best known for the cookware it stopped making in 1998, has shed its old-economy ties and bet the company on the new-economy world of high-tech innovation. Corning is now the world's largest maker of optical fiber to manipulate more data in the form of pulses of light through fiber more pure than wilderness air, with 1,500 scientists and engineers who apply for an average of one patent each working day.

"Corning has transformed itself." At 149 years old, Corning may seem too stodgy to be competing in the high-tech arena. Businesses that are growing today are growing because of new technologies. "That's a truism," says Corning CEO Roger Ackerman. Since bottoming out at $23.50 a share in 1998, the stock has shot up as high as $226.44. Ackerman describes Corning's culture as "confident nervousness." "We have too many ideas," says Charles Craig, Corning's vice-president of strategic planning and innovation. He laughs at the thought of other companies offering employee courses in idea generation. The nervous part of Corning's culture springs from the realization that its products have a commercial life of less than one year.

Growth depends not only on selling more fiber, but coming up with the photonics to transmit more data over each strand. Corning has increased research-and-development spending from 5% to 8% of revenue. A walk through Sullivan Park [research center] reveals a profusion of foreign accents. The company boasts that there are more researchers named Wang than Jones. Corning hired 700 more people with Ph.D.s in the past three years. So many scientists in one place stir big dreams. One day it will be possible to transport information via a combination of light and DNA genetics, says Lina Echeverria, a Ph.D. from Columbia who runs a division of Corning scientists. "Biotech and optics will eventually converge," she says.

Activity 2: Discussion Questions

1. Corning had been successful in the past selling Corning Ware. Why did the company decide to sell its cookware division and start a new program? Compare and contrast Corning's change in search of greater effectiveness in a changing world to your school and district. How does your school explore and invent the best practices to boost student learning?
2. Corning has a culture of "confident nervousness." What does this mean to you? Discuss the "confident nervousness" at your school about changing practices in a changing world of education, students, parents, communities, careers, and job skills.
3. Compare Corning's culture to what Senge describes as a learning organization. Why is Corning likely not to just survive but to prosper in the future? Compare and contrast Corning's culture as a learning organization with the culture at your school.
4. Why might Corning have more Ph.D.s as research scientists named Wang than Jones and so many workers with foreign accents? Why do so many high-tech jobs in America go unfilled each year?
5. Corning officials knew and used their quarterly earnings to justify practices and plan improvements. These frequent results were used as feedback about what was effective and what was not and as proof to the public that Corning's management team was effective and deserving of investor confidence. What lesson can schools and districts learn from Corning about reporting and using results frequently?

Activity 3: Parables about Change

Arrange the staff to sit in small table groups. Read the text in the box below. Then answer the discussion questions in one of two ways. Option One: small groups to discuss the first question and follow with whole group reporting and comments and then move onto the next question. Option Two: assign one question to each table group for discussion and report on to the whole group, allowing for whole group comments.

Parable 1

Change is inevitable. Change is something you do or something that happens to you. Change in life is like water flowing downstream in a river. You can try to stay in one place by swimming upstream, but eventually that effort will be futile, and you will grow tired and likely drown in the current going against you. Or you can swim with the current, avoid crashing into rocks jutting out of the water by flowing around them, and explore new places downstream.

Discussion Questions

1. What is the lesson to be learned from this parable about swimming downstream and avoiding the big rocks instead of swimming against the "current of change"?
2. All facets of life are constantly changing, including business, neighborhoods, and students. What changes in the world and school neighborhood, whether gradual or sudden, can you identify? What has been the reaction of staff to these changes? Why?
3. How have teaching practices changed over time in response to changes in the student clientele or the world of work?

Parable 2

A person builds a raft of logs with a cloth sail and crosses a river. Upon reaching the other side, he encounters a desert, so he hoists the raft on his shoulders and walks across. Soon he tires, puts down the raft, and makes an umbrella out of the sail and splinters of wood to shield himself from the scorching sun, leaving the heavy logs behind.

Discussion Questions

1. What is the lesson to be learned about a tool or practice that was effective in one situation, at one point in time, but becomes a burden when the situation changes?
2. The whole raft was not discarded. The sail was kept and modified into an umbrella. What examples do you have that staff frequently reflects on "where it is now" and decides if a strategy need to be let go of or is useful enough to be saved and modified?

Activity 4: Understanding the School Change Process

This activity strengthens understanding about the value of ongoing accountability and the ideas that meaningful change is centered at the school level and building the culture of a learning organization is the foundation for any instructional improvements.

A common characteristic of improving schools is the frequent use of results to inform program decisions. Meaningful change in the education of a student is the result of schoolwide change. Change is best attempted and accomplished as a team effort. A school culture that nurtures change builds a solid foundation on which best instructional practices can be built and endure.

Ask staff to read the three statements on the following pages, which describe (a) ongoing accountability, (b) the school as the unit of change, and (c) the school as a learning organization, and respond to the related set of discussion questions. We suggest that if a staff is large, assign or ask small table groups to read a particular topic and engage in dialogue about its meaning and application. Ask each small group to report to the whole group by highlighting statements about the topic (for the benefit of those who did not read about that topic) and the group's responses. Two questions per topic are given below to help frame the dialogue.

Topic 1: Ongoing Accountability

- Why is it better for a school staff to look at results frequently during the year rather than just at the end or the beginning?
- How public should accountability be? Should individual teacher, grade/department, or school results be made public? Some schools share results with just the district administrators, and some also share results with the school board and parents/community. What is right for your school, given that you have a choice?

Topic 2: School as the Unit of Change

- What are the benefits to the individual teacher when all teachers are involved in a common change initiative? What are the long-range benefits to the students?
- In systems thinking, the classroom, school, and district are important and interdependent, but some people think the school is the "the unit of change." Why?

Topic 3: School as a Learning Organization

- Why is school culture important to school improvement? How is school culture related to program implementation and improvement?
- Some schools work on developing a positive school culture before attempting changes in classroom instruction. Other schools work on both at the same time. What is right for your school? Why?

Topic 1: Ongoing Program Accountability

In the self-renewing organization, educators in all positions in the system create a better learning environment for themselves and students by studying education and how to improve it. The resulting initiatives for educational improvement propel the students into more active states of learning; and the greater activity of the students, in turn, stimulates the educators to engage in more study and create even more vigorous learning environments. An enriching spiral is generated. (p. 3)

A system of tracking effects was put in place early and used to confirm or modify the innovation while it was in progress. The effects on students were examined at regular intervals spaced fairly closely together. . . . some assessments were as frequent as weekly [discipline]; others were as far apart as quarterly [writing]. . . . successful school improvement programs do not wait for the standard "test scores" to come in. Those are used for confirmation of what has already been documented. (p. 54)

Joyce, Wolf, and Calhoun (1993)

School improvement is not a mystery. Incremental, even dramatic, improvement is not only possible but probable under the right conditions. . . . We have to acknowledge that people work more effectively, efficiently, and persistently when they work collectively, while gauging their efforts against results (Rosenholtz, 1991). Results goad, guide, and motivate groups and individuals. . . . In this sense, all results—good or bad—are ultimately good because they provide feedback that can guide us, telling us what to do next and how to do it better. (pp. 1–3)

cont.

Why do we avoid data? The reason is fear—of data's capacity to reveal strength and weakness, failure and success. Data almost always point to action—they are the enemy of comfortable routines. By ignoring data, we promote inaction and inefficiency. Fatalism feeds fear. Teachers have limited confidence in their ability to "raise achievement." In such a climate, any expectation for improvement seems unrealistic—and generates fear. (p. 39)

Schmoker (1999)

"Formative evaluation" is a reflection by a school staff of the impact of instruction on student achievement in an ongoing cycle to recognize successes and plan improvements. "Ongoing local accountability for school improvement" is a synonymous term. Ongoing assessment feedback helps students to adjust and accelerate their learning.

Ongoing assessment results help teachers to adjust and improve their teaching. For both students and teachers, feedback and the use of results need to happen at critical points during the year to pinpoint corrections while there is an opportunity to act and to recognize successes along the way.

Carr (1999)

Topic 2: School as the Unit of Change

Successful school improvement requires the participation of all, or nearly all, of the people involved. In whatever segment of the organization that is trying to improve, all personnel need to participate in the initiative. A few enthusiastic volunteers do not a school-improvement program make. Schoolwide participation is essential where the school is the focus; and districtwide participation, where the education agency is the focus. (p. 53–54)

Joyce, Wolf, and Calhoun (1993)

When Thomas Edison was asked why he was so prolific an inventor, he replied that it was the result of what he called the "multiplier effect." He placed his team of inventors near each other to encourage them to consult with one another so that

cont.

each member of the team benefited from the collective intelligence of the group. His teams not only worked better but faster.
(Smith, 1995, p. 9)

Teachers at Donaldson Elementary School in our district were reluctant to spend large chunks of their early-out times in meetings supposedly intended to promote "continuous improvement." But when they began to see collective progress, a direct result of their focused collaboration, the meetings became more meaningful. A good example is what happened when we discussed a key weakness in 2nd grade writing: students' difficulty in writing descriptive settings. After the team brainstormed, a team member proposed having students first draw then describe in writing the setting they imagined for their stories. The number of students able to write high-quality descriptions went from just a few to almost the entire 2nd grade class. (p. 11–12)

Schmoker (1999)

It is obvious that teams outperform individuals, that learning not only occurs in teams but endures. Teams bring together complementary skills and experiences that, by definition, exceed those of any individual on the team . . . bringing multiple capabilities to bear on difficult issues.

Katzenbach and Smith (1993)

An African saying is that it takes a village to raise a child. Think beyond the mental model of "my classroom" to the whole educational experience of each child. How many teachers does it take to educate a child? Can one teacher do it alone in one year, or is it a cumulative effect? It is not so much *this year* that matters as *kindergarten through twelfth grade* for a student. It takes all teachers within a school working as a team and teams across school levels, to truly educate a child to be a contributing member in a global village and successful in the world of work.

Carr (1999)

Topic 3: The School as a Learning Organization

School improvement is moving away from highly targeted innovations intended to solve specific problems toward a fluid inquiry into how to make education better day to day. The intent is to make all schools learning communities for faculties as well as students—making use of the most powerful models of learning with both groups.

For many years and through many different reform movements, our schools have been hampered by structural characteristics that make innovation laborious: no time in the workday for collegial inquiry, no structures for democratic decision making, a shortage of information and the absence of a pervasive staff development system. Essentially, we have tried to engage in school improvement with a series of Catch-22s designed into our organization. (p. 51)

Joyce and Calhoun (1995)

A learning organization is an organization in which people at all levels are, collectively, continually enhancing their capacity to create things they really want to create. Our fundamental challenges in education are no different than in business. They involve fundamental cultural changes, and that will require collective learning. They involve people at multiple levels thinking together about significant and enduring solutions we might create, and then helping those solutions come about. (O'Neil 1995). "The most successful corporation of the 1990s will be something called a learning organization" (Senge, 1990).

When a school becomes a learning organization, all members of the school community participate in long-range planning, implement the best practices for the success of all students, and evaluate progress toward the common vision. A learning organization is proactive, it anticipates the need for change and plans for it.

Carr (1999)

5 Improving Instructional Practice

Good teaching matters.

—*Kati Haycock*

Teaching not only is important, but it is more important than all demographic characteristics combined.

—*Douglas Reeves*

Overview

Good teaching practices evolve into best practices when teachers expand their repertoire and concentrate schoolwide on a core set of the most effective strategies to help all students reach or exceed standards of excellence. There is always more to learn about how to teach. A new and better way to reach a child is always waiting to be discovered. The third wheel of the School BUS is about accountability for continually improving the school's instructional practice. Elements in the cycle of instructional improvement are professional development to learn new strategies, time and support to practice, and assessment of schoolwide implementation and improvement.

The previous chapter was about fostering a culture for school change of instructional practices. This chapter focuses on making the changes in instructional practices that lead to dramatic, sustained improvement in student achievement. A *comprehensive instructional program* is defined as all of the strategies to help students learn the (quintessential) standards that a school staff has agreed to implement schoolwide. A comprehensive instructional program has three components:

- A cohesive set of *core classroom instructional strategies* practiced schoolwide
- A set of *school interventions* that support classroom instruction for students who need extra help to reach proficiency on at least the quintessential standards
- A set of strategies that the school uses to build *a partnership with the family and community* to support classroom instructional strategies and school interventions.

All three components are important, but teachers have the most control over their classroom instruction and, therefore, the greatest impact on student achievement. Meaningful improvement in a student's education is not the result of one teacher's efforts one year, but all teachers working together throughout the life of the student in the educational system. School staff engages in adult learning—professional development—that largely mirrors their own students' learning. In effective professional development, teachers frequently and actively participate in analyzing results, problem solving, and constructing new knowledge and skills with one primary focus.

A new approach to lesson planning and delivery is called *standards-based instruction*. It starts with identifying the content standard and the assessment to measure student mastery, planning a variety of learning activities and instructional strategies to help students learn and practice the standard, and then using assessment feedback to strategically assist struggling students to master the standards. Starting with the standard and final assessment in mind, the teacher designs "a straight row of instruction toward mastery of the standard" that often is lacking in traditional instructional approaches. Teachers must understand the standards and how to use information from student assessment to select appropriate instructional strategies. Improving teacher's content knowledge and pedagogy rests on effective professional development embedded in a system of accountability. The School BUS provides this accountability structure.

The Basic and Advanced School BUS models describe the focus of instructional program improvement in the two school districts and give an example of a school's Instructional Practices report form. Teachers use a scoring guide to self-assess their own level of instructional implementation at the beginning of the year and agree on an action plan to support improvement. At the end of the year, teachers assess their progress and celebrate collective improvement in their teaching.

The Staff Development Activities section provides four activities:

- an optional form and scoring guide for assessing general classroom instruction across a school
- an optional form and scoring guide for assessing professional development at a school
- a discussion about the relative impact of various "research-based" instructional strategies
- a dialogue about truths and myths that can influence a teacher's approach to instruction and change

A Comprehensive Instructional Program

A comprehensive instructional program has three components listed in order of how important their impact is on student learning: core classroom instructional strategies, school interventions for students who need extra help, and family and community partnerships.

A *comprehensive instructional program* is defined as all of the instructional strategies that a school staff has agreed to implement schoolwide. Many schools have school plans mandated by either federal Title I or state regulations or by a voluntary decision that a business plan makes good business sense. School plans list or describe a set of strategies that form the school's instructional program. In some schools, a plan is produced annually as required but "put on a shelf to gather dust." In other schools, the plan is an important tool that school staff uses to build consensus, set goals or objectives, and check implementation throughout the year. A comprehensive instructional program has three components, as shown in Figure 5.1.

- A cohesive set of *core classroom instructional strategies* practiced schoolwide is at the center of school change initiative
- A set of *school interventions* that support classroom instruction for students who need extra help to reach proficiency on at least the quintessential standard that is the focus for school–wide improvement
- A set of strategies that build *a partnership between the school and the family and community* that support classroom instructional strategies and school interventions targeting the focus for schoolwide improvement

The term curriculum has been defined as content (concepts and skills to be taught), instructional materials, and instructional strategies, or some combination of the three. This book defines curriculum as the materials used to teach the content standards. The curriculum can be taught in many different ways, with rigid or flexible pacing, and with or without the requirement that a student reach some level of mastery before moving on to the next topic or grade level.

While curriculum materials are important, they are not considered in the discussion of improving instructional practice in this book. The School BUS does allow examination of any factors that influence improving student learning, but when time and simplicity are crucial, instructional practice is the primary consideration. All too often, a school staff quickly blames curriculum materials for the failure in student learning and expends a huge amount of money to change materials. They believe that no improvement is possible if no funds are available for more or different materials. This chapter will provide a rationale for targeting improvement in schoolwide classroom instructional practices before examining other possible areas.

FIGURE 5.1

Comprehensive Instructional Program: Circles of Impact, Sequence of Decisions

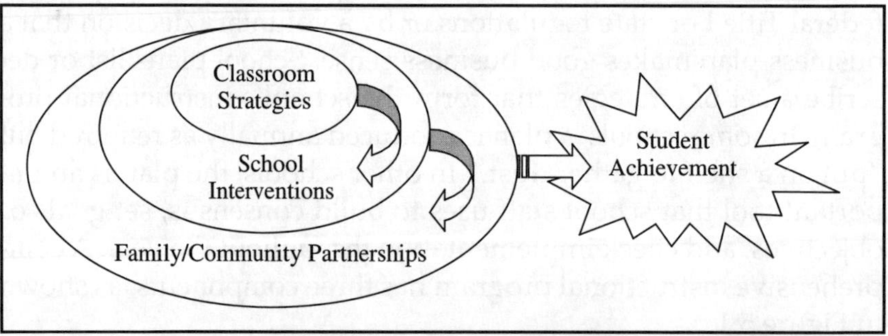

Core Classroom Instructional Strategies

Foremost in a school's comprehensive instructional program are the *classroom instructional strategies* that form a set of core practices implemented by all teachers at appropriate grade levels in a school or district. Shown at the center of Figure 5.1, classroom strategies are the primary focus of a school staff using the School BUS to make informed decisions about improving student learning. In other words, improving classroom teaching strategies has the biggest single impact on changes in student learning and is the component over which teachers have the most control.

The School BUS does not expect that all teachers "teach exactly the same details in the same way all day, every day." The School BUS does expect a school staff to agree to teach certain quintessential standards using a core set of instructional strategies that all teachers have learned or are learning through ongoing professional development. If there is a school plan, this core set of strategies should appear as the instructional program element of the plan. A school beginning to use the School BUS might select one complex, multi-faceted instructional strategy, such as cooperative learning (Johnson et al, 1994) or reciprocal teaching (Rosenshine et al, 1994), or a cohesive cluster of specific strategies to learn to teach a certain quintessential standard all year. This one complex strategy or cluster of strategies may be the year-long focus of assessment and accountability in the School BUS approach.

Reeves refers to rejecting some teaching practices in favor of best practices as "pulling the weeds before planting the garden" (2000a). A school might throw out some practices that do not appear to have a big impact on student learning and add a few practices that promise a greater impact. Another school might throw out most or all practices and import an entirely new instructional program, such as Success For All. Both schools are embarking on the journey for instructional program improvement.

School Interventions

The second most important component of a comprehensive instructional program is the set of *school interventions* to support, but not replace, classroom instruction. This component is shown as the second ring in Figure 5.1. Good first teaching in the classrooms reduces the number of students needing extra instructional services. Some students have personal or family conditions that are especially challenging and require more intensive instruction than any classroom teacher can give in a room of 20 or more students. The School BUS attempts to identify these students, identify appropriate interventions, and monitor results.

Students at the Partial and Minimal performance levels are candidates for school interventions (see chapters 2, 3, and 6). "MI" students at the Partial level might be offered one or more *moderate interventions* around mid-year, for example, small group instruction a few days per week. "II" students at the Minimal level are candidates for *intensive interventions* such as one-on-one daily instruction by a trained professional. An improvement in an effective system of interventions can reduce the number of students referred for special education.

Professional literature (e.g., Barr & Parrett, 1995) suggests that there is sufficient knowledge about what does work to help all students learn successfully, especially those considered at-risk. Levin suggests that educators discard practices that have proven not to work, such as many remedial programs, and try strategies that are proving to excite students and accelerate their learning, such as strategies for gifted and talented students (Brandt, 1992). Slavin (1992/93) emphasizes early intensive intervention with continued support and compares this to bringing a stew to a boil and then letting it simmer to thoroughly cook. Too often, intensive help is given and then all supports are taken away and the student slowly regresses, or "tepid" remedial help fails to accelerate learning and close the achievement gap.

Schools must determine the need for and implement interventions (especially preventive and early interventions) before a student is so far behind that catching up is almost impossible. Professional literature also suggests that the effectiveness of an intervention largely hinges on its link to classroom practices. A student will likely be confused when taught one way to read by the classroom teacher and a very different way by a reading specialist in a pull-out program. A student taught to block letters into a sound by a Reading Recovery tutor will more likely master the skill when the classroom teacher uses the same technique.

School interventions do not take the place of classroom instruction and may be offered before or after school, on Saturdays, during intersessions at year-round schools, or as an elective in secondary schools. Teachers as a whole school staff have control over school interventions. Best first teaching in the classroom aligned with research-based school interventions can accelerate student learning to a sufficient level of proficiency.

Early intervention within the classroom is far more successful and less costly than later attempts at remediation or special education services. Prevention of failure remains the most cost-effective and holds the unrivaled promise of long-term success (Barr & Parrett, 1995). Before/after/within school reading programs (e.g., Reading Recovery), homework tutorials, cross-age tutoring (Gartner & Reissman, 1994), and HOTS (Pogrow, 1990) are a few examples of moderate and intensive interventions to accelerate student learning.

Family/Community Partnerships

The third component of a comprehensive instructional program is a set of family and community strategies that build a partnership with the school to support classroom instruction and school interventions. This component forms the outer circle in Figure 5.1 and is the area over which teachers have the least influence and control.

There are many strategies that increase home and community involvement in educating students and supporting classroom teachers. Some schools and districts have prevention programs, such as infancy and preschool educational programs for parents and guardians. Some schools recognize alternative family situations such as grandparents with primary care responsibility or foster care homes. Some schools provide homework centers and special bus stops for homeless students. One principal gave a mother a map of the school boundaries and urged her to keep her child in the same school when she was unable to pay her rent and forced to move from apartment to apartment.

Rather than complain that many parents do not have books in their home and do not read to or with their children, a school created "book bags" with leveled books in English and Spanish that parents exchanged weekly. Parents received instruction about how to read to their children and ask "thinking" questions during and at the end of a story. Joe Johnson of the Dana Center in Austin, Texas, talked about a school that invites illiterate parents to come to the school, listen to a "struggling reader" orally read a book with success, ask questions of the student, and then give applause for the performance. This gives both the student and parents a feeling of pride and self-worth. Henry Levin mentioned an Accelerated School Project school's simple "respect and communication" strategies, which resulted in increasing PTA meeting attendance from virtually zero to hundreds and motivating migrant parents to do all they could to ensure that their children continued their education at that same school. Every school from any type of neighborhood does or should have its own success stories of strategies that made families and the community active collaborators in students' education.

Parents do not have to be English speakers or literate readers and writers in order to help their children learn and show support of the classroom teacher and the school. Professional literature does point to critical parent behaviors, such as daily asking about and discussing what happened in school, asking critical thinking questions during parent-child interactions, and providing a set place and time for homework. Anthony Alvarado (2000), chancellor of San Diego City Schools, tells the story of growing up in a home where his father expected his children's homework to be neatly done and in a tidy pile on the dining room table when he came home late at night from work. If homework was not neat or not there, the child was awakened and told to do it. It wasn't until middle school that Tony realized his father could not read English. Barr and Parrett (1995) identify ways for parents to influence their children's learning in school:

- Help children to learn to read by holding, cuddling, and reading to small children; encourage older children to identify words or talk about the story that they have read.
- Talk with children, ask questions that involve critical thinking in English or the home language, and encourage children to make decisions.
- Provide a stimulating environment for children, excursions that involve learning and dialogue.
- Encourage responsible television viewing, especially educational shows; children who watch more than 20 hours of television a week usually do poorly in school.
- Be interested and involved in children's school.
- Provide a safe, loving environment ...

Barr, R. D., and Parrott, W. H. *Hope at Last for At-Risk Youth*, pp. 69-70, copyright 1995 by Allyn and Bacon. Reprinted with permission.

These three components—school unity around core classroom strategies, supportive school interventions for students who need extra help, and home/community partnerships—form a school's comprehensive instructional program. The School BUS considers how to improve all three components and realizes that the integration of services often has an indivisible impact on student learning.

Determiners of Student Achievement

Yes, socioeconomic status (SES) does matter when looking at test results for schools and districts. Higher SES students as a group outperform lower SES students as a group on state and national achievement tests. Many students from affluent families enter kindergarten with the "high home capital resources" of language arts and math knowledge and skills, grow up with computers at home, and have enriched background experiences. Many students from high poverty families enter kindergarten with "low home capital resources" or are recent immigrants with little or no English skills. Other home capital resources that influence a student's readiness to learn include health and nutrition and feelings of safety and ownership of personal property (e.g., toys, books, clothes, home/bedroom).

Teachers in schools in highly affluent neighborhoods do not face the same instructional challenges as do teachers in schools in high poverty neighborhoods. "Low home capital resources" is not a barrier to learning, but does present a greater difficulty for a school staff to find the ways to meet and beat the challenges. It is the responsibility of the staff at a school in a high poverty neighborhood to find ways to narrow the achievement gap between the "high and low home capital resource" students. Many "high home capital resource" students have parents with college degrees. Some schools with "low home capital resource" students take the students to visit colleges or find college professors and students to mentor the "low home capital resource" students.

SES does not cause student achievement to be low or high, but there is an association. SES is not a "determiner" of achievement—coming from a low SES family does not determine that a child will have low test scores now and forever—but it is associated with factors that do have an impact on student achievement. Schools cannot change a child's SES, but they can influence some of those factors associated with SES that have a link to academic achievement.

The example above of giving bags of books weekly to parents who cannot afford a home library is one of many strategies that schools in high poverty neighborhoods can use to influence home capital resources. Teachers with high student expectations and a determination to take on the challenge can reduce the negative impact of low home capital resources. There are schools from high poverty neighborhoods with test results that rank among the highest in the state or show some of the greatest gains.

Reference was made above that SES is associated with "group tendencies." Some high SES students are low achievers and have two parents who spend little time with them. Some low SES students are high achievers with single parents or grandparents who are intensely concerned that the children get into the best universities. Some students from rich families fail, drop out of school, "turn on to drugs and tune out school" and some students from poor families excel and graduate.

The school can inspire and guide parents to read to their children, to listen to them read, to talk with them about their school day and the importance of an education, and to ensure that they complete their homework and get enough sleep. Schools can find ways to work with many parents and the community to support their children's learning. It is much more likely that a student from a low SES background will excel in education when that student has a series of teachers who demand excellence, not a series of teachers who demand little and expect failure.

Now we look at a few research studies that compare the relative impact of different factors on student achievement. These are not "single research studies," but summaries of many research studies. For example, what is more important, quality of teaching or background factors of students and parents? The preponderance of evidence is that teachers matter more than any other single factor (Brophy, 1984; Darling-Hammond and Ball, 1997; Haycock et al, 1999; Reeves, 2000; Wang et al, 1993/94). It is not that other factors do not matter—they do. But a highly qualified professional teacher who is educating a student for many hours a day five days a week does tend to be more important in how much a student learns and in how much a student improves in achievement, than any other factor in that student's life.

Darling-Hammond and Ball (1997) summarized various research studies that support the importance of teaching quality on student achievement. Figure 5.2 presents a pie graph showing the relative influence of four categories of factors on changes in students achievement test scores. Test score change was on the NAEP (National Assessment of Educational Progress) scores for eighth grade mathematics from 1990 to 1996 (taken from *NAEP 1996 Mathematics Report Card for the Nation and the States*, Table 2.3, p. 30). The four categories were: small classes and schools, student and family background (e.g., poverty, English as a second language), parent education level, and teacher qualifications (e.g., credentials, years of teaching experience).

Figure 5.2

Categories Influencing Change in NAEP Grade 8 Math Scores (1992-96)

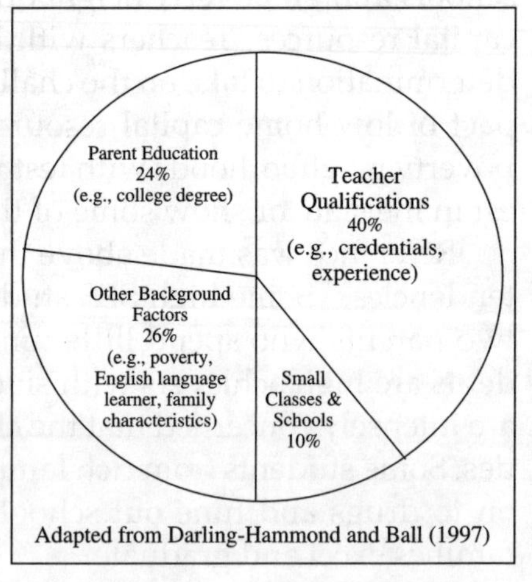

Adapted from Darling-Hammond and Ball (1997)

What was the relative impact of each of these four categories of factors on changes in test scores over the six-year period? Small classes and schools accounted for 10% of the variance in test scores. Parent education level explained 24%, and other background factors accounted for 26% of test score variance. Compare that with teacher qualifications, which explained 40% of the test score differences. Note that "teacher qualifications," such as possessing a full credential and years of teaching experience, is a gross indicator of true quality of teaching, yet this factor still had the largest impact on changes in student achievement. The authors also reported that the large achievement gap between black and white students was almost entirely accounted for by teacher differences. The same or very similar percentages were reported in pie graphs from other NAEP achievement tests and in findings by other researchers.

Darling-Hammond and Ball cited a study by Sanders and Rivers (1996) that the average student assigned to ineffective teachers three years in a row scored fifty percentile points lower on achievement tests than those assigned to the most effective teachers. As teacher quality increased from low to high, so did test scores. However, because Sanders and Rivers defined teacher quality in terms of student test results, the circular definition introduces some controversy about the strength of the findings (Bracey, 1999).

Darling-Hammond and Ball (1997) also reported that teachers with higher levels of education were more likely to use literature-based reading and writing assignments that tap higher level performance skills. "Teachers who spent more time studying teaching are more effective overall, and strikingly so for developing higher order thinking skills and for meeting the needs of diverse students," according to Darling-Hammond and Ball.

In 1984, Brophy summarized the prior 25 years of research on teacher effects and offered several conclusions. Teachers who elicit greater gains in student achievement than other teachers establish high expectations, use most of classroom time on activities to foster mastery of the curriculum, effectively organize and efficiently manage their classrooms as learning environments, and actively instruct students with fewer lecture-presentations to the whole class. Effective teachers use "think aloud" demonstrations to model for students the usually covert strategic thinking used in problem solving (this is a part of strategies called "scaffolding" and "reciprocal teaching"). These teachers realize that students actively construct new meaning; students are not passive learners, and teachers do not pour new information into "semi-empty brains." They create "a learning community where dialogue promotes understanding." They use curriculum materials as a resource and teach fewer topics but more in-depth.

Brophy found that highly effective teachers teach reading as a process for extracting meaning from text and teach decoding skills within that context. Students often work in collaborative groups reading to each other and discussing answers to questions implied by the text. Writing is taught as a means to organize and communicate thinking to particular audiences for particular purposes. To learn mathematics, students explore, conjecture, reason logically, and use a variety of models to solve non-routine problems. Science is not just memorizing facts about dinosaurs but requires engaging in hypothesis-testing and data analysis. Instead of working first through basic skills and then getting to experience the fun of real world application, students start with authentic problem solving to learn low-level skills and spend more time on discussions about meanings of concepts and operations and less time on computation skills sheets.

Wang, Haertel, and Walberg (1994) performed a meta-analysis of 179 handbook chapters and reviews, 91 research syntheses, and surveys by 61 researchers to create a database of 11,000 statistical findings. (A meta-analysis is a way of summarizing trends across many single studies or sources.) They formed a list of the relative importance of 28 categories on student learning. Figure 5.3 is an adaptation of their bar graph showing 19 of the original 28 categories. (Numbers in the table refer to effect size multiplied by 100 as an indicator of a category's impact on student achievement.) Classroom management (group alerting strategies to maintain students' active participation) and metacognitive and cognitive processes are at the top of the graph. Home environment/parental support, the next in importance, is mostly about parents ensuring that their children complete homework. At the bottom of the graph are various categories about policies and demographics. Classroom instructional strategies matter more than school demographics in student learning, but building parental support is also important.

Kati Haycock (1998) states that about half of the achievement gap would disappear if poor and minority students had teachers of the same quality as other children. "If we went further and assigned our best teachers to the students who most need them . . . there's persuasive evidence to suggest that we could entirely close the gap." In short, good teaching matters. Reeves (2000) has studied high performing schools with high poverty and high minority student populations and is convinced that a growing "mountain of evidence demonstrates that successful teaching progress substantially mitigates the impact of the demographic factors . . ." (p.170).

This section of research studies supports the claim that good teaching does matter for all students and matters more than many other factors. Teachers are most important in the education of students, but some students need extra support beyond the classroom,

FIGURE 5.3

Relative Influences on Learning (Effect Sizes x 100)

Classroom Management/Alerting	65
Metacognitive Processes	63
Home Environment/Parental Support	61
Student/Teacher Social Interactions	58
Motivational Affective Attributes	55
Peer Group	54
Quantity of Instruction	54
School Culture	53
Classroom Instruction	52
Curriculum Design	51
Academic Interactions	51
Classroom Assessment	50
Community Influences	49
Curriculum and Instruction	48
Parental Involvement Policy	46
Student Demographics	45
School Demographics	41
State-Level Policies	37
School Policies	37

30 40 50 60 70

19 of the 28 categories adapted from Wang, Haertel, and Walberg (1994)

especially in cases of severe learning difficulties, dysfunctional homes, or unsafe neighborhoods. Teachers do not abdicate their central role and responsibility—they work in a team to give intensive care to those students with intense needs. Some students need extra support in addition to what the classroom teacher can give. Those school interventions, which may involve family and community partnerships, should be intensive, early, and integrated with individual classroom strategies.

The School BUS draws from research and professional wisdom about the relative impact of different factors on student learning to define a comprehensive instructional program in a school. The School BUS identifies three components of a comprehensive instructional program—core classroom instruction strategies, supportive school interventions, and family / community partnerships, and targets each in order of importance for making decisions about school improvement (see Figure 5.1).

Many Bullets, None Magic

A school may choose to change one or a few instructional strategies or the whole instructional program. Instructional strategies have three parts: understanding the standards, learning pedagogy, and standards-based instruction.

Should a school change one or a few instructional strategies, the whole classroom instructional program, or the whole school comprehensive instructional program? There are no silver or magic bullets or easy answers to school improvement. No one strategy or program has been found to be best for all students. Some methods work better for certain types of students, and some methods may depend on teachers' disposition and style.

Stories about how a staff in some schools accomplished dramatic improvements in student achievement in high poverty schools point to integrating simple solutions rather than throwing out an old program and purchasing a whole new program. Staff began with the high expectation that all students can and will succeed, and the assumption that methods exist or could be invented to help every student succeed. Then they started the ongoing, collaborative work of taking stock of what was effective, discarding what was not effective, and experimenting with new ideas about how to teach more students more effectively (Wheaton and Kay, 1999; Berman, Cross, and Evans, 2000; and Calwelti, 2000). A school does not lead students to success alone nor can it sustain improvement alone. District staff must support school efforts. Parents, the community, and local universities are part of the comprehensive, sustainable solution (e.g., Navarro and Natilicio, 2000).

Approaches to improving student achievement range from comprehensive school reform programs to subject area franchise (i.e., "home-grown") programs to the accumulation and integration of specific strategies for topics and types of students. The federal government encourages local adoption of Comprehensive School Reform Demonstration (CSRD) programs through $50 million from the Obey-Porter legislation. Many schools have posted impressive gains after adopting a CSRD program. Other schools adopted a CSRD program but did not realize meaningful gains, perhaps because there was not full staff commitment to change itself or to the particular new program model. Fullen (2000) believes that "reculturing"—developing professional learning communities in the school—is most important to starting and sustaining school improvement.

Reeves (2000a) and his staff at the Center for Performance Assessment have been studying "90/90/90 schools," that is, schools in which more than 90% of its students come from low-income families, more than 90% of students are from ethnic minorities, and more than 90% meet at least high academic standards. Reeves found that none of the schools used a specific program or any other proprietary model to achieve their success. These schools achieved dramatic improvements in student learning because everyone united around a common vision of high expectations, inquiry-based staff development and meetings, essential common curricula and pedagogy, and relentless accountability.

Wheaton and Kay (1999) report on a network of schools that created the theme "1000 Days to Success" to show its commitment that 100% of students who enter a school in kindergarten will be literate by the end of third grade. Teachers at these schools weave together best strategies inside and outside the classrooms to accomplish their goal. They have been able to change a history of disjointed workshops and failed improvement efforts by keeping effective methods, discarding unproductive techniques, and adding promising methods from external sources to form a comprehensive package of services tailored to individual student's needs. Reeves calls this "weeding the garden before planting the flowers."

Improving classroom instructional strategies can be divided into three topics. First, teachers must have a firm understanding of the content standards to increase the likelihood that students will come to understand the standards. Second, teachers must continuously add to and refine their pedagogy, so that more students learn at greater levels of mastery. Third, teachers must strategically plan lessons, streamlining instructional strategies to target a specific standard at an expected level of mastery on a specific assessment. Discussion of these topics is expanded in the following three sections.

Understanding the Standards

Teachers must understand the exact meaning of broadly stated content standards and the fundamental concepts or skills embedded in the standards. Some teachers may need to learn the fundamental concepts that they are expected to teach, such as reviewing multiplication as a "short-cut" strategy of addition, not just as memorizing a multiplication table and routinely applying an algorithm to computation problems on a page.

Bracey's study (2000) cited findings from TIMSS (Third International Mathematics and Science Study) comparing teaching practices in America with those in Germany and Japan. During math lessons, American teachers presented about twice as many definitions from much thicker textbooks than did German and Japanese teachers. Consequently, American teachers tended to superficially cover topics with few proofs and show little interrelation between lessons.

> In a typical American lesson, a teacher would review homework, demonstrate how to solve the problem of the day, give students practice in seatwork, correct seatwork, and assign homework. In Japan, the teacher would review the previous day's problem, present the problem of the day, and set the students to working on its solution either individually or in groups. The whole class would then discuss the solutions, usually with students who thought they had solved the problem leading the discussion from the blackboard—something that almost never happened in American classes . . . American teachers see math as a set of procedures, and they want their students to become skilled in using the procedures. Japanese teachers "act as if mathematics is a set of relationships between concepts, facts, and procedures. [They] wanted their students to think about these relationships in new ways. (p.474)

After teachers thoroughly understand the content standards, they can facilitate class discussions so students can understand the meaning in the statements and translate the adult language into "kid-friendly" wording. The kid-friendly standards are posted on classroom walls and teachers point to them as they begin a lesson on the standard. A visitor should be able to enter the classroom during a lesson, ask a student what he or she is learning, and expect the student to point to the standard on the wall and state what it is.

After teachers thoroughly understand the district performance standards and performance levels, they can facilitate class discussions so students can understand expectations of their achievement (and how they will be graded). Students transform adult language performance levels and scoring guides into kid-friendly language and post them on the wall next to models of student work, as appropriate. Students engage in self-assessment and peer assessment and create scoring guides for classroom assessments. When teachers understand and target standards to learn and standards of performance, teaching becomes powerful. When students understand what they are to learn and take responsibility for assessing their own learning, instructional power is intensified.

Learning Pedagogy

Research shows that some instructional strategies are more effective than others. Later in this section, a variety of instructional strategies will be compared in terms of their relative impact on learning. Why use Strategy A when research has shown that Strategy B can be twice as effective? A teacher can learn "the basics" of a strategy and then gradually learn nuances, refinements, and adaptations to use it more effectively with more success for a greater diversity of students. The professional teacher continually reflects on current instructional practices and explores other techniques that are potentially more powerful.

Computer users get used to the fact that software programs are continually updated and decide when it is time to install and learn the more advanced program. In every grocery store, many products are labeled "new and improved." It's not that the product was bad before, but now it is even better because food researchers found ways to enhance the product.

There is no one instructional strategy that works wonderfully for all students. People have different learning styles, strengths and weaknesses, and interests. Some people are global learners—they want the global idea, the big picture at the end of the lesson, before beginning the sequence of steps in the lesson. Other people are sequential learners—they want one step presented at a time and opportunity for reflection on the whole at the end of the lesson. There are learners whose primary strength is auditory, visual, spatial, musical/rhythmic, tactile, and kinesthetic. Consider a spelling lesson for the word cat. The teacher who wants to reach all students will have auditory learners orally spell the word and visual learners write the word on the chalkboard. Tactile learners will trace the letters on their forearms, spatial learners close their eyes and imagine a cat with the letters revolving around it, musical learners create a song, and kinesthetic learners form letters with arm gestures.

The teacher who uses the one-size-fits-all approach aimed at the "middle student" bores many high achievers who already understand the topic, satisfies some middle range students, and frustrates low achievers. No wonder test results illustrate a bell-shaped curve in those classrooms. The teacher who teaches one way according to his or her learning strengths and interests fails to provide equity to all students, that is, equal access to the curriculum for students with different learning strengths and interests. The professional teacher strives to grow in her breadth and depth of pedagogy and reach all students.

Because a typical classroom contains a diversity of learning needs and interests, the teacher must differentiate instruction to meet those diverse needs and interests. This does not mean individual lesson plans for each student, but it does mean diversification for subgroups of students to the degree that the teacher can manage it. All students in the classroom are expected to learn the same content standards to the same performance standard, but there are alternative pathways to the standards.

The master carpenter does not attempt to build a house using one hammer. He or she has a tool belt with various instruments and a toolbox with a wider variety when the basic set is not enough. Likewise, the master teacher builds a lesson with a variety of strategies in mind and goes to his or her toolbox of alternative strategies when he or she finds that some students need something other than those originally planned. Both the carpenter and teacher are prepared to meet a variety of conditions and to change tools as they work. Both frequently reflect on their work, use formative assessments (the teacher checks for understanding; the carpenter observes for task completion), and, if necessary, take corrective action.

Moving from the "one-size-fits-all" approach to differentiated instruction is not easy, but it is rewarding. Fortunately, there are wonderful models in many classrooms, from kindergarten with learning centers to multi-graded classrooms to high schools with alternative group projects. Tomlinson (1999) describes the differentiated classroom and strategies that teachers can use to meet all students' needs in the elementary, middle, or high school classroom. For example:

- Stations are placed at different locations in the classroom where students work on various tasks on a theme or subject area. Students self-select (or are assigned to) one or more stations depending on their learning needs.
- Centers with self-instructional materials are set up in the corners of a classroom for different subject areas. Children rotate through all the centers and might have choices based on learning styles or difficulty levels.
- Orbital studies (Stevenson, 1992) provide independent investigations around a curriculum theme. Students select their own topics, develop their own study plans, and select from a variety of performance options.

Silver, Strong, and Perini (2000) encourage teachers to differentiate instruction and assessment for students with diverse learning styles and intelligences. It is not practical or appropriate that every lesson contain multi-modularity variation. The authors offer a commonsense approach to teach "so each may learn."

Shulman et al (1998) offer 16 case studies of "groupwork" and cooperative learning in diverse classrooms. Groupwork activities might be problem solving, discovery learning, or research investigations in which tasks within a group complement one another and include an assessment component. The teacher facilitates and constructively intervenes only when appropriate. Trumbull et al (1998) discussed individualism versus collectivism as rooted in different cultural values and norms and explained how collaborative groups can support communication for the English learners in the groups. For example, students from Asian cultures may feel more comfortable working on a collaborative group task because it is a common method of learning in their native countries, and English-proficient students in the group can negotiate language that would be a barrier to reading and writing if students worked alone.

If we can agree that teachers should use *diverse teaching strategies* to address the strengths of a diverse student population, then it follows that teachers should use *diverse assessment strategies* to ensure that all students demonstrate accurately what they have learned. It is only fair and equitable to give all students equal opportunity to learn the standards and show what they have learned. The content standards remain constant; the performance standards remain the same. Assessment accommodations (e.g., more time, rephrasing directions) and alternatives (e.g., oral responses to support or amplify written responses for English learners) give students the equal opportunity to perform to their true achievement level on an assessment. Poor performance on an assessment should indicate an instructional need, not a problem with a poorly designed or "one-size-fits-all" assessment (Koelsch, Trumbull, & Farr, 1995; Farr & Trumbull, 1997). Effective, professional teachers keep trying different methods with a student until they find what works.

School staff may find it worthwhile to view a brief scene near the end of the movie, *Mr. Holland's Opus.* While playing chess with his friend, the football coach, Mr. Holland says that one student (who happens to be the star football player) just cannot learn to play the drum. The coach, angry that Mr. Holland thinks "his one way of teaching" is the only way, tells Mr. Holland that *he* is the failure for not trying to find the way that works for every student, not the student who was already giving his best. After trying all sorts of methods to "get rhythm into the student's head and body," Mr. Holland and the student are successful and beam wide smiles full of pride in their accomplishment.

It takes time to develop a full repertoire of teaching methods. But it is easier when teachers collaborate on lesson planning and "team teach." It can help to have a critical friend.

Standards-Based Instruction

When teachers have an adequate understanding of content and pedagogy, they are ready to engage in "standards-based lesson planning" (Western Assessment Collaborative, 2000), also called "backward design" (Wiggins & McTighe, 1998). Standards-based instruction is defined as mapping backwards from a desired outcome to define a variety of instructional strategies so that all students are likely to reach the performance standard. Figure 5.4 compares the approaches of traditional and standards-based lesson planning.

In the traditional approach to lesson planning, a teacher plans instructional strategies and student learning activities for a selected unit or topic. After instruction, an assessment is selected or created to measure how well students learned the topic. Sometimes the test measures exactly what was taught, but sometimes more or slightly different topics were taught or tested, partly because the design and delivery of instruction preceded the design of the assessment. Students are left guessing about what is expected of them or how the teacher will assign grades. Some teachers use the assessment for grading and move on to the next topic. Others provide additional teaching and retesting for students not reaching competency.

FIGURE 5.4

Traditional Lesson Planning	Standards-Based Lesson Planning
• Select a curriculum unit/topic	• Select standard(s) and become familiar with required content knowledge and skills
• Plan instructional activities	• Design assessment and scoring guide
• Select/design and give assessment	• Plan learning activities and instructional strategies
• Give grade, feedback	• Articulate standard and scoring guide to the students
• Move to next unit/topic	• Administer assessment; give feedback and extra opportunities to learn; move on to next standard

Adapted from Western Assessment Collaborative at WestEd, 2000

In standards-based lesson planning, the teacher identifies the content standard(s) and selects or designs an assessment to measure the level of mastery of the standard(s). This "up front" selection of standards and assessments before teaching helps the teacher to target exactly what and how students need to learn. The teacher designs which aspects of the Civil War will be assessed and then ensures in-depth instruction is planned for those aspects. In standards-based lessons, students are informed at the outset about the standard that will be taught and the scoring guide that will be used to judge achievement.

Teaching strategies and learning activities are then developed. Curriculum materials are identified to support instruction. Teachers build in differentiation to accommodate multiple learning styles and needs so that all students have equitable opportunities to learn the standards. Activities are planned that actively engage students individually and in collaborative groups to construct new knowledge and skills.

The teacher explicitly states and articulates the content standard to be learned and the scoring guide to judge achievement. Exemplars of student work and scoring guides (rubrics) from past years or similar tasks help students see the expected outcome and self-assess their progress. To accurately gauge their own performance, students need to see what good work looks like. The scoring guide becomes a more powerful tool when students participate in developing the guide and engage in self- and peer-assessment.

During the lesson, formative assessment informs the teacher about adjustments for students having difficulty. At the end of the lesson, the summative assessment is given. Standards-based teaching does not end with the assessment. Information from the assessment helps the teacher plan follow-up lessons and reassessment for students not meeting a required level of proficiency. Teachers may give follow-up lessons within the normal day, or students may be offered before/after school interventions. When given the option, many, but not all, students choose to continue learning and be reassessed when they do not reach the proficient level.

Inside Out Improvement

School staff starts with core classroom instructional strategies to make improvements, then moves outward to school interventions, and, finally, to family/community partnerships.

As discussed previously and illustrated in Figure 5.1, research indicates that quality of teaching is the most important determiner of student achievement. But it is unrealistic to expect that regular classroom teachers can provide all the instruction each student needs to master the standards. Some schools are experimenting with ungraded classrooms, allowing students to master sequentially core standards at their own "developmentally appropriate" pace while still trying to accelerate progress (Sumner, 1993). However, the vast majority of schools expect students to move one grade per year with their chronological age peers. Educators and policymakers are cautioned not to push or rush curriculum beyond students' developmental capacities (Orlich, 2000).

In the School BUS approach, a school staff concentrates first on how they can improve classroom instruction, in particular, a core set of strategies that addresses the quintessential standards or the one standard with the greatest need for improvement, as indicated by assessment results. Next, the staff examines how school interventions can be improved or added to support classroom instruction for students identified as needing extra help to accelerate their learning. Last, staff explores how family and community partnerships can be strengthened to support instruction, especially for students who need extra help. The School BUS takes an inside-out approach to improving the school's comprehensive instructional program. The School BUS is a bottom up approach where the school staff has control of and responsibility for reflecting on results, making decisions about improvements, and continually learning and practicing the discipline.

Who is Invited to the Meeting

School BUS staff meetings do not prohibit others from joining the team meetings to discuss issues about program implementation. The principal and other school support staff should rotate attendance at grade level or departmental meetings. School leadership team members facilitate the meetings. Educators and other stakeholders (students, parents, community members, board members, and union representatives) might be invited as occasional or permanent members.

Persons who are not part of the school staff can bring diverse perspectives, knowledge, and experience to school staff meetings, enriching discussions and deepening critical examination of school practices. They can serve in a variety of roles, such as critical friend, coach, or consultant. The Accelerated Schools Project encourages external people to serve on school cadres to help generate alternative hypotheses about causes of and solutions to school challenges. An external person who is tactful yet undaunted by the challenge of exploring classroom instruction can help a school team that is reticent, impeded by mental models, or just "too close to the microscope" to critically examine classroom practices.

Effective Professional Development

Effective professional development is a series of sessions planned and led by staff to review pedagogy, explore improvements, and learn new strategies.

Professional development is the primary vehicle for teachers to examine past practices, explore new approaches, and learn and practice new strategies. When a school agrees to adopt a new program, or even a new strategy with some degree of complexity, the answers to several questions will determine whether the new program will be a success or another failure. After just one workshop, are teachers expected to proficiently implement the new program in their classrooms? Does the school schedule a different topic for each staff development day? Both practices are traditional models of staff development, but neither is considered a powerful model. The effective model of professional development is based on how students learn best—related topics integrate prior lessons until a comprehensive concept is constructed by the student and practiced with feedback over a long period of time until mastery is achieved or surpassed.

Leiberman (1995) states, "What everyone appears to want for students—a wide array of learning opportunities that engage students in experiencing, creating, and solving real problems, using their own experiences, and working with others—is for some reason denied teachers when they are learners" (p. 591). Teachers must create a culture of inquiry and participate in reciprocal learning experiences. "[P]eople learn best through active involvement and becoming articulate about what they have learned" (p. 592).

Sparks and Hirsh (1997) speak about professional development as constructivist learning done *by* teachers, not *to* teachers.

> [They] seek a form of professional development that prepares teachers "to see complex subject matter from the perspectives of diverse students" and they point out that understanding cannot be developed only through traditional top-down teacher-training strategies limited to teachers' acquisition of new knowledge and skills. Professional development today also means providing occasions for teachers to reflect critically on their practice and to fashion new knowledge and beliefs about content, pedagogy, and learners. (p. 3)

Staff development that supports true school renewal embodies three practices in workshops (Sparks & Hirsh, p. 9). *Results-driven education* requires teachers to use results to inform school improvement decisions. *Systems thinking* seeks to understand the interrelationships and long-range cause-and-effect links in a complex system or organization. *Constructivism* acknowledges that "learners create their own knowledge structures rather than merely receive them from others."

The new, effective approach to staff development for Sparks and Hirsh involves "the creation of learning communities in which everyone . . . are both learners and teachers" (p.17). Colorado State University matches professors, teacher candidates, and high school teachers for the purpose of connecting theory to practice. Each of the three groups learn from one another in a partnership to improve teaching methodology (Middleton, 2000).

King and Newmann (2000) contended that effective professional development at school sites must consist of three elements—teachers' knowledge, skills, and dispositions; the school as a professional community; and program coherence. Teachers must be "professionally competent in instruction and assessment appropriate to the curriculum for their students, and they must hold high expectations for all students' learning." The strong professional community has clear, shared goals for student learning, and staff engages in collaboration, reflective inquiry, and decision-making about the school's activities and policies. The school's program must be coherent, focused on clear learning goals, and sustained over time. "Teacher learning is most likely when they have sustained opportunities to study, to experiment with, and to receive helpful feedback on specific innovations."

A survey of over 1,000 teachers by Birman et al (2000) disclosed three structural and three core features of effective staff development. The study found that effective staff development has the *form* of reform activities, sustained *duration*, and group *participation* of teachers representing the same site if it was a district or regional workshop. Core features of effective professional development included: a *content focus* on subject matter knowledge; *active learning* through meaningful analysis of teaching and learning; and *coherence* over time and across levels with state standards and assessments.

The National Foundation for the Improvement of Education published a clear, straight forward, comprehensive 97-page report, *Teachers Take Charge of Their Learning*, that underscores what is known to be highly effective and most important:

- *Student Achievement*—Teachers' foremost concern in their own learning is student achievement; working toward this goal should be the top priority.

- *Time*—Reallocating existing time and finding new opportunities for teachers to prepare themselves daily and yearlong through individual and group studies
- *Empowerment*—Nurturing responsibility and skills for teachers to work with colleagues, develop a shared vision, and make important decisions
- *Community Involvement*—Teachers need partners to help them enhance their knowledge and skills (e.g., parents, universities, businesses, and museums).
- *Funding*—Additional funds and reallocation of existing funds to build high-quality, ongoing professional development

Staff Meetings as Staff Development

In some schools, staff meetings consist of listening to the principal read a news bulletin and discussing daily operations, such as copier use and paper supplies. These schools rarely find time to explore the more important issues of curriculum development and instruction reform. Teachers rarely get the opportunity to discuss teaching and learning. It is common for staff in Accelerated Schools to agree to read the bulletins the principal places in their mailboxes and use precious staff meeting time for professional dialogue about instruction.

Schools that are improving use a majority of staff meetings, or a portion of each meeting, to examine curriculum, instruction, and assessment issues. It is common for the beginning of one meeting to be a discussion about how teachers implemented the action decision made at the end of the previous meeting. Using a series of meetings to make decisions for instruction and evaluate implementation and impact on student learning is the heart of ongoing accountability.

Suppose a staff decides to concentrate on the interaction strategy of allowing "think time"—pausing five seconds after asking a question during a lesson—before calling on a student for an answer. The next day, the principal wanders through classrooms to observe implementation. At the staff meeting two weeks later, a discussion about the impact on students is prompted by the question, "Did 'think time' lead to more students raising their hands with an answer to the question?" The resulting responses may include some teachers saying it was effective, while others relate observations that many students do not *listen* to the answers. Because the teachers want students to be good listeners *and* critical thinkers, the staff decides to have students use hand gestures to signal agreement or disagreement with an answer given by a student in class. At the start of the subsequent staff meeting, teachers discuss the impact of that strategy—is there evidence it was a good decision?

In summary, effective professional development is being defined by many of the same terms used to define accountability. Both entail reflecting on current practice and impact on student achievement, identifying challenges, exploring solutions, implementing and monitoring progress of a planned solution, and then recognizing and celebrating success when it happens.

Instructional Practice Accountability

In the School BUS, teachers self-assess core classroom instructional practice using a scoring guide and complete a form with a mini action plan twice a year. During the year, staff implements the action plan, primarily by professional development activities. Corroborating evidence from other sources builds confidence in the accuracy of self-assessment data and soundness of planned actions for improvement.

Accountability that serves improvement of a school's instructional practices involves formal assessment and use of results to inform decisions about further improvement. The focus of the third wheel of the School BUS is on improving instructional practices. The school selects one or a few instructional strategies or a whole new instructional program as their focus for improvement. It will likely take all teachers several years of adding, deleting, and enhancing individual strategies or learning a whole new program to reach or exceed the Proficient level.

Implementation of the school's comprehensive instructional program should be reviewed at least at the beginning and end of the school year, and informally throughout the year. A formal assessment using a scoring guide targets the primary component of the school's program, the core classroom instructional strategies. Figure 5.5 presents a five-point scoring guide for teachers to self-assess their level of implementing the core classroom instructional strategies.

The scoring guide is developmental, progressing from a Novice who is beginning to learn new strategies to the Expert teacher who is fully proficient and has made adjustments and supplements to address the learning needs of all or almost all students. The expectation is that teachers might start at the Advanced Beginner level and, with effective professional development, gradually learn and progress to the Proficient level or higher, perhaps by the end of the year. The scoring guide borrows performance level labels (e.g., Novice, Advanced Beginner) from David Berliner's (1988) description of the five stages of teachers' skill development.

FIGURE 5.5

School BUS Scoring Guide for Instructional Practice Implementation

	Core Classroom Instructional Practice Scoring Guide
5 Expert	▪ I use the core instructional strategies daily and extensively along with supplements to enhance certain topics or for certain subgroups of students. ▪ Instruction is differentiated to meet the learning needs/styles of all, or almost all, students. Formative assessments inform my ongoing decisions about adjusting strategies for subgroups of students. ▪ For each unit, I build in opportunities for reteaching and reassessment for students not yet proficient on all quintessential standards and all or most of the other essential standards. ▪ Students are challenged to achieve at higher levels and they rise to the challenge. The teacher and students exemplify a passion for learning.
4 Proficient	▪ I use the core instructional strategies extensively and some supplements to enhance certain topics or for some students. ▪ Instruction is differentiated to meet the learning needs/styles of many students fairly often. Formative assessments inform my ongoing decisions about adjusting strategies for subgroups of students. ▪ There are opportunities for reteaching and reassessment for students not yet proficient on quintessential and some of the essential standards. ▪ Students are challenged to achieve at higher levels and most respond. The teacher and most students exemplify a passion for learning.
3 Competent	▪ I use the core instructional strategies. I need more practice to supplement strategies and increase pacing. ▪ Formative assessments help me to adjust lesson delivery, but I am not yet able to differentiate instruction for all student subgroups. ▪ Reteaching and reassessment opportunities are limited and apply to quintessential standards in language arts and math; sometimes it is necessary for "underperforming" students to move on to the next topic.
2 Advanced Beginner	▪ I use the core strategies with some success but need more practice and coaching. I am limited in my ability to differentiate strategies to meet the needs of students. ▪ I use informal formative assessment; it helps me adjust whole group lesson delivery and target strategies for one or two subgroups.
1 Novice	▪ I am starting to practice with some core strategies with help from a coach. Classroom management and discipline are major concerns.

Carr (2000)

Staff rate their individual practices at the beginning and again at the end of the year. It is expected that teaching practices will improve as a result of continuing forms of professional development and practice. However, it is sometimes the case that ratings show a decrease over time because the staff has reached a more critical understanding about proficient practices and become more critical in their self-assessment. One is reminded of the adage "the more I know, the more I know what I do not know." Group dialogue and cross-validation such as classroom observation ratings by others can support self-ratings on the scoring guide.

Process

The process of self-assessment and creating a mini action plan can be accomplished within a one-hour staff meeting. The first session is conducted at the beginning of the year, perhaps following the staff meeting when school culture was assessed (see chapter 4). The second session is conducted at the end of the year in the same staff meeting when the school culture is reassessed, providing that the principal thinks there will not be much need for extended discussion and planning future improvement actions. Otherwise, this assessment of classroom instructional strategies requires its own one-hour meeting. The principal or other leadership team member facilitates the meeting.

Prior to the meeting, the school leadership team reviews the scoring guide in Figure 5.5 and makes appropriate adjustments in wording. The model scoring guide uses the general term "core instructional strategies," but the leadership team may want to substitute the names of one or more specific strategies. Also, the team may want to modify statements in other ways, but it is suggested that the district accountability committee, not individual schools, make any changes in rigor of the performance levels.

1. *Distribute the scoring guide* and ballots to teachers to rate their own performance level. Remind teachers that it takes time to learn a new program and develop strategies to meet the needs of all students. They might be at the Novice or Advanced Beginner stages. The purpose of the self-assessment is to measure the current level of implementation to inform staff development planning and, at the end of the year, to measure progress.
2. After teachers have submitted their ballots by recording one performance level number, immediately *tabulate the number of*

teachers at each performance level for all to see on a wall chart.

3. *Discuss and reach agreement* on a description of the data, teacher's strengths, team challenges, and action plan. Draft statements.
4. *After the meeting*, a member of the school leadership team converts the number of teachers at each level to percentages and writes final statements on the Classroom Strategies Implementation Form (see Figure 5.6). Copies of the form are posted on the faculty room wall and distributed to all staff. The forum stays at the site or is submitted to the district office according to a prior agreement.

Figure 5.6

Core Classroom Instructional Practice Report Form

Core Classroom Instructional Practice Report Form

School: ____________ Date: ________

Strategies: ______________________

	1 Novice	2 Advanced Beginner	3 Competent	4 Proficient	5 Advanced
#					
%					

Description (major finding):

Strengths:

Challenge:

Action Plan:

5. Recall that space was reserved on the bar chart on the wall of the faculty room for additional bars to be entered for the beginning and end of the year. *Write the following percentages on the vertical line* next to the numbers 1–4 that were entered for the school culture bar: 1–25%, 2–50%, 3–75%, and 4–100%. Create a bar for the beginning rating (e.g., September) that shows the percentage of teachers at or above the Proficient level. At the far right is space for the year-end bar when teachers reassess implementation (see Figure 5.7).
6. *Anecdotes on Post-It™ notes* as evidence of implementation of the action plan are added above each month, perhaps using a color different from notes for school culture.
7. *Significant progress* implementing the action plan—improving instruction of core classroom strategies—is celebrated at year-end.

Figure 5.7

Partial Bar Graph Including Strategies Ratings

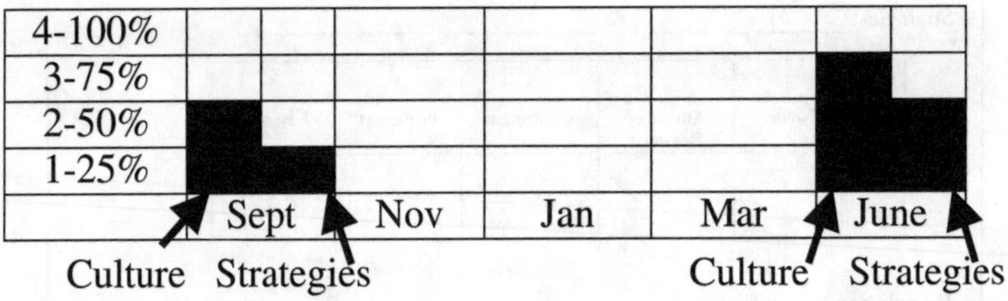

4-100%			
3-75%			
2-50%			
1-25%			
	Sept	Nov	Jan	Mar	June

Culture Strategies Culture Strategies

More to the Process

This section discusses why it is important for teachers to self-assess their instructional practices rather than leave the task to some external observer(s) to rate the teachers and report summary findings. It does not mean that "external eyes" are not valuable, but teachers must reflect on their own practice in earnest before contemplating observations and suggestions from others. Several options are given for corroborating self-assessment results with observations by others, especially when the data will be reported publicly and carry some level of high stakes, or importance.

Too often, a school has a formal school plan that lists instructional strategies or a proprietary program all teachers are expected to implement. However, when asked if all teachers are truly implementing what is stated in the school plan, no one at the school can say for sure. When few or no teachers at the school change their practices and ignore planned changes, student achievement results likely will stay the same. If student results are quite low, the school may be asked or told to change their school plan. But the strategies in the plan may not be faulty or ineffective; rather, the school plan was not implemented wholly and effectively. Either it was just assumed everyone would do what was written, or the plan was viewed as a bureaucratic formality that no one really intended to implement. Some schools make a few changes in their plans every year and submit the plans to the district office, however, each teacher continues to teach whatever way he or she wants and has been doing for years. In these cases, it is no surprise that the plan keeps changing but classroom teaching never changes and, consequently, neither does student achievement.

In a school that seriously practices the culture of a learning organization, teachers *want* to keep gradually changing as part of a team because they realize that is the only way students will become educated adults. Teachers honestly reflect on and talk about their progress in the long-term, continuous process of learning to improve teaching to improve student learning.

Peters (1987) said, "What gets measured gets done." That is why elements very important to "get done" are assessed in the School BUS. A school culture of a learning organization, the theme in Chapter 4, is so important in the School BUS that it is the second wheel of the model and gets assessed by staff using a scoring guide. A culture of change is the foundation for exploring and making changes in classrooms and supportive interventions. In this chapter, continually improving research-based, core classroom instructional practices is the third wheel of the School BUS. Progress implementing core practices is assessed because improving teaching schoolwide has the most leverage to improve student learning. Knowing that practice will be assessed spurs implementing practice. The assessment results are not used as a "gotcha," but as formative feedback that informs decisions that support further learning by teachers. Similarly, teachers use formative assessment of students during their learning to identify student needs and modify instruction accordingly so that all students are successful.

Consider the humorous saying, "To err is human, but it is against company policy." Teachers are likely to be honest in their self-assessment in a climate that supports them as learners—a climate in which it is okay to make mistakes as long as effort and progress are being made. Students are not admonished for making mistakes as they learn and neither should teachers.

Learning to teach better so that all students are successful is extremely difficult. To compound this difficulty, conditions, students, and world information are always changing. Making a mistake can be a wonderful opportunity for learning. Beverly Sills said, " You may be disappointed if you fail, but you are doomed if you don't try. " It is the responsibility of the school principal to both establish a risk-free environment for adult and student learning, and to demand that everyone engage in learning. When teachers see themselves as learners and know the principal expects that they learn from their mistakes, teachers are more likely to be honest in their appraisal of learning new pedagogy.

In the School BUS, teachers and other school staff take responsibility for "bottom-up" reflection and analysis about what is working well, what is not, and how to improve it. It is very important that teachers self-assess their own practice in the School BUS in order to encourage change from within, from the bottom up. The School BUS helps build capacity and expertise within the school through a bottom-up approach.

Teachers are likely to be accurate in their self-assessment if they have a deep understanding of what proficient performance looks like. As students need to see what a proficient writing sample looks like to see where they are in relation to the standard, so also do teachers gain an understanding of what proficient teaching looks like from watching others teach proficiently.

A scoring guide and professional standards can serve as exemplars and goals. Learning comes from practice in the classroom preceded and followed by continual, incremental professional development activities. It is not at all easy for any teacher simultaneously to teach and reflect on how well she is teaching. Feedback from students and a coach or colleague can give a fresh perspective or validate what the teacher "sees in her own practice."

Why do professional athletes have so many professional coaches watching and advising? The athletes need someone to observe closely while they concentrate on the performance of the moment. Coaches can see things that the athletes cannot see for themselves. In *Mr. Holland's Opus*, the football coach saw what Mr. Holland was unable to see in himself because of his mental model about what good teaching looks like or because he had never seen truly proficient teaching. The coach jarred Mr. Holland's mental model and challenged him to experiment with a new belief that every student can learn if the teacher can only find the right way for each student.

This example may create some concern about why there are not many coaches for professional teachers, but that is a discussion beyond the realm of this book. Money and time for human resources are important, but a culture of "opening classroom doors" and peer coaching is the bottom line. Some schools establish the culture and rearrange schedules to create peer coaching. Including the information from coaches into the introspection process can help teachers deeply, objectively see their level of performance and determine where improvement is needed and how to improve.

Teachers in some schools have become so used to teaching "where students are" that over time, instruction and expectations have drifted far below grade level. Indeed, the gap between instruction and (state) grade level expectations may widen across grade levels. Students being presented with essentially the same level of math from second grade to high school should be taken as an indication that something is seriously wrong. Curriculum specialists external to the school must be invited to observe lessons, examine student work, compare findings to external sources of grade level expectations, and then discuss the results with the school staff.

When teachers stop assigning homework because "students won't do homework," something is seriously wrong, and someone from outside the school must challenge the mental model the staff has developed over time. There are schools in high-poverty, high-minority neighborhoods where students do hours of homework, where children hold a flashlight under a blanket on their bed to keep reading after their mothers tell them to turn out the lights and go to sleep. The difference in schools is culture, expectations, mental models, and excitement in teaching and engagement in learning.

It is paramount that teachers' self-ratings be corroborated by other evidence especially in situations where the school is undergoing a formal state program review or is applying for recognition as a distinguished school. Formal student feedback is one means for obtaining corroborating evidence. For example, if teachers say that their lessons are exciting adventures in learning, corroborating evidence might come from interviewing a random sample of students or from ratings on a written survey completed by all students. If a teacher says he or she is using a variety of strategies to meet the needs of all students, then all students in the class should agree.

Trained observers using a process and scoring guide known to the staff might report on findings for public accountability or an awards application, corroborating teachers' self-assessment findings. One option is for pairs of school leadership team members to accompany external observers into classrooms, observe together, talk with students and the teacher, examine student work, and reconcile observations after they leave the room. When the feedback is given to staff, the leadership team and external observers report the findings together. This collaboration alleviates staff mistrust or disbelief in negative findings and increases acceptance when colleagues affirm problem areas. When staff works as a team to explore options and find their own solutions as a team rather than rely on recommendations given by an outsider, defensiveness and helplessness give way to empowerment and effective problem-solving.

Sometimes teachers in a school and district with historically low student achievement need to go out and see other schools with similar student demographics but much higher achievement in order to raise their expectations and see other ways of "doing business." Sometimes the low-performing school needs to invite teachers from high-performing schools with similar student demographics to observe and discuss differences between the two schools.

Corroborative data builds confidence that the self-assessment results are accurate. When a discrepancy occurs, sources must be examined closely and a sound rationale given for why one set of data appears more accurate or why additional sources must be explored and reconciled. Corroboration of teachers' self-assessment of their classroom instruction is necessary to garner acceptance by people external to the school who read the school's accountability report.

While the School BUS emphasizes a bottom-up approach to collecting and using results, as data rise to the top it should be cross-validated (corroborated) to be confident that the reported data appear to be accurate. It is not recommended that a school staff "be observed or be assessed" any more than "be held accountable." They should "*be* observing and *be* self-assessing" and "*be* accountable." When public high-stakes accountability is involved, it is important to include outsiders' observations.

Although the School BUS advocates a bottom-up approach, the process is truly a balanced approach. District administrators have the right and responsibility to review a school's findings and action plan contained in the report form (see Figure 5.6), question any statements that appear unsound or inaccurate, and reach a resolution with the school leadership team. Confidence that a school truly is implementing "best, research-based" practices with proficiency in all classrooms comes from corroborating evidence from district staff and, in high-stakes or very formal situations, "expert" educators external to the district. That a school is improving its instructional effectiveness is best proven by meaningful improvements in student achievement results: "The proof is in the pudding." Examining student results to determine instructional effectiveness and plan further improvement is the fourth wheel of the School BUS and the topic of the next chapter.

Basic School BUS Model

Ms. Wright, a third grade teacher on the leadership team at Countryside Elementary School, attended a workshop last year in which reciprocal teaching was presented along with the Rosenshine's (1994) research findings. Reciprocal teaching is especially appropriate for teaching reading comprehension and was found to improve dramatically both internal CRT and external NRT test results.

Ms. Wright explained the strategy to the leadership team, which then discussed it with the whole staff. They agreed to focus professional development throughout the year on learning to implement reciprocal teaching in all intermediate grade classrooms. A modification of the strategy would be tailored to students in the primary grades. The subparts, or specific strategies, that comprise reciprocal teaching were spread throughout the yearlong series of staff development hours and staff meetings.

Reciprocal teaching starts with the teacher asking questions that involve prediction, facts, and inferences at the end of increasingly longer sections of text. After modeling, students form small groups and take the reciprocal roles of "teacher and student." Answers may be verified by locating exact statements in the text. Students learn that reading is not just decoding a string of words, but also constructing meaning, using personal experiences as background knowledge, and exploring their relationship to stories with a moral. Gradually increasing the amount of text read before reflection builds memory.

Members of the leadership teams at Countryside Middle School and Countryside High School attended the same workshop that Ms. Wright attended the previous year. They all had the same concern about students' poor reading comprehension. Teachers outside the English department saw how the strategy could be applied in their subject areas to enhance students' understanding of textbooks. Reciprocal teaching became a schoolwide innovation at all three schools in the district as a bottom-up decision by teachers about how to improve student learning of a quintessential standard in greatest need for improvement.

After attending the reciprocal teaching workshop, the teachers representing each school were so impressed and excited that they decided to try reciprocal teaching during summer school. They coached and consulted each other to learn how to apply the technique at various grade levels. When the whole school staff decided to adopt the strategy, the teachers who had attended the workshop became the facilitators and the county office provided additional support.

All staff participated in a one-day "overview" workshop on reciprocal teaching at the start of the school year. Workshops on specific strategies within reciprocal teaching and time for teachers to discuss problems and resolutions were planned throughout the year. The leadership teams substituted the specific term "reciprocal teaching" for "core classroom instructional strategies" in the scoring guide.

Staff meetings in September were set aside for concentrating on the school culture and assessing that wheel of the School BUS. At the staff meeting in the second week of October, staff used the scoring guide to self-assess their starting level of implementation and used the action plan to address professional development. Predictably, the only teachers at the Competent or Proficient level in October were the teacher-trainers who had practiced reciprocal teaching during summer school. The remaining staff rated themselves at the Novice or Advanced Beginner stage. It was discovered during staff discussion that teachers who professed to be at the Novice stage tended to be new to the profession of teaching and struggling with classroom management. Experienced teachers were assigned as mentors, and this strategy was added to the action plan.

Principals of the three schools scheduled part of staff meetings in other months for grade levels and departments to meet separately and as a whole school to discuss their successes and challenges using reciprocal teaching and help each other overcome the challenges. Leadership team members facilitated their grade or department meetings and placed on the wall chart Post-It™ notes on which they'd written anecdotes as evidence of significant, concrete improvements in implementing reciprocal teaching.

In June, each school again self-assessed using the scoring guide and found that all teachers were at least at the Competent performance level. Anecdotal notes on the wall chart indicated many examples of their steady improvement. Ongoing reflection and discussions throughout the year alerted the leadership teams that progress was being made, and they prepared to have a success party at the June meeting.

Advanced School BUS Model

As stated earlier, Cityscape USD is a mid-sized district that had already completed their first year using the School BUS and was moving from a focus on reading comprehension to an integrated approach to reading and writing. Each school reviewed and selected core classroom instructional strategies, tailored to local conditions. At the end of year, results across schools showed a range of percentages of teachers at or above the Proficient level on the assessment of core classroom instructional practices.

District administrators convened a principals' meeting to review the previous year's results for both school culture and instructional practices. A chart called a scattergram showed the relationship between each school's consensus culture rating and the percentage of teachers at or above proficiency. Figure 5.8 shows the scattergram with a culture rating (scale 1–4) on the horizontal line and a practices rating (zero to 100%) on the vertical line representing each school. Dots showed how school scores intersected. Because each school was shown only as a dot, schools maintained anonymity. Everyone saw that the "swarm of marks" formed a fairly narrow diagonal pattern. This indicated a fairly strong relationship between culture and practice—the higher the rating on school culture, the higher the percentages of teachers at or above proficiency on core instructional practices.

Figure 5.8

Scattergram for 38 Schools in Cityscape USD
Trend for Instruction to Improve as Culture Improves

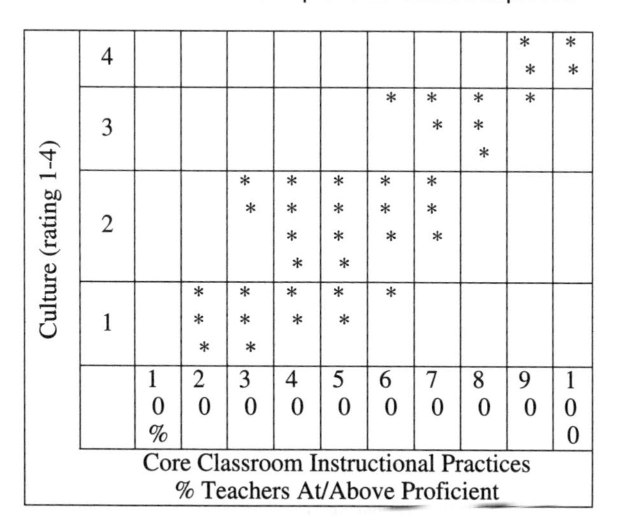

This finding led to a renewed collaboration between the district and lower performing schools to concentrate on professional development and other actions to improve the school culture to support changes in teaching practices. The district grouped into clusters, some schools by location and some to bring together schools in the lower and upper ranges of the scattergram for informal coaching. These clusters met each quarter to discuss progress and share ideas for meeting and overcoming challenges. Just as some students need extra support and differentiated instruction, some schools (principals, leadership teams, and staff) need extra support and differentiated supervision to learn how to make certain changes.

For schools in the higher range (e.g., rating of 3 on culture and at least 70% Proficient on practices), the goal was to continue improving school culture through team learning of an expanded set of schoolwide instructional strategies. Schools in the lower range continued to focus on the one set of reading strategies before attempting to expand to integrated writing. Process results informed process decisions.

Schools self-assessed core classroom practices at the beginning of their second year using the School BUS for two reasons. First, almost all schools had at least a few new staff. Second, year-end results for Year 1 were reconciled with the results for the beginning of Year 2 to establish a new baseline for improvement. Schools also assessed at end of the year and held staff meetings to discuss progress. The district found that ratings using the scoring guide improved and were bolstered by anecdotes of qualitative changes. The district held a success celebration for leadership teams, and each school celebrated with all staff at their respective sites.

Staff Development Activities

Activity 1: Optional Scoring Guide

This scoring guide is a four-point scale with descriptors adapted from WASC rubrics. If a district is highly critical of the scoring guide presented in the main body of this chapter (see Figure 5.5), the district might consider using this scoring guide instead. The descriptors in this optional scoring guide are more general and apply to a comprehensive instructional program rather than a specific set of strategies. It is likely "overkill" to use both assessment tools in a school. The reporting form is shown below, followed by a two-page optional scoring guide.

Powerful Teaching and Learning Report Form

School: ____________________ Date: ____________
Strategy/Program: ______________________________

	1 Traditional Lecture	2 Traditional Repetition	3 Meaning-Centered Teachers as Guides	4 Research- Based Interactive
#				
%				

Description (major finding):

Strengths:

Challenge:

Action Plan:

Powerful Teaching and Learning: Teachers design learning experiences that involve students actively in rigorous learning and use diversified methods that enable more students to succeed at high levels. Teachers focus on active learning strategies, such as inquiry, demonstration, collaborative learning, and effective use of technology.

	4 Advanced	3 Proficient
CURRICULUM	Everyone in the diverse student population receives a thinking, meaning-centered academic foundation that reflects current educational research and practice.	Students receive a thinking, meaning centered academic foundation aligned with district/state content standards.
COURSEWORK	Standards closely aligned with state frameworks emphasize learning about subjects in depth, connecting new learning across disciplines, constructing new knowledge, and applying learning in real-world contexts. Inquiry is made the norm in all subjects by focusing on such goals as depth of knowledge, student collaboration, long-term projects, and revision of work in progress. Teachers are coaches and facilitators of student learning.	Teachers regularly review and revise their courses to make them more effective and more closely aligned with the district standards.They use a variety of information sources (e.g., current research and assessment results) as a basis for redesigning lesson plans.They attempt to challenge many of their students intellectually, and they also try to guide all students' learning through direct instruction and interaction.
ROLE	Teachers utilize state curriculum frameworks as standards for assignments, instructional activities, the development of a classroom learning community, and accomplishing the expected schoolwide learning results. They frequently try innovative methods encountered through research and professional development activities.	Teachers see themselves as guides and learners who continue to develop their knowledge about both their subject area and their teaching practices.
TECHNOLOGY	The use of technology is well coordinated and aimed at helping all students to achieve the expected schoolwide learning results. All teachers are able to guide their students in using technological tools to enhance skills or work on projects.	The use of technology is coordinated to focus on student learning. Many teachers are skilled in using technological tools to enhance instruction to help students improve verbal and computational skills and work on projects.

Powerful Teaching and Learning: Teachers design learning experiences that involve students actively in rigorous learning and use diversified methods that enable more students to succeed at high levels. Teachers focus on active learning strategies such as inquiry, demonstration, collaborative learning, and effective use of technology.

	2 Partial	**1 Minimal**
CURRICULUM	Students receive a curriculum based on traditional expectations for skills and knowledge, but there is little depth or application of learning across disciplines in the academic foundation. Primarily, learning is textbook-oriented and abstract, emphasizing the accumulation of facts and concepts.	All students receive a curriculum based on ability level and traditional expectations for skills and knowledge. The learning is textbook-oriented, emphasizing the memorization of facts and the acquisition and practice of basic skills.
COURSEWORK	Teachers present consistent but repetitive coursework year after year, changing approaches, activities, and assignments only when they are given ideas or directives through staff development programs or textbook instructional guides. They refer to textbooks to prepare and sequence instruction, reinforce students' learning, and serve as a basis for judging students' achievement.	Teachers rely on the same course work year after year. Their methods focus on covering the material, helping students learn factual information, testing, and grading final products. They act as sources of information and judges of student performance.
ROLE	Teachers see themselves as content area experts, and they encourage their students to learn as much as they can.	Teachers see themselves as content area experts who present their knowledge through lectures and presentations and expect the students to learn what has been covered.
TECHNOLOGY	The use of technology in the school is primarily focused on staff needs, such as record-keeping. Other uses of technology are the result either of grants or individual staff projects. Computer teachers and other staff are often available to help students learn how to enhance verbal and computational skills and produce technology-aided projects.	Technology is used primarily for record keeping and data collection.

Adapted from Accrediting Commision for Schools, Western Association of Schools and Colleges Self-Study Document

Activity 2: Scoring Guide for Professional Development

This activity contains an optional report form and scoring guide (adapted fromWASC four-point rubrics) that a school might want to use to assess its professional development practices. It is not an essential tool in the School BUS, but it can be useful for schools undergoing dramatic change in their planning and implementation of professional development, especially when the change is written into the action plan of a formal school program review.

Professional Development Report Form

School: ______________ Date: ________

Strategy/Program: ______________________

	1 No Plan Fragmented	2 Ad Hoc Unfocused	3 Research-Based Focused	4 Continuous Collegial
#				
%				

Description (major finding):

Strengths:

Challenge:

Action Plan:

Professional Development: There is an organizational structure for and commitment to professional development and staff utilization, monitoring, and support that facilitates greater achievement of the expected schoolwide learning results.

	4 Advanced	3 Proficient
PLAN	The school has an effective, collegial, and continuing staff development program that focuses on improving staff skills and promoting quality innovations that will help all students to accomplish the standards. Staff is committed to personal and team mastery. Although the staff already has expertise about effective teaching approaches and how these approaches can be adapted to meet the needs of all students, they continue to learn.	The school has a staff development program based on research and data about the school and its programs, and a team approach is generally used in implementing it. The staff understands the techniques and practices that lead to better instruction, and there is evidence of effective teaching and improved student learning across the entire program.
DECISION MAKING	The staff development exemplifies shared decision-making and links resources to school improvement and to student results.The plan promotes both formal and informal interdisciplinary discussions of current educational research. When staff development activities are held off-campus, they are attended by interdisciplinary teams with the expectation that they will return to provide ongoing leadership to the rest of the staff.	The staff development plan is guided by clearly identified needs, and current thinking and programs related to those needs are encouraged. There is a focus on the study of the art of teaching and experimentation. Staff members engage in both short-term and long-term planning with a focus on the school's vision and goals. Teachers are encouraged to attend—and share any valuable information or ideas upon their return from—off-campus workshops.
MENTORING	Because improvement, growth, learning, experimentation, research, and risk-taking are organizational norms, coaching and mentoring are systematically promoted within and across disciplines.	Coaching and mentoring are regularly encouraged and practiced. Current educational research documents have been the subject of at least one staff development program, as well as numerous formal and informal discussions, with the principal serving as facilitator and leader.

Professional Development: There is an organizational structure for and commitment to professional development and staff utilization, monitoring, and support that facilitates greater achievement of the expected schoolwide learning results.

	2 Partial	**1 Minimal**
PLAN	In the absence of a comprehensive plan, staff development is implemented on an ad hoc basis to address particular problems. The results are sporadic, unfocused inservices with uncertain effects and little staff involvement or follow-up.	Staff development at the school is not driven by a formal, coherent plan. It is instead based on individual or department interests and availability of training, workshops, and conferences; thus, staff development appears random and fragmented.
DECISION MAKING	The schoolwide staff development program introduces staff to new approaches that are in vogue each year, but implementation is limited. When staff development opportunities are offered, teachers participate as individuals and work independently to implement programs in their own departments and/or classes.	Staff members are sent to off-campus staff development training either because they are viewed as exemplary or because they are in desperate need of remediation. When they return to work, information from the workshop is shared within a narrow circle of colleagues.
MENTORING	Coaching, mentoring, and other forms of staff support are limited by resources, time, and workload.	Coaching, mentoring, and other forms of staff support rarely occur.

Adapted from Accrediting Commission for Schools, Western Association of Schools and Colleges Self-Study Document

Activity 3: Bloom's Search for Best Practices

The purpose of this activity is for teachers to compare some strategies in the research literature in terms of their impact on student learning. The question is whether teachers are using any of the most effective research-based techniques.

In an article for *Educational Leadership*, Benjamin Bloom (1984) described the findings from research studies about the effects of a variety of teaching strategies on student achievement. Bloom discussed his quest for the most effective teaching strategies that were feasible in a regular classroom of about 30 students.

Bloom reported that mastery learning was dramatically more effective than conventional instruction. Mastery learning involves the use of formative assessment (e.g., formal tests, such as quizzes, or informal feedback, such as hand gestures) to provide feedback to teachers during the teaching process to make adjustments and target strategies to students in need. Conventional instruction involves teaching a unit of study, testing students, and then moving on to the next topic. (This was discussed in Chapter 3 in the section on Formative versus Summative Assessment and illustrated in Figure 3.1.)

Bloom was interested in "effect sizes" as he reviewed many research studies to find which factors had the biggest impact on student achievement. An effect size is a statistical term that is beyond the scope of this book to fully explain. It will suffice to say that an effect size is used to compare the results from different research studies using different student assessments. An effect size of 1.0 means the average student in the experimental group outperformed 84 percent of the students in the conventional group. An effect size of 2.0 means the average student in the experimental group outperformed 95 percent of the students in the conventional group.

Bloom found that mastery learning had an effect size (ES) of 1.0; the average student in the mastery learning classroom outperformed 84 percent of students in the conventional instruction classroom. When a teacher uses formative assessment to guide the selection of strategies to target student subgroups, the impact can be dramatic.

Bloom then explored other factors in the research literature as well as some factors that might have an additive effect. Leyton (1983) found that initial cognitive prerequisites had an ES = .7, and nearly an additive 1.6 ES when combined with mastery learning in a 10- to 12-week period of instruction. Initial cognitive prerequisites involve assessing students on crucial fundamental concepts and skills needed for a course of study and then giving intensive instruction on prerequisites before or during the course (e.g., after-school instruction).

The table in Figure 5.9 shows the "effect sizes" for some of the strategies reported in a study by Walberg (1984) and discussed by Bloom (1984). Bloom included socioeconomic status in the table to provide contrast with the instructional strategies that teachers can use in regular classrooms.

The activity facilitator asks teacher-participants:

- Some teachers are quick to label curricula, student background variables such as socioeconomic status, or parental support as foremost reasons for low achievement. What does Bloom's research indicate about the relative impact of instructional strategies versus other factors, such as socioeconomic status? Why might some teachers blame non-instructional variables instead of identifying where and how to improve their teaching strategies in order to improve student achievement?
- Which of the factors listed in Figure 5.9 do you use? Which factors have a greater impact that you are not using? (Participants interested in factors with greater impact might refer to Bloom's article that describes many of these strategies further. Several copies might be made available at the workshop for reference.)

FIGURE 5.9

Effect of Selected Alterable Variables on Student Achievements

		Effect Size
Reinforcement of Correct Answers	************	1.20
Mastery Learning	**********	**1.00**
Cues & explanations	**********	1.00
Student classroom participation	**********	1.00
Student time-on-task	**********	1.00
Cooperative learning	********	.80
Homework (graded)	********	.80
Initial cognitive prerequisites	******	.60
Home environment intervention	*****	.50
Peer & cross-age remedial tutoring	****	.40
Homework (assigned, not graded)	***	.30
Higher order questions	***	.30
New science & math curricula	***	.30
Teacher expectancy	***	.30
Advance organizers	**	.20
Socioeconomic status	***	.25

Adapted from Bloom (1984) who cites Walberg (1984)

Activity 4: School Mythology

Barr and Parrett (1995), in Hope at Last for At-Risk Youth, identified seven myths that some people have about at-risk students. Consider the perspective that it is not the student who is at-risk of failure but that the schools are at-risk of failing youth, and the school must change to fit the student, rather than the student fit a narrow, unchanging school instructional program. Yes, students and parents should accept their responsibility, but teachers are the professionals whose impact on student achievement is influenced by mental models, some truths and some myths. Dialogue with introspection is an avenue for becoming aware of mental models and dealing with those that are myths.

Engage in dialogue about these seven myths. Keep in mind that ample research and case studies of exemplar schools in Barr and Parrett's book as well as other literature sources indicate that these myths are just that.

Why do some people not recognize that these statements are myths?

Seven Myths about At-Risk Youth

- At-risk youth are slow learning.
- At-risk youth should be retained during the early grades until they are ready to move forward.
- At-risk youth can be educated with the same expenditures as other students.
- Classroom teachers can adequately address the needs of at-risk youth.
- Some students can't learn.
- The most effective way to improve instruction for at-risk youth is to reduce classroom size.
- Students who are having learning difficulties probably need special education

6 Using Student Results to Make Decisions

If all students aren't learning, we've got to try another way.

—Mel Riddile (principal at J.E.B. Stuart High School in Fairfax County, Va.)

We take all of the excuses off the table and have committed ourselves to working with the kids that walk through the door.

— Principal (Thayer Elementary School, Kansas)

Overview

The School BUS needs all four wheels to proceed along the road to school improvement. Chapter 3 covered the first wheel, the development of at least one standards-based assessment to measure student progress during the year on the school's primary target for improvement. Chapter 4 emphasized the second wheel, the importance of building a foundation of the school as a learning organization, continually looking for ways to improve the discipline of teaching. Chapter 5 discussed the third wheel, professional development as ongoing learning and problem solving and described the comprehensive instructional program as having three components, core classroom strategies, school interventions, and family/community partnerships. This chapter describes the fourth wheel, how to examine student results to evaluate the impact of the instructional program and make decisions at key times during the year to continually improve practices.

Staff must have the will and capacity to learn as a team, making best use of limited time in a systematic, organized way. Standards-based assessments yield data that is quick and simple to summarize, minimizing data-crunching and maximizing time for professional dialogue ending in decisions about action.

According to Schmoker (1999), one reason staff at some schools avoid data about student results is that they expect the results to "look bad or make them (teachers) look bad." Being "data-driven" or "results-driven" should imply that the staff wants to travel in a better direction in a common vehicle. When staff do not want to change their practices or have no hope that students can achieve at a higher level, they will continue to avoid data. If a school staff is *willing* to look at student results as a team and *willing* to change instructional practices it will use student data to determine how staff can improve, not to blame students and others. The School BUS provides a process for a school staff that wants to change, a systematic way to see student learning improve in response to adult learning.

At the other end of the spectrum are schools that feel they are drowning in data—they want to analyze results often to inform decisions but just do not see a feasible way to do it. Converting assessment raw scores to performance level data and using the tools and process described in this chapter is an answer. When all teachers at all grade levels in elementary schools and across all departments in secondary schools are speaking the same language, the professional dialogue is laser-like in its focus on improvement. Productive dialogue and decisions about students at Advanced, Proficient, Approaching, Partial, and Minimal performance levels and strategies to accelerate learning for students at each level are the engine of the local accountability process.

Forms and a process described in this chapter enable a school and district to quickly tabulate student academic achievement data from the standards-based assessments. Information gleaned from the data assists staff to reach agreement on where and how the next program improvements should take place. Easily tabulated performance level data leads directly to program decisions for groups of students with different levels or types of instructional needs. Accountability meetings are scheduled each grading period (this chapter uses quarterly periods as an example).

Before describing the process for using data to make school program decisions, it is necessary to lay the groundwork. Making decisions that effect student achievement and finding solutions to existing problems start with a bottom-up, or inside-out, approach.

Decisions are first made about core classroom practices, where a teacher's influence is greatest, and then extend out of classrooms to include school as well as family and community strategies to support teaching in the classrooms. Teams of teachers become the decision-makers, and decisions flow from the bottom up, from the school to the district.

Four Phases of Using Student Results

Student results are the percentage of students at each performance level on the assessment. Describe any key differences or patterns. Identify key challenge for students at Minimal and Partial levels. Interpret causes, focusing first on core classroom instructional strategies and next on school interventions. Find a solution and make a mini-action plan.

The School BUS model uses a four-phase process to analyze student achievement. All four phases might occur within a single staff meeting to analyze school achievement data, make decisions about where in the system improvement is needed, and where there is cause for celebration.

- *Description:* Staff develops a descriptive statement to summarize patterns, key differences, or particularly high or low student achievement results. The description is a nonjudgmental factual statement about "what is." The lowest result is identified as the foremost challenge for improvement.
- *Interpretation:* Staff explores and reaches agreement on the chief causal factors that likely influenced student achievement results. Highest priority should be given to causal factors upon which teachers have greatest influence and that are most within teachers' control: first and foremost, classroom teaching; second, school interventions; and third, family and community partnerships. Found within these three components are all of the important factors that affect a school's comprehensive instructional program. The most important factors contributing to the lowest student results establish the direction for finding solutions.
- *Solution:* Staff explores alternatives and reaches agreement on the best feasible solution to the identified problem. Solutions

may be short-term, long-term, or a combination, but all are directly controlled by the teachers.

- *Resolution:* Staff translates determination to improve into a plan of support systems and success indicators to build its capacity to reach a shared vision of a desired outcome.

Ground Rules

The first ground rule for *interpreting* student results is that individual teachers are not blamed for low results. One or a very few teachers generally do not have much impact on whole school results, that is, the summary of results for all students in the school. No one teacher has a great enough impact positively or negatively to change whole school results, but the combined action of all teachers moving in one direction can have tremendous impact. Blaming individual teachers is counterproductive in a learning organization. Performance of an individual teacher is a "personnel matter" between the principal and a teacher. The collective team performance is what matters in the School BUS because whole staff performance is what has an impact on whole school student results. Chapter 4 stated that professional literature (e.g., Joyce, Wolf, and Calhoun, 1993) indicated that it is the team, the school as a unit, that affects school improvement and the long-term education of a child.

The second ground rule is that students and their parents should not be blamed for poor results but should be recognized for achievements made. *Blaming* students or their parents fails to recognize possible opportunities for making improvements over which teachers do have control. When students and their parents share responsibility for teaching and learning, student achievement is significantly improved. However, the teaching staff has the primary responsibility for educating students. All students can learn, and ample research shows that feasible classroom strategies and school interventions do work. Chapter 5 discussed research literature (e.g., Darling-Hammond and Ball, 1997; and Wang, Haertel, and Walberg, 1993/94) pointed out that while many factors have an impact on student achievement, quality of teaching is certainly the most important factor.

The two previous chapters explained building shared vision, sharing responsibility for all students in the system, and learning to improve a common set of instructional strategies as a school team. Responsibility for student results is shared among all stakeholders in the educational system. A school team uses systems thinking to explore causal relationships within the complex system that the school team can change. Individual student results are important, but the School BUS concentrates on whole school results as an indicator of the impact of a whole school change initiative.

Interpretation of schoolwide student achievement results and the search for solutions to improvement begin with classroom teachers who examine their core instructional strategies and then move outward to supportive school interventions and family/community partnerships. Classroom teachers take primary responsibility for the learning of students in their classrooms. They do not give away that responsibility to instructional aides or specialists or anyone else inside or outside the school. Figure 6.1 repeats Figure 5.1 here as an important illustration of the relationship between levels of impact and steps towards solutions.

Figure 6.1

Comprehensive Instructional Program: Order of Impact, Sequence of Decisions

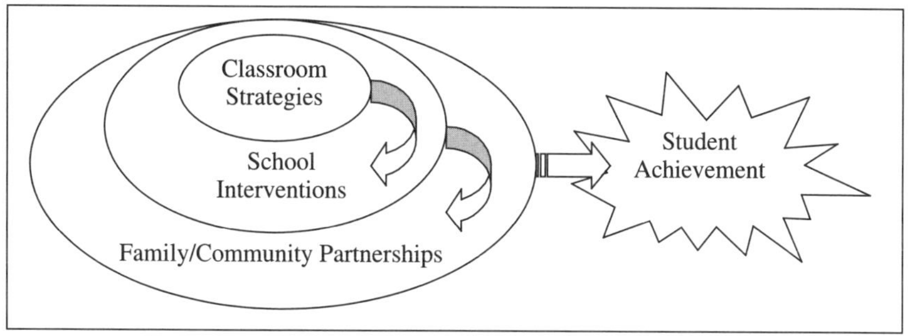

Chapter 2 introduced the idea that five performance levels are linked to five types of instructional program decisions. In chapter 3, content and performance standards were "operationalized" by establishing standards-based assessments. A school beginning the School BUS might start with just one assessment or set of grade level assessments that measure the quintessential standard that is the school's primary target for improvement. Figure 2.7 illustrated that student results at the Approaching level inform decisions about improving core classroom instructional practices. At the Partial and Minimal levels, student results inform decisions about improving classroom practices as well as whether to add moderate interventions and intensive interventions, respectively.

The interpretation of student results is done in terms of processes, not individual people. To interpret why student results increased, decreased, or stayed the same, one must understand how group actions, or inaction, affected students' learning. From interpretation flows exploration of possible solutions that are within control of the school team, which resolves to act on one or more particular solutions. How can instructional strategies be improved schoolwide to improve student achievement? How can school interventions be improved to support classroom practice? How can family and community partnership strategies support classroom practice?

Identifying the Best Solution

The School BUS assumes that a school team is much more likely to identify a very promising solution when the decision is informed by an analysis of its impact on student results. When a staff is forced to accept a decision by one influential entity (e.g., principal, district, or state) or they make a decision without information from student results and professional literature, one of two outcomes is likely. First, a decision rooted in politics or emotions and not in sound research will probably not be implemented by all staff members. Second, when the decision is not supported by research, it likely will not have the impact of a best practice best suited for staff and students in that school.

Student results point school staff toward students' greatest learning needs. Discussion of instructional practices points staff towards what appears to have worked and away from what appears to have little or no positive impact. Students may receive so many classroom strategies and school interventions in various combinations and varying levels of implementation over a year, that it becomes impossible, or nearly so, to use even sophisticated statistical analyses to determine separate effects of each "treatment." Many schools have neither the expertise nor the time for sophisticated research methodology that may not be decisive anyway. The School BUS assumes that a school team has ample time to review student results at each performance level, look at their instructional practices, and reach sound conclusions about what did or did not work.

A solution might come from the school staff, educators who are external to the school, or the professional literature. There should be some empirical evidence that the solution is likely to have a meaningful impact on students in "this school." In the Accelerated Schools Project, the chosen solution is treated as a "hypothesis" to be tested. Staff agrees to try earnestly to implement the solution for an ample period, examine the impact on student learning, and decide whether it is indeed a "better" or "best" practice, should be modified, or dropped in favor of a competing solution. A school can only be faulted for not trying anything, not for trying something that looked promising.

The process of reviewing student results and making decisions about instructional practices can be done within a one-hour staff meeting, but more time might be require to interpret results, explore potential solutions, or reach agreement on the next course of action. Decisions can be reached when staff gains experience using systematic thinking and when it engages in discussions about "best practices out there" on an ongoing basis. For the sake of simplicity, this chapter describes the process in terms of making decisions within one normal staff meeting, but that should not be construed as the norm. Some types of decisions can be made fairly quickly, and practice with the process can shorten the time. Decisions are made on action to take—ways to improve instructional practices or, at least, to create avenues for further exploration of likely causes or potential solutions.

Source of Student Results

Student data can be recorded in fairly traditional teachers' grade books and quickly summarized upward from grades or departments to the school and district with percentages calculated with an inexpensive calculator. Student data can be entered and extracted from an electronic (computer) database and reported using sophisticated software at the school or district or via the Internet. Because the School BUS does not require sophisticated or "high tech" resources to obtain and use student achievement data, any school in any locale can start the School BUS, but technology can enhance the process.

It is imperative that school staff has student results shortly after administration of the assessment so that timely decisions can be made about improving instruction on what was assessed before "it is too late to do anything about it for these students." Timing is almost everything when it comes to making periodic decisions during the school year to improve incrementally instruction. If district personnel can quickly send data back to schools, schools can use district-generated summary reports. Otherwise, teachers should tabulate the results themselves so that data can be used immediately. This chapter describes the bottom-up approach, which can be very quick and simple when student scores are reported as performance levels.

The Teacher's Grade Book

Staff program decisions based on student data start with each teacher's grade book. Recording performance level data in the grade book makes it simple and easy to combine data across teachers in the grade/department meetings that will be discussed later. Figure 6.2 shows a partial example of a teacher's grade book in a standards-based assessment system.

FIGURE 6.2

Teacher's Sample Grade Book:
Student Information on the Left, Assessment Results on the Right

Student Name	Demographic			Program			1st Quarter			
							A1		A2	A3
	G	E	S	EL	SE	T1	RS	PL	PL	PL

Students' names and key demographic and program data are entered on the left side of the grade book. Student demographic information is necessary for at least state and federal requirements for data analysis and use of results for certain student subgroups. Instructional program information identifies services (e.g., Title I tutoring after school); symbols may indicate multiple services for some students. This format helps when results for subgroups are compared to explore achievement gaps. Setting up the grade book to show key demographic information for each student makes it fairly easy to analyze data for student subgroups later on. Some teachers prefer color-coding instead to letter or number codes because they can more readily see results for different subgroups.

Key demographic and program data symbols, as shown by columns in the teacher's grade book in Figure 6.2, might be:

- (G) Gender
- (E) Ethnicity
- (S) SES, Socioeconomic Status (confidential in many districts/states)
- (EL) English learner status (category or current proficiency level)
- (SE) Special Education designation
- (T1) Title I with symbols for specific service(s)

Assessment data are on the right side of the grade book. The right side might include a subject area, global standard with specific benchmarks, or cluster of standards. Standards-based assessments—A1, A2, and A3 are used in Figure 6.2—might be included as well as space for reassessment if students are expected to continue learning until reaching some level of mastery. In the sample grade book (see Figure 6.2), RS stands for Raw Score and PL indicates Performance Level. A1 is an assessment with a raw score converted to a performance level, while A2 and A3 are performance assessments that directly yield performance levels.

In one grade book format for elementary school teachers, four or more pages are attached to the right side of the grade book so that teachers can use separate pages for subject areas or standards. Students' names and demographic and program information are visible on the left side, and assessment is visible on the right side. Indicators of effort, attendance, behavior, and homework completion might be entered somewhere on the left or right side of the grade book but are kept separate from measures of "pure" academic achievement. Excluding these other indicators from report card grades is important in a standards-based grading system (Carr, 2000b; Marzano, 2000), but this issue is beyond the scope of this book. The School BUS uses specific assessment data, not report card grades.

The School BUS is concerned only with standards-based performance level data (PL in Figure 6.2) that represent status at the end of each quarter (or trimester) when staff meet to make periodic decisions about the school's instructional practices. In the first year of implementing the School BUS, the school might focus on one subject area, such as reading or, perhaps even more narrowly, reading comprehension. In the beginning, the school may consider the results from only one assessment instrument (if the assessment was administered multiple times during the quarter, the school should consider only the last and highest achievement results). A case was made in chapter 3 that staff can have more confidence in the accuracy of results when a variety of assessments are used, but administering multiple assessments may be too much to ask of a school in the first year of using the School BUS. During the staff discussion of student results from one assessment, it is assumed that teachers will consider other information from formal or informal assessments of student achievement before drawing conclusions and making decisions.

Overview of Using Student Results

Collect and examine student results each grading period (e.g., quarter). Start with a grade or department meeting to examine results and complete report form. The school leadership team drafts the school form and leads a whole staff meeting to finalize the schoolwide action plan the next week. District receives school forms, develops district report form, and discusses results at principals' meeting the following week.

Assume a traditional school calendar with one-hour staff meetings twice a month every other Tuesday. Meetings twice a month may be the minimum for a school undergoing meaningful, major improvements. School BUS meetings are held at the end of each grading period (e.g., quarters or trimesters). This chapter assumes a district is on a quarter system and the third quarter is used to just assess and examine results for students at the Minimal and Partial levels. In the first, second, and fourth quarters, or each trimester for districts on that system, all students are assessed and results examined for all performance levels.

In the month ending a quarter grading period, the two monthly meetings are scheduled during consecutive weeks. At the first meeting, grade level or department teams summarize, analyze, and report data and decisions at their level. At the next week's meeting, the whole staff discusses schoolwide results and decisions. In the School BUS, a school must have a school leadership team composed of teacher representatives and school administrators to facilitate these meetings and complete report forms.

The week following the schools' whole staff meetings, the superintendent meets with principals and district support staff to discuss districtwide results and decisions. (If a school has only teacher per grade level, only a whole staff meeting is held; if the district has only one school, only the school or district meeting is held.

Figure 6.3 illustrates the flow of decisions from the bottom up, from the teacher to the district level (or even state). The individual teacher might use detailed assessment information for each student to target instruction to subgroups of students according to their particular needs. Raw scores are converted to performance levels. These results are used by teams of teachers at higher levels to make decisions about core instructional practices at the grade, department, school, and district levels.

FIGURE 6.3
FLOW OF DECISIONS IN THE SCHOOL BUS

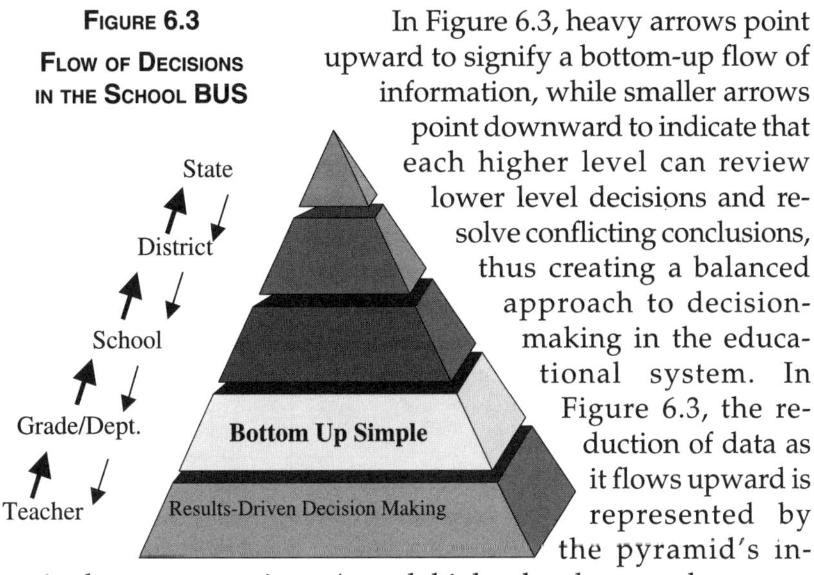

In Figure 6.3, heavy arrows point upward to signify a bottom-up flow of information, while smaller arrows point downward to indicate that each higher level can review lower level decisions and resolve conflicting conclusions, thus creating a balanced approach to decision-making in the educational system. In Figure 6.3, the reduction of data as it flows upward is represented by the pyramid's increasingly narrow sections. At each higher level, teams do not create new ideas—they summarize student results and reduce information to descriptions, interpretations, and decisions. For example, grade level results are summarized schoolwide and actions are indicated that pertain to all teachers. The school and district actions will often involve adjustments in professional development plans as teachers step back or move forward as a group, learning and implementing new instructional strategies.

The School BUS is not strictly a one-way, bottom-up approach. Rather, it empowers teachers in teams to make decisions that flow upward, while oversight and guidance responsibilities, which remain with leaders at a particular level, flow downward to the next lower level. Persons at the next higher level might review descriptions and decisions in a report form submitted by the team at the lower level. In case of a disagreement, the two teams must discuss the issue and reach agreement before the report form continues upward.

Figure 6.4 shows a more detailed flowchart of the decision-making process used in the School BUS. The individual teacher uses the detailed information found in informal and formal assessment results to make daily and weekly lesson plan decisions. In chapter 3, this was referred to as Tier 1 assessment results information. Tier 2 data, called performance level results, are used for making instructional program decisions. The strength of the School BUS process of team decision-making begins with Tier 2 data analysis. Decisions flow upward from individual students or classroom subgroups to the whole school and then to the whole district. Teachers summarize their classroom data to tally grade or department results. Grade or department results are summarized into school results which, in turn, are summarized into district results.

FIGURE 6.4

Using Student Results in a System of Standard-Based Accountability

School BUS Student Results Flowchart				
Flow	**Data Level**	**Decisions**	**Data Results**	**Time**
Teacher	Students	Subgroup Strategies	Student's score	Daily
	Group/Class	Lesson Plans	Students' scores	Daily/Wkly
Grade/ Dept	Classes	Common Lessons, Teaching Strategies	% of Students at Performance Levels	Twice a month
	Grade/ Department	Core Classroom Instructional Practices		Grading Periods
School	Grades/ Departments	School-wide Core Classroom Practices & Interventions	% of Students at Performance Levels	Grading Periods
	School			
District	Schools	District-wide Practices & Policy	% of Students at Performance Levels	Grading Periods
	District			

Figure 6.5 presents the schedule of meetings for a year in a district with several schools and several teachers at each grade level or secondary school department. In quarters one, two, and four, grade or department teams summarize their results and decisions on the appropriate report form at the Tuesday meeting. On Thursday, the School Leadership Team (SLT) meets to draft the school report and decide if any discussions with certain grade or department teams on particular issues are warranted. The following Tuesday, the draft school report is discussed with the whole school staff before it becomes the final report, which is then submitted to the district office. District administrators might discuss a school report with an SLT before formal acceptance. The Friday of the second week, the superintendent holds the principals' meeting to discuss district results.

At the end of the third quarter, when many districts and states conduct external assessments, the schools may assess only those students previously at the Minimal and Partial levels to inform group decisions about interventions. At this time, districts and states with promotion and retention policies might begin final identification of "at-risk" students, notification to parents, and summer school plans. As suggested in Chapter 2, students at the Minimal level are candidates for retention decisions (or decisions about extended interventions, such as summer school).

FIGURE 6.5

Sample Schedule of Student Results Meetings

Quarter	Day, Week	Group	Product
1st	Tuesday, 2	Grade/Dept.	Grade/Dept. Report Form
	Thursday, 2	Leadership Team	Draft School Report Form
	Tuesday, 3	Whole School	Final School Report Form
	Monday, 4	Principals/District	District Report Form
2nd	Tuesday, 2	Grade/Dept.	Grade/Dept. Report Form
	Thursday, 2	Leadership Team	Draft School Report Form
	Tuesday, 3	Whole School	Final School Report Form
	Monday, 4	Principals/District	District Report Form
3rd	Tuesday, 2	Grade/Dept.	Report on Minimal/Partial
	Thursday, 2	Leadership Team	Draft School Report
	Tuesday, 3	Whole School	Final School Report
4th	Tuesday, 2	Grade/Dept.	Grade/Dept. Report Form
	Thursday, 2	Leadership Team	Draft School Report Form
	Tuesday, 3	Whole School	Final School Report Form
	Monday, 4	Principals/District	District Report Form

This schedule shows decisions flowing from grade/departments to the district in about two-and-a-half weeks. Grade or departments might make a decision Tuesday and begin action to improve instruction on Wednesday. Whole school common action could begin as early as the following Wednesday. Whole district action might occur by the following Monday. Decisions can be made one day, and action can start the next. The probability of slight delays in decision-making increases as the process moves up through the levels. Teachers are the first "to know, decide, and act," and district administrators are the last—as it should be in a professional organization in which teachers are empowered and administrators provide guidance and support.

The School BUS forms used to report student results at the grade/department, school, and district levels for each quarter of the year are presented in Figures 6.6 to 6.8. Forms contain sample data for Countryside USD, the district used in prior chapters to provide an example of the Basic School BUS Model. The forms are intended to be one page in length unless an actual school or district needs more space to write brief statements describing and interpreting results and then to outline a mini action plan. The mini action plan includes core classroom instructional practices, school interventions, and, possibly, family/community strategies. Classroom strategies particularly target students at the Approaching performance level to accelerate them to the Proficient level. Moderate interventions target students at the Partial level, and intensive interventions target students at Minimal level.

The report forms should be used to capture agreements from staff meetings, put decisions in writing for accountability, and minimize time spent on paperwork. Only a few minutes should be needed to tabulate student results, calculate the percentages of students at each of the five performance levels, and draft statements (e.g., bullet points) after discussion. Quickly summarizing results and comments leaves about 50 minutes of a one-hour meeting to discuss professionally the results and make decisions about how next to improve practices. Recording time can be almost eliminated when the leadership team member collects classroom results and calculates grade/department results before the meeting, leaving more time for discussion.

Notice that somewhat different decisions are made each quarter. The description of Countryside's process in the Basic Model that follows provides examples of the types of decisions made at each reporting period. Different results might lead to different types of decisions.

Each quarter, the school and district report forms add a row of results so that staff can easily note any indications that students are moving upward to higher performance levels. All students are included in the results each quarter, not just the students who have been enrolled since the beginning of the year, which "muddies the water" slightly. When teachers bring their grade books to the meeting, they can identify any partial-year students and still analyze student movement throughout the year. A school with computer software might choose to produce two sets of results, one for all students and one for students enrolled since the beginning of the year.

Basic School BUS Model

Now in their first year using the School BUS model, the staffs at Countryside Elementary School and Countryside Middle School are learning to use student achievement results to inform decisions about instructional program improvement at key points in the school year. Their goal is to improve classroom instruction and school interventions to accelerate learning for students at the Minimal and Partial performance levels. Ideally, every student in the school at the Minimal level in the first quarter will be at the Proficient level in the fourth quarter.

At the very least, the schools's goal is to find ways to accelerate student learning so that no student is at the Minimal level by the end of the year and a candidate for retention. Ideally, all students will move from the Minimal and Partial levels to the Proficient level. When the Proficient level is set at a rigorous yet reasonable achievement level, the ideal goal is attainable. High rather than minimal expectations are more likely to yield high gains. Continual improvement in the instructional program each year will bring results closer and closer to the ideal.

First Quarter Results

Focus is on the student group at Minimal level and classroom and extra help strategies to accelerate their learning.

The School Leadership Team (SLTs) at Countryside Elementary and Middle Schools reminded teachers to complete reading comprehension assessments of all students by the Friday before the Tuesday grade or department meeting. Teachers were concerned that a safe, respectful dialogue about effective teaching practices might be hindered if some teachers were known to have much higher score results than others. Sharing assessment data would be a new experience for teachers who had never even shared grade books.

Districts with a promotion and retention policy may require early identification of at-risk students, notification to parents, and interventions, all of which might be accomplished at the end of the first quarter. The district might identify at-risk students as students at the Minimal performance level, which correlates to the School BUS process of focusing on the group of students at the Minimal level to ensure best practices in the classroom and supportive school interventions. Teachers could use parent conferences normally held at the end of the grading period to discuss the at-risk identification process, classroom and school strategies to accelerate the child's learning, and what parents can do to help.

Grade Form & Meeting

At Countryside Elementary School, the SLT collected data from each teacher prior to the first meeting to make sure scores recorded correctly, to summarize results before the meeting, and to keep classroom results confidential. The SLT's grade level summaries may lack detail, but this approach allowed the meeting to run efficiently and trust to be established.

SLT members decided to encourage the sharing of teacher-level results by showing sample work by struggling students and asking other teachers on the team to suggest effective strategies. Later, all teachers might feel comfortable with this type of sharing which also has the "natural advantage" of helping teachers establish and maintain grading consistency.

All grade levels held their meeting on Tuesday. On Monday, each SLT teacher went to each teacher's classroom and collected the count of students at each of the five performance levels. To encourage dialogue at the next day's meeting, leaders asked each teacher to reflect on the teaching strategies that were effective with students at or above proficiency and the challenges facing students at the Partial and Minimal levels. Teachers were reminded that the school wanted to identify those best practices that accelerate learning, especially for students beginning at the Minimal and Partial levels.

Each SLT teacher recorded the number of students at each performance level in the first row of the grade level form and computed the percentages for the grade level on the School BUS Grade Level Form prior to the grade level meeting. SLT teachers wrote the results on overhead transparencies or on the chalkboard to focus everyone's attention on the same results and encourage interaction. Figure 6.6 shows the results entered onto the School BUS Grade Level Form for three fifth-grade classes of 30 students each. The short diagonal lines denote that more space is provided on the actual full-page form. A computer word processor must be used to replicate and complete forms so that writers are not restricted by the space allotted for each section.

The three fifth-grade teachers brought their grade books to the meeting, in order to reference actual students, not just percentages of students in a performance level. The SLT teacher facilitated the grade level meeting, starting with a summary description of the data to highlight findings and include observations of student progress during the trimester not explicitly shown in the data table. The description is a factual summary of student performance; it does not contain value judgments.

FIGURE 6.6

Condensed Example of School BUS Grade Level Form

Countryside Elementary School

School BUS Grade Level Form

Standard 2: Reading Comprehension   Assessment: Reading Inventory

Grade Level: 5   Date: 1st Quarter

	1 Minimal	2 Partial	3 Approach	4 Proficient	5 Advanced
# (90)	20	49	14	7	0
%	22	54	16	8	0

Description:
//
Interpretation
Strength:
//
Challenge:
//
Action Plan
Classroom Strategies:
//

Next, the team began the interpretation phase by focusing on the fact that 8 percent of the students (7 out of 90) were at the Proficient level by October (end of the first quarter). They compared students who started school at this level with students who progressed to this level and identified strategies that affected student performance. They agreed on a draft summary statement entitled "Program Strength," which will recognize teaching effectiveness and remind teachers that their strengths are the keys to overcoming challenges.

The students who entered at the Approaching or Partial levels will likely still be there at the end of the first trimester, but, with normal progress, should be at the Proficient level by year-end. In the first quarter, the team focused on the learning challenges of and possible instructional solutions for students at the Minimal level. The team discussed individual classroom strategies that could help these students to learn better and that could accelerate learning, not slow it down. Discussion about *school* intervention strategies to support classroom learning and the acceleration process might wait until the whole staff meeting.

The fifth grade teachers agreed on one classroom strategy to improve. Although they were learning "reciprocal teaching" the teachers decided they needed more modeling and guidance before using the strategy with lower achieving students. At the next quarter meeting, they will judge how effectively they have used the strategy by analyzing students' progress.

They finished the one-hour meeting by drafting a short "professional development" action plan that described how and when the reading specialist and teachers would work together to improve their use of the reciprocal teaching strategy. After the grade level meeting, each SLT teacher summarized the discussion and wrote statements about program strengths and challenges and composed an action plan to complete the grade level form.

Department Form and Meeting

At a small- to medium-size middle school where teachers are assigned to multiple grade levels, teachers might meet as a department and complete the department form to list results for each grade level. At a large middle school, the process might be altered so that grade level teachers meet and complete a grade level form and then attend a department meeting to complete a department form.

At Countryside Middle School, English teachers are assigned to multiple grade levels. At their department meeting at the end of the first quarter, they used a department form to compile results by grade level, and then they created a mini action plan. As teachers entered the department meeting, they wrote on the chalkboard the number of their students at each performance level. This "worksheet" activity gave teachers some anonymity because they were not associated by name with any particular results.

Pairs of teachers were assigned to calculate the sums and percentages of students at each performance level for the assigned grade level and were instructed to write the results on the chalkboard. The Worksheet in Figure 6.7 shows an example.

To calculate the percentage, the sum of students at a performance level is divided by the total number of students in the grade. The sum is multiplied by 100 and rounded to the nearest whole number. For sixth grade for example, 25 + 27 = 52; 52 divided by 260 times 100 = 20 percent. Rounding to a whole number makes the data table easier to read; fractional differences are not meaningful differences. Either a remaining pair of teachers or all teachers calculate the bottom row, which will show the number and percentage of students at each performance level for the "Total" school.

Figure 6.7

Example of Middle School Department Form

Grade		Worksheet				
	#	1 Minimal	2 Partial	3 Approach	4 Proficient	5 Advanced
6	260	25+27= 52# 20%	76+70= 146# 56%	18+21= 39# 15%	13+10= 23# 9%	0+0= 0# 0%
7	250					
8	240					
Total	750					

Countryside Middle School
School BUS Department Form

Standard 2: Reading Comprehension Assessment: Reading Inventory

Department: English Date: 1st Quarter

Grade		% Students at Performance Levels				
	#	1 Minimal	2 Partial	3 Approach	4 Proficient	5 Advanced
6	260	20	56	15	9	0
7	250	25	58	12	5	0
8	240	34	58	5	3	0
Total	750	26	57	11	6	0

The results from the worksheet were copied onto the Department Form (see Figure 6.7). Initially, this process takes a few minutes, but with practice should take less time. The department chair might choose to collect the data and calculate the results before the meeting, as was done at Countryside Elementary School, to give staff more time to discuss the results and agree on a plan of action to improve instruction. At the department meeting, the teachers reviewed the bottom row of results for the total school and then looked for patterns or differences across grade levels. (If all grade levels have similar results, teachers can discuss schoolwide findings; if grade levels have different results, teachers can discuss grade level patterns and differences.)

Teachers proceeded from discussing to interpreting the results and identified reasons why some students were performing at or above the Proficient level. Teachers then focused attention on students at the Minimal level, discussing alternative solutions and reaching agreement on a mini action plan to improve learning for those students. (Discussion about school intervention strategies to support classroom learning and the acceleration process might occur here or wait until the whole staff meeting.)

Staff at Countryside Middle School had started staff development on reciprocal teaching, but many felt they were struggling to use the strategy effectively. Their mini action plan described further professional development activities to improve the use of the strategy. They were concerned about the increasing percentages of sixth to eighth graders at the Minimal level (see Figure 6.7) and wanted to do more. The previous month, staff had read and discussed research literature about the effectiveness of cross-age tutoring as an intervention strategy. They talked with their neighbors at Countryside Elementary School about creating an after-school tutorial program in which middle school students at the Minimal level could work on reading with elementary grade students at the Minimal level. The Title I coordinator had experience with and training in cross-age tutoring and accepted the responsibility of coordinating the program. The principal promised she would remove any resource barriers, such as busing, location, and materials.

The other departments at Countryside Middle School met that same day to talk about applying strategies of reciprocal teaching and making textbooks and supplemental materials accessible in their subject areas. Reciprocal teaching became a schoolwide strategy. The SLT teacher in each department used the department form to list strengths and challenges to describe an action plan (same as the example in Figure 6.7, although assessment results are not shown).

SLT Meeting and Draft of School Form

The SLT at each school met to draft a school form on Thursday. The SLT at Countryside Elementary School combined grade level achievement results and agreed on schoolwide strengths and challenges and an action plan. The SLT at Countryside Middle School did the same by looking for *common* statements across departments. At this point, the form was a draft version that needed to be approved by all staff before becoming the school's official school form.

At the SLT meeting, discrepancies between results and solutions (actions) can be resolved and questionable statements can be discussed. If necessary, further discussion with the grade or department team can be scheduled at some time during the next day as part of the "checks and balances" system of bottom-up and top-down management. Each level reviews reports by the next level down, and both levels must reach agreement on final statements. Problems with describing or interpreting results or stating an action plan are avoided or minimized when school administrators and support staff participate in team meetings.

Calculations for Total School

When a data table shows the *percentages* for each performance level and the total number of students for each grade level, calculating the *percentages for the total school* can be done in one of two ways: the simple method and the method of weighted average.

Simple Method of Averaging: When the numbers of students across grade levels are very close, as they are Countryside Elementary School (grades K-5 range from 87 to 90) the following steps are recommended:

- Sum the percentages in a column for a performance level.
- Divide by the number of grades, which yields the percentage for the total school at that performance level. Round to the nearest whole number.
- Repeat for each column (performance level).

Method of Weighted Average: When the numbers of students are fairly different across grade levels, the *method of weighted average* should be used to yield percentages for the total school.

- Multiply the number of students in the grade level by the proportion in the column (e.g., 20% = .20). (The difference between a percent and proportion is placement of the decimal point.)
- Sum the products down a column (across grade levels within a performance level).
- Divide the sum by the total number of students in the school, which yields the percentage for the total school at that perfor-

mance level. Round to the nearest whole number.

- Repeat for each column (performance level).

Although the number of students at each grade level is fairly close at Countryside Middle School, their calculations provide an example of how to find the percentage of students at the Minimal level (26% as shown in Figure 6.6).

260 times .20 = 52.0
250 times .25 = 62.5
240 times .34 = 81.6
TOTAL = 196.1 divided by 750 = .26 = 26 %

School Meeting and School Form

The following Tuesday at the whole staff meeting, the SLT presented the draft School Form and facilitated a dialogue to reach agreement on final ideas, particularly the schoolwide action plan. (To reach agreement, teachers concentrate on the *ideas* in the report, not on "wordsmithing" sentences.) One person or a team wrote simple, clear, and concise final statements after the meeting. Figure 6.8 shows the data table from the school form for Countryside Elementary School. Notice the similarity between the grade/department form and the school form (as well as the culture and program implementation forms)—similarity and simplicity of report forms is a hallmark of the School BUS process. The number of students at each grade level is included in the school form for a special purpose. When the report is sent to the district office, the method of weighted average will be used to calculate districtwide percentages across all schools for each grade and for the total district.

The whole staff meeting provides an opportunity for all staff to see student achievement results for the whole school in a succinct format; the data table shows percentages of students at each performance level by grade level and displays results for the total school. The strengths, challenges, and action plans described in each grade level/department form become part of the schoolwide set of statements in the school form. During this meeting, staff recognize and celebrate their strengths and unify their efforts for improvement.

Staff then reaches agreement on a draft that becomes the official school form, which contains succinct summary statements about schoolwide strengths, challenges and actions for improvement. Grade levels or departments might retain their individual forms to help them pursue any specific actions not contained in the schoolwide action plans.

FIGURE 6.8

Condensed Example of School Form

Countryside Elementary School
School BUS School Form

Standard 2: Reading Comprehension
Assessment: Story Retelling (kindergarten), Running Records (grades 1-3), Reading Inventory (grades 4-5)
Date: 1st Quarter

Grade	#	Minimal	Partial	Approach	Proficient	Advanced
K	87	40	50	10	0	0
1	88	30	45	20	5	0
2	89	20	40	27	8	5
3	87	10	37	33	15	5
4	88	14	44	31	11	0
5	90	22	53	20	5	0
Total	529	24	46	22	7	1

Description:
//
Interpretation
Strength:
//
Challenge:
//
Action Plan
Classroom Strategies:
//
Intervention Strategies:
//

District Form and Meeting

The day after the whole staff meeting, school principals sent the official School Form to the district office. The district person responsible for assessment calculated the districtwide results across grade levels and created the data table and Description section in the District Form. The person responsible for instructional guidance and support in language arts wrote the Interpretation sections, focusing on actions the district office would take to support the schools (e.g., additional workshops and coaching opportunities).

The superintendent's district team met a few days before the next principals' meeting to review the draft district form and reach agreement on final statements. At the principals meeting on Friday, district staff presented the districtwide results, celebrated strengths, and, based on challenges most frequently mentioned in schools' action plans, discussed the actions the district would take to support school improvement. Principals then distributed copies of this district form to their staff so that all stakeholders were informed of progress in the entire educational system and discussed districtwide findings at the next school staff meeting.

Second Quarter Results

Focus is on student groups at Minimal and Partial. Are students moving to higher levels? Are classroom strategies and school interventions starting to be effective in accelerating learning?

The second quarter forms are essentially the same as the first quarter forms except that the data tables include the results for both quarters, so that staff can readily see what progress has been made. Figure 6.9 shows the 1st and 2nd quarter data table for a grade or department form. Students should either stay within a performance level or move upward, not downward to lower levels. Any decreases usually involve a small number of students and are best dealt with on an individual basis. Teachers might comment on students who achieved more accelerated performance than expected and explore reasons for the increase.

FIGURE 6.9

Second Quarter Grade Level Data Table

Quarter	% Students at Performance Levels				
	1 Minimal	2 Partial	3 Approach	4 Proficient	5 Advanced
1st					
2nd					

In the 2nd and 4th quarters, the school or district or both must decide whether their primary purpose is to show static or progress results. When the primary purpose is to show *static results*, that is, results at each point in time, staff should be aware that some students included in the 1st quarter report may no longer be enrolled in later quarters. Even so, students should make progress from the 1st to 2nd quarter, even in schools with a moderate amount of student mobility in a school year (up to 30% mobility for most schools). When the primary purpose is to show *progress results*, staff may want to exclude data for students who do not have assessment scores for both 1st and 2nd quarters. We suggest that schools begin by using the simple static process, which keeps all students "in view" and in the accountability system. Schools can use static results at successive points in time to approximate progress results. This topic will be discussed fully in chapter 8.

Figure 6.10 presents the school form's data table for an elementary, middle or high school's record grade level results for the 2nd quarter in the top part of the table, which is followed by two rows at the bottom for student totals for both the 1st and 2nd quarters; this allows a quick comparison of quarters and makes it easier to review schoolwide results and make school improvement decisions. Presenting results for both quarters for each grade level yields double the number of rows in the data table and tends to engage in "data drowning." Analyzing grade level progress results is appropriately reserved for grade level meetings, not whole staff meetings, at least when starting the School BUS.

FIGURE 6.10

Condensed Second Quarter School Data Table

Grade	2nd Trimester: % Students at Performance Levels				
	1 Minimal	2 Partial	3 Approach	4 Proficient	5 Advanced
K					
5					
Quarter					
1st					
2nd					

The School BUS data tables do not show individual students who remained in a performance level, but teachers infer this from looking at percentage shifts and concluding that a certain percentage appeared to remain in a performance level. For this reason, teachers should bring their grade books to the meeting. They can scan the two columns of data, see which students did not progress, look at more detailed raw scores to gauge progress, and then discuss program effectiveness with actual students in mind.

Framing Questions for Interpreting Results

Strengths

Certain percentages of students progressed to the Proficient and Advanced levels. What strengths in teaching likely had a major impact on student learning? What strategies in the comprehensive instructional program (classroom instruction, school interventions, and family/community partnerships) most likely are the reason that students progressed?

Challenges

Certain percentages of students did not progress to the next level. Certain percentages of students in the Minimal level are not accelerating and might not reach the Proficient level by the end of the year. What strategies can we improve or add for these students? If potential strategies are not obvious, staff may need to engage in deeper inquiry and consult with others.

Corroborating Evidence

Potential causal factors and a direction for improvement were identified. Staff wants to make results-based decisions, not rash judgments. What other assessment or observational data can bolster confidence in the validity and accuracy of their primary assessment results? What other sources of information can bolster confidence that they are pointed in the right direction? What do students say? What do the people whom they invited to observe student learning in classrooms say? Do people with different perspectives agree?

Third Quarter Results

Focus is on students at the Minimal level. Are instructional practices effective? What more can be done to help these students accelerate learning?

One option is to repeat the forms and process used in the second quarter and to examine the degree to which students are advancing. A second option is not to repeat the process when resources and time already are stretched thin from state testing programs or other reasons. A third option is to assess only those students who were at the Minimal and Partial levels in the second quarter and examine the impact of interventions.

Some districts may implement promotion and retention policies at this time to identify students at-risk of retention, to notify parents, and to plan staff needs for summer school programs. The students at Minimal level at year-end do not have the requisite concepts and skills to begin learning the next grade level's standards. Countryside USD selected the third option in this first year in the School BUS.

Fourth Quarter Results

Examine three or four rows of results for each quarter, looking for movement to higher performance levels. Is the comprehensive instructional program effective? What improvements will be made next year? Celebrate this year's success (i.e., meaningful improvements).

The 4th quarter forms are the similar to those used for the 2nd quarter but have an additional row to show 1st, 2nd, and 4th quarter results for the total school or district. Meaningful improvement from beginning to end of the year is cause for celebration. While the mini action plans for earlier quarters address that year's school plan, the action plan in the final quarter should address the next year and give more consideration to dropping ineffective practices and adding strategies that will likely be more effective. If results look good, the action plan may only need refinements. This discussion may take longer than a regular one-hour staff meeting and the principal might schedule several hours as a professional development activity.

A bar graph showing the percentage of students in the school at each performance level each quarter can be created from the data table. A simplified bar graph is based on the percentage of students at or above Proficiency each quarter. With a little creativity, the bar graphs for Culture, Program Implementation, and Student Achievement can be combined to form one large graph. Figure 6.11 shows a consensus performance level on the Culture scoring guide (ratings 1-4), the percentage of teacher at or above the Proficient level on the Classroom Instructional Practices scoring guide, and the percentage of students at or above the Proficient level on the assessment scoring guide. As mentioned in chapters 4 and 5 a wall chart created for display in the staff meeting room graphs the results for each quarter, and teachers post anecdotal notes on the chart to show evidence of the action plans' effectiveness in improving culture and instructional practices.

Now the School BUS program theory is complete. An improvement in culture is expected to lead to an improvement in the quality of teaching (i.e., classroom instructional strategies). As quality of teaching improves, student achievement is expected to improve. Figure 6.12 illustrates this program theory by rearranging the bars of the graph in Figure 6.11. The one-way direction shown in the figure illustrates the simple program theory of the School BUS; the more likely reality is that an interdependence among the three elements exists. For example, an increase in student achievement may lead teachers to feel enthusiasm that their efforts have been effective and inspire them to try even harder to improve teaching. As teaching and student learning improve, teachers feel their efforts have been rewarded, which reinforces the school culture of working as a team to continually learn and improve itself.

FIGURE 6.11

Bar Graph of Culture, Strategies, Student Results

Quarter	1st		2nd	3rd	4th
	Sept	Oct	Jan	Apr	June
4-100%					
3-75%					
2-50%					
1-25%					
	Culture Strategies	Students	Students		Culture Strategies Students

FIGURE 6.12

Example of Program Theory Graph of Results

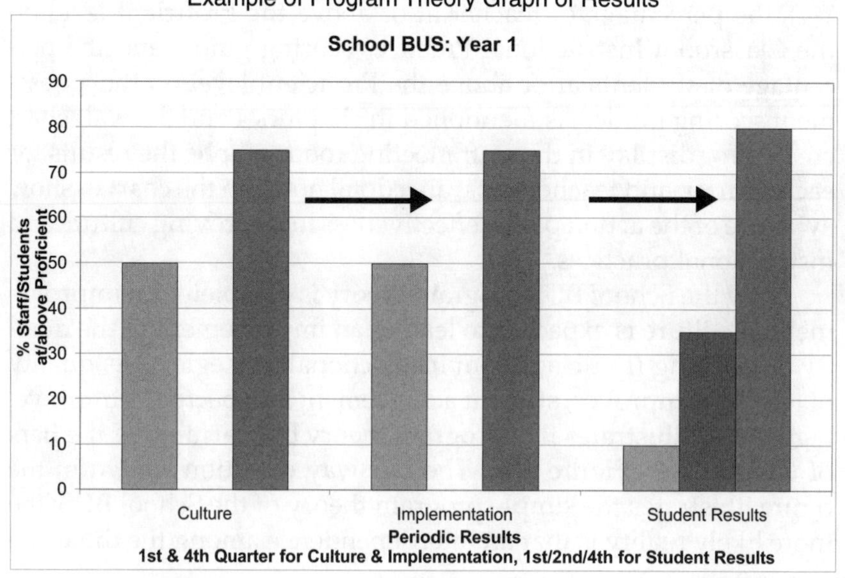

The school should celebrate when the School BUS helps it move in the right direction on the never-ending journey of school improvement. The district office, board of education, parents, and community should rejoice in their team effort as stakeholders in and contributors to the educational system. Teachers should be praised as the central agents of change. Teachers should recognize that they could not have been successful without the support of school administrators, parents, district staff, and the board of education. Each student has become a success story.

Advanced School BUS Model

Advanced users of the School BUS integrate staff meeting and professional development time, holding frequent, longer meetings during which teachers can examine results, plan improvements, and learn new strategies. Standards as well as the instruction and assessment of standards are integrated in the classrooms. Learning flows seamlessly among teams of adults and students.

Cityscape USD is in its second year of using the School BUS. Many schools have expanded from just assessing reading comprehension to also assessing student writing. A few schools are piloting a new integrated assessment of reading and writing. Many schools have progressed from examining the results of single assessments to comparing results from a variety of assessments. Professional development and accountability are intertwined. The district reached agreement with the teachers union to allow schools to divide state-allowed staff development days into segments of hours which each then can be scattered throughout the year and used as the school wishes.

Many schools have three-hour professional development meetings about once a month or 90-minute meetings every two weeks by combining staff meeting and staff development time allotments. All schools have staff meetings at least twice a month. Restructuring meeting time is essentially a bottom-up decision made by teachers in order to have more time for adult learning.

Some schools in their second School BUS year expanded data analysis from summary results for all students to subgroup analysis. The district provided subgroup results at the end of the first year that showed certain achievement gaps. Principals checked staff placement patterns to ensure that the more experienced teachers were matched with the groups of students who have the greatest learning needs. Principals checked that classrooms of students were reasonably heterogeneous in terms of abilities, interests, and ethnicity. Staff engaged in dialogue to ensure that they indeed had high expectations for all students. They were resolved to determine new ways to accelerate learning for student subgroups that appeared to be performing lower than expected. (Chapter 8 will describe methods for student subgroup analysis.)

One wall in the faculty meeting room shows the bar chart of progress on culture, implementing classroom strategies, and student results. Anecdotal notes show evidence of how teachers are implementing the mini action plans each month. A part of each staff meeting is devoted to culture, instruction, and assessment topics. The school leadership team looks for successes along the way (on the wall) and celebrates with the whole staff.

District administrators guide and support expansion and refinement of the School BUS model. All schools are expected to move forward but not all at the same pace. Schools not making ample progress are given extra guidance and support to accelerate change and learning. The administration models a learning organization and the School BUS's primarily bottom-up, simple-steps approach. The district provides leadership training and formally recognizes the accomplishments of each school leadership team and rotates members to avoid "burn-out."

Staff Development Activities

Activity 1: Practice Using the 1st Quarter School Form

This activity gives a staff practice in and a deeper understanding of using the School BUS to describe, interpret, and make improvement decisions informed by student results. It might be used with principals and school leadership teams to prepare them to lead and facilitate school faculties with confidence and some degree of prior experience.

Set a time limit of perhaps 20 minutes for respectful dialogue and to brainstorm a few possible improvement actions linked to the results without making any value judgments on any of the suggestions. Allow table groups to exchange ideas before opening the discussion to the whole group.

The remainder of this chapter discusses issues of *context* and *impact* in a school's comprehensive accountability report. Context refers to a description of school characteristics, such as student and staff demographics, that may help to explain or provide perspective on student results but that do not necessarily have a direct, causal impact. For example, if a school in a highly affluent suburb achieves 90% of its students at proficiency, that is well and good; however, when a school in a high poverty area achieves the same results, it is extremely impressive. Impact information refers to student results and causal factors, such as actions to improve school culture and the schoolwide instructional program.

Student Achievement Results

In the School BUS model, student results are reported as the percentage of students at or above the Proficient performance standard. Systematic analysis gives way to the examination of change across years and within student subgroups.

Schools receiving federal Title I funds and public schools receiving certain state funds may be required to produce a report of student results showing summary data over several years and for student subgroups. Subgroup categories might be gender, ethnicity, socioeconomic status (e.g., economically disadvantaged based on free or reduced lunch program status), English proficiency (e.g., English learner or Limited English Proficient), special education designation, or Title I designation. Some states produce reports of state test results broken down by student subgroup categories and set comparable goals for all subgroups of sufficient size.

A suggestion is to include the federal and state requirements in a school's annual comprehensive accountability report. The district office, especially in medium to large size districts, can identify required elements and produce the achievement data reports for schools. Student subgroup results are required, at least in part, to provide evidence that equitable education is offered to all students and that all student subgroups are making comparable progress. A corollary suggestion is to organize the data in the report to allow readers to easily make visual comparisons, for example, placing data in rows or columns and rounding to whole numbers (decimals can be distracting and usually do not identify significant differences).

Consider whether to include two types of data in the same table or in separate tables; for example, numbers of students tested and percentage of students at or above 50th percentile. Consider which data tables have information important enough to be presented as a graphic chart (e.g., pie chart, bar graph, or line graph) for readers who prefer data presented visually. Be sure to label data tables and graphic charts to inform the reader about what the numbers represent. Sequence the tables and charts to "tell a systematic story." Start with the global picture or bird's eye view of the school, and then present more detailed levels of analysis. For example, start with the percentage of students at or above the Proficient level in the whole school, and then show data by grade level or student subgroups. Or start with the percentage of all students at or above the Proficient level, and then show percentages at each performance level. Chapter 9 will explain how to systematically dig deeper into data.

Figures 7.1 to 7.5 show data tables and one bar graph of a school's state test results for which the 50th percentile on a nationally norm-referenced test (e.g., SAT-9) serves as the "criterion for grade level proficiency." Figure 7.1 shows the numbers of students tested at each grade level on each subject area test (reading, language, and mathematics). If any anomalies "pop out," such as far fewer students tested at a particular grade level, then they are highlighted in the text description of the results to raise reader awareness that test results may not fully represent the true student population at the school or be completely accurate.

FIGURE 7.1

2000 SAT-9: # Students Tested

# Students Tested	Grade Levels			
	2	3	4	All
Reading	159	187	170	516
Language	161	153	172	486
Math	160	185	173	518

FIGURE 7.2

2000 SAT-9: % Student At/Above 50th Percentile

% Students At/Above 50th Percentile	Grade Levels			
	2	3	4	All
Reading	45	26	27	32
Language	39	31	30	33
Math	38	37	46	40

Figure 7.2 presents test results in a way that allows the reader to compare results across rows and down columns (e.g., differences or patterns across subject area tests or grade levels). The data table in Figure 7.2 is considered important enough to include a bar graph of the results, as shown in Figure 7.3. For the benefit of the reader, Figure 7.3 also includes the actual Microsoft Excel spreadsheet used to create the bar graph. All data tables and graphs are accompanied by text descriptions in the body of the report to explain important differences and patterns in the data tables or graphs.

FIGURE 7.3

Example of Bar Graph Showing Excel Data Table

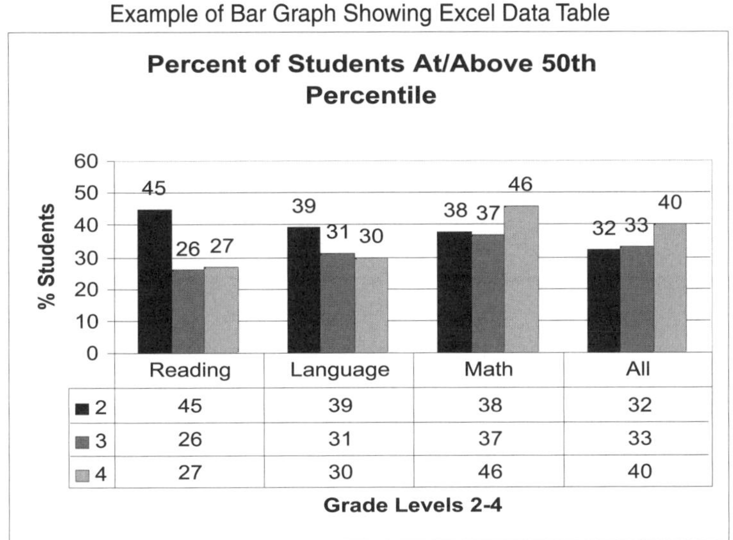

	Reading	Language	Math	All
2	45	39	38	32
3	26	31	37	33
4	27	30	46	40

The Excel spreadsheet shows three rows for reading, language, and math results with columns for each grade level. By positioning the data results for All (combined grade levels) as the last row and then changing bar colors, it was possible to show the three bars for reading, language, and math to the far right in the bar graph. This layout makes it easy for a reader to examine the subject area test results for All grades on the right, and then look to the left at results for grade levels within each subject area test.

Because the state mandates subgroup analysis, subgroup results are reported in Figure 7.4, although data are omitted when the subgroup size is not a sufficiently large part of the school population. Significant differences among subgroups are mentioned in the text. Figure 7.5 presents results on the state test for the last three years along with the one- and two-year changes in the percentage of students at or above 50th percentile for the whole school. "Results across years" are often presented and analyzed this way, but it is not the best approach for making inferences about how changes in a school's instructional practices have led to changes in student results because some percentage of students enter or leave the school each year. Results across three years represents some but not all of the same students. Chapter 8 will explain a more sophisticated method.

FIGURE 7.4

2000 SAT-9: Student Subgroups
Percent of Students At/Above 50th Percentile
(example table format, data not entered)

	#	Reading	Language	Math
All				
Not English Learner				
English Learner				
Higher SES				
Lower SES				
African-American				
American Indian				
Asian-American				
Filipino				
Hispanic				
Pacific Islander				
White (not Hispanic)				

= Total number tested in Reading * = Group size too small

State test results, where available are usually required elements in state and federally funded project reports. Schools applying for special awards or project funding often are required to submit state test results. Local district or school assessment results might be required but usually are optional for state and federal reports. State or national results might be presented first, followed by local assessment results. A description and interpretation of the external and internal results should identify similarities or differences in the two sets of results and likely reasons for any discrepancies.

Evidence of the validity and reliability of local assessments supports conclusions about the accuracy of internal data. The school or district that uses some form of double-scoring of performance assessments can compute the average percentage agreement among raters with relative ease (75 or 80% is an acceptably high level of agreement). The greater the public visibility of the school's comprehensive accountability report, the more care should be taken to present empirical information about the degree to which the internal assessment meets standards of high quality (see chapter 3). People external to the school should be confident that the school's internal assessment results are accurate and valid.

FIGURE 7.5

SAT-9 Change from 1998 to 2000
Percent of Students At/Above 50th Percentile

Reading					**Change**	
Grade Levels	2	3	4	All	1 Yr	2 Yr
1998	28	18	17	21	+3	
1999	36	16	19	24		+11
2000	45	26	27	32	+8	
Language					**Change**	
Grade Levels	2	3	4	All	1 Yr	2 Yr
1998	25	16	14	18	+4	
1999	28	21	18	22		+15
2000	39	31	30	33	+11	
Math					**Change**	
Grade Levels	2	3	4	All	1 Yr	2 Yr
1998	20	22	25	22	+12	
1999	32	37	33	34		+18
2000	38	37	46	40	+6	

Context and Causal Factors

Contextual information provides a comparative perspective for interpreting student results for a school. The contextual information helps when making judgments about school effectiveness, although the contextual factors may not be causal factors that have a direct impact on student achievement. Research literature and logic support the idea that changes in causal factors connect to changes in student achievement. Given their intimate knowledge of the school and students, school staff can make professional judgments about what practices were or were not effective in improving student learning.

School Demographics

Student achievement results are grounded in information about students and staff at the school. No demographic factor is reason to accept very low student results and refrain from trying to improve, but differences among schools' demographics do help to explain, at least in part, differences in student results. Chapter 5 discussed research studies that compared a variety of instructional and demographic factors and indicated that all had important influences, but quality of teaching had the greatest impact on student learning.

School demographics include descriptions about the student population, such as ethnicity, socioeconomic status, English language proficiency, languages spoken, mobility, dropout rates, special education, and Title I designation. Demographic factors about staff include gender, ethnicity, languages spoken, mobility, years of teaching experience, credentials and licenses and in the subject taught, professional awards, and advanced certification (e.g., National Board for Professional Teaching Standards). The quality of the physical building, textbook, library resources, and technology, including Internet access in classrooms, are informative about school environment and material support for instruction.

When teachers serve on state curriculum committees and assessment scoring teams, advise textbook companies, write books, and create educational videos, they bring back to the classroom a wealth of information and experience. These accomplishments should be mentioned in the contextual information section of the report.

Description of enrichment programs, such as GATE and AP courses at the high schools as well as common enrichment activities in all classrooms, provide some background information for understanding student results and the percentage of students who reach the Advanced level on assessments. Class scheduling (e.g., block plans in secondary schools with common teacher prep periods, structures for "houses or academies" within large schools, and looping and multi-age classrooms at elementary schools) tell part of the story about a school's climate for learning and teacher-student bonding.

One page can list by source all of the funds that a school receives, with or without some degree of discretion for use. The ratio of dollars per student might be included. Comparison to other schools in the district might also be included to indicate equity in terms of financial and other resource allocations and staff qualifications. Staff inequalities, especially between schools with a mostly affluent or impoverished population base, may lead to a description of the district policies and union contracts that might address such inequities.

Climate and Culture

Information from surveys and focus group interviews can provide data about staff, parent, community, and student attitudes toward the school, the quality of teaching and learning at the school, and the joy of being a part of the school and learning community.

Results from the assessment of the staff about how well their school culture reflects a learning organization (see chapter 4) indicate the degree to which there is a strong foundation for initiating any change in the school. Results over time indicate that the staff is engaging in continual improvement of the organization and team learning in ways that will benefit students. Do anecdotal records on the wall chart corroborate assertions?

Comprehensive Instructional Program

Many schools have a school plan that lists or describes intended core instructional strategies or comprehensive programs. Perhaps the intended implementation matched real implementation, or perhaps the school plan is not a "living resource" and is largely ignored by teachers. The plan of action needs to be compared to evidence of action. If changes in the school plan were made, but staff did not change practices and student results stayed the same, then it is inappropriate to call for a change (yet again) in the school plan.

This section of the comprehensive accountability report should recount the school's moderate and intensive school interventions and relate them to the ability of the school to serve students in need, as indicated by numbers of students at the Minimal and Partial performance levels. This section should also describe family and community activities, services, and education programs that give extra help to students, especially those below proficiency. Family and community strategies directly linked and supporting the school's primary focus for academic improvement should be in place.

Information on actual implementation can come from the assessment of core classroom instructional strategies discussed in chapter 5. What is the relationship between changes in schoolwide instruction and changes in student achievement results? Is there a relationship between changes in school culture and changes in program implementation? Do anecdotal records on the wall chart corroborate assertions?

The integration of professional development activities and staff meetings is described here, especially because it is the engine that drives teachers toward acquiring the skills they need to learn and implement the strategies for instructional improvement. The School BUS accountability process of using these meeting times to reflect on assessment results, explore options, and make decisions about continual refinements might be mentioned in this section. Or it might be included in the first section by broadening the label to "student achievement results and accountability" to indicate results and how they are used in the school.

A suggestion is to begin the comprehensive accountability report by presenting student results, the most important information. Then follow with categories of factors that may have had a positive or negative impact on student results. Figure 7.6 is an example of a "summary causal relationship chart" that highlights important changes in student achievement results from 1998 to 2000 and factors that likely had a positive or negative impact. Figure 7.6 shows the various factors that school staff believed had an impact on changes in student achievement from 1998 to 2000. The body of text in each section of the report provides specific evidence and examples to support each assertion.

FIGURE 7.6

Summary Causal Relationship Chart

Student Results	1998-2000	**Significant Changes**
		Math +12 pts. 1998-99 Reading +8 pts. and Language +11 pts. 1999-2000
	Impact	
Student Demographics	slightly negative or none	Poverty Index 50% 1998, 55% 1999, 58% 2000 (association, not causal factor)
Staff Demographics	positive	10% mobility 1998-2000; 7 more advanced certifications; 5 completing advanced degrees
Climate & Culture	positive	From rating of "2" in 1998 to "high 3" in 2000 on Culture scoring guide
Instructional Program	positive	Math program change 1999, language arts change in 2000; increased ratings of staff instruction at proficient level 1998-2000; after school interventions in math 1999, language arts in 2000
Family Community	positive	Family-oriented homework projects; parent education; book bags; community reading tutors

Special Qualities

Ritchey (2000) encourages teachers to go beyond the yardstick measurement of their worth in terms of student achievement on once-a-year tests and to embrace additional indicators of their professionalism and their deep concern for developing well-rounded, wise, caring citizens. A mark of a great teacher is the student who carries lifetime memories of special, wonderful events that opened doors of educational opportunity and heartfelt experiences. A good teacher does so much more than just teach.

What are the things about this school that make it a wonderful place for teaching and learning? What students participate in science camp, Young Authors' Faire, speech contests, daily school news broadcasts, school and community service activities, leadership programs, marching band, and social clubs?

Some schools have outstanding special education inclusion programs, team teaching, parent organizations and resource rooms, respect for diversity that goes far beyond "celebration days," and signs around the school written in the primary languages of students and parents.

Some schools have received recognition awards for making sustained, dramatic improvement in academic achievement, and staff members have been invited to present at professional conferences. More teachers should be giving presentations to administrators, consultants, and researchers at conferences and institutes. Mr. Tran in Alhambra Middle School (California) described the multimedia research reports done each month in his social studies class by student teams and how students were informed of the specific expectations, coursework plan, and assessment scoring guide. Not only did Mr. Tran follow what research says is best teaching and have extremely high expectations for student performance, but his students were mostly English learners from poverty backgrounds. Some districts post model lesson plans and other teacher products on the district's Internet site; schools should mention work accepted for public display.

Azzara (2000) advises principals to "make your school unique, even if it isn't." When she was principal in East Harlem, the community theme was "Rain, sleet, or snow—the sun always shines at Louise Archer School." She said, "It's corny, but everyone buys into it. The sunflower has become our official flower." Sunflowers decorate walls, courtyards, and the shirts and hats of students and teachers. Azzara drew upon the history of the school—formerly an all

African-American school where the first principal transported her students to school—to build themes and norms of a caring family.

Figure 7.7 presents a comprehensive accountability map that illustrates the sources of different pieces of information about the school and places the relationship or impact on student results in the center of the map. Results from one area might need corroboration from results from another area. Information is not included in the accountability report "just to fill pages," but to form correlationals and causal links among different elements of a school's comprehensive program. If teaching practices are said to have improved, that should be supported by data showing improvement in student learning. If student results change from one year to the next, they should be linked to instructional program changes and show that student demographics did not change appreciably in that time. In other words, changes in student achievement are linked directly to changes in teaching.

FIGURE 7.7

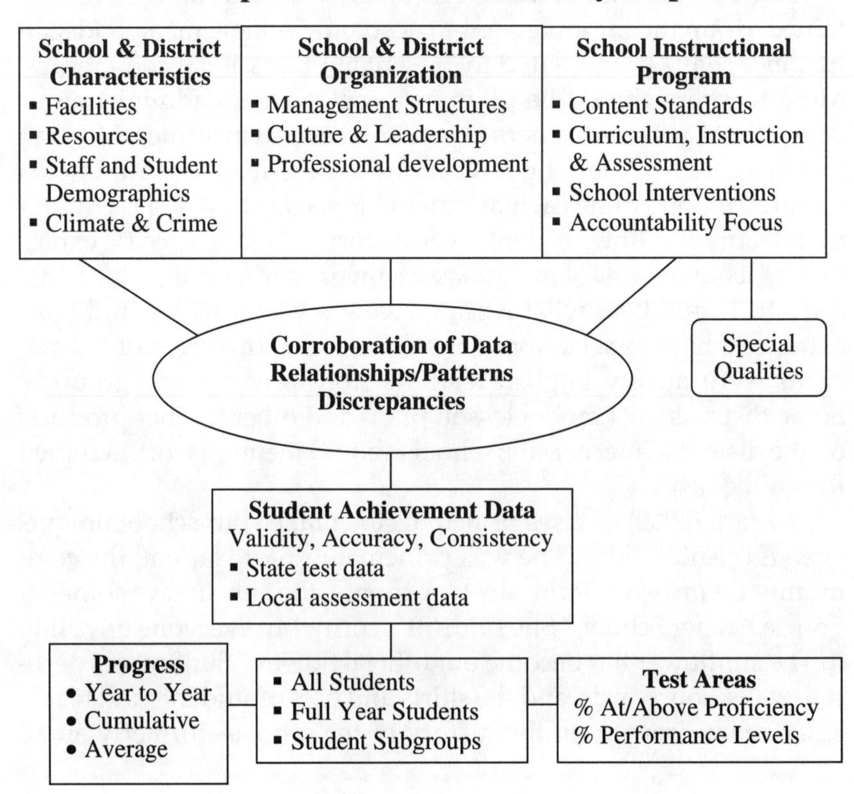

Report Presentation

Writing a comprehensive accountability report is not as daunting a task as it seems. District staff can provide some parts, such as data tables and "boilerplate" text sections that are common to all schools in the district. The School BUS forms and wall chart that are developed throughout the year provide much quantitative and qualitative information that can be "dropped into" the annual report. Much of the information, such as demographics, just needs updating in successive years. The thrust of the report is to show changes in schoolwide student achievement from one year to the next. Information (demographics, the instructional program) provides a context and gives details about factors that had an impact on any improvement in student achievement.

In a small to medium size district, schools might set up displays around the boardroom for everyone to review. Perhaps the principal, a teacher, or a student could stand beside each school's display and answer any questions. The required presentation to the board by a district administrator could be brief and reference the displays. After the board meeting, the displays are returned to each school's office for parents to see when they come to register their children or request information about the school. The displays and reports are an entry point for newspaper reporters looking for facts as well as positive success stories.

Up to this point, the discussion of the use of results has been limited to a single assessment for all students in a grade level or school during a school year. Chapter 8 describes how to calculate and report results for student subgroups and analyze trends over years. It should not be assumed that all students are succeeding when summary results indicate meaningful progress—most students may be progressing but a minority group may not be making progress or closing an achievement gap. States such as California, Texas, and Kentucky embed an expectation that all student subgroups make comparable progress within the state's accountability system.

A novice in student data analysis is cautioned that some concepts in Chapter 8 can overwhelm the reader initially, but an effort is made to present complex, highly sophisticated concepts in as basic and clear manner as possible. The novice might find specific topics that are immediately relevant such as student racial/ethnic and gender subgroup reporting for a single year and wait to tackle other topics until data analysis skills become stronger through practice and then return to these remaining topics. Activities at the end of the chapter in the Staff Development section provide additional practice with data sets.

8 Deeper Data Analysis

Nothing in life is to be feared. It is only to be understood.

—*Marie Curie*

Effective management means always asking the right question.

—*Robert Heller*

Overview

The system and techniques of data analysis presented in this chapter are extensions of the School BUS approach. The system of digging deeper into data is simply a logical, sequential thinking process. Simple, fairly easy ways for school staff to explore deeper into student achievement data can unearth hidden information about specific test content and student subgroups or discover patterns across years. Targeting a specific teaching strategy for a specific concept or skill can achieve what Schmoker (1999) called "rapid results." Examining data for student subgroups might indicate achievement gaps among student subgroups, perhaps the result of differential opportunity to learn. Results can fluctuate from one year to the next due to chance rather than actual program effects, so it is wise to look for patterns of rising or falling test scores across at least three years.

Deeper data analysis for student subgroups follows a systematic process of first looking at results for all students, then looking at results for students attending the school most or all year, and lastly looking at results for student subgroups based on gender, ethnicity, or other demographic factors. The school is accountable for providing a full year of program services to assist all *full year* students to reach proficiency, regardless of their starting performance level.

The obligation to full-year students does not mean that highly mobile students are ignored or that the school should not include "short-term" services to meet their needs. At Waitz Elementary School, over 90% of students pass Texas's state tests, yet many students from migrant worker families enter school a month late and leave before the end of the school year (Calwelti, 2000). Other schools give students "study packets" to take with them to Mexico in December, or they coordinate lessons with Mexican schools. One principal gave a map of the school's boundaries to a highly mobile mother in an attempt to keep the child in the same school all year. Individual principals, teachers, schools, and districts are making heroic efforts to assist all students. Accountability for highly mobile students, those attending a school for a few months or less, is important but beyond the scope of this book.

Looking at year-end data in terms of the deeper layers of what the test measures—from the general subject area (e.g., reading), to subareas (e.g., decoding, fluency, or comprehension), to specific concepts and skills (e.g., making inferences from informational text)—can pinpoint specific teaching strategies that are effective or need improvement. Nationally norm-referenced tests (e.g., SAT-9, Terra Nova, and ITBS) allow this type of deeper analysis. Many criterion-referenced tests allow for deconstruction into more detailed information; for example, running records yield book levels but also miscue word analysis information.

Staff examines the results for different types of students to see the degree to which the school program is meeting diverse student needs. There are two types of student characteristics: *demographic* (e.g., gender, economic status, and ethnicity) and *programmatic* (e.g., Title I, special education, English proficiency, and type of school intervention program). Are there achievement gaps among student subgroups, and are "underperforming" subgroups closing achievement gaps?

What can staff learn from looking at data across several years? Is student achievement improving over time? Looking at the same group of students over many years can be futile if the group is highly mobile or can be too difficult if computer software cannot be used. A variety of methods are presented, but Diagonal School Analysis is perhaps the most appropriate and feasible method for a school that has only year-end results for all students, not year-to-year data matched by students.

A school may need to phase in expansion of deeper data analyses over several years. A school or district might design student and teacher databases for immediate use that eventually will be able to yield data for a variety of inquiries.

This chapter starts with a discussion about who should be involved in creating and presenting data results. The approach to creating and presenting results should build ownership and understanding by teachers. A variety of ways to dig deeper into student data results are presented, but all methods start with a global perspective and are followed by disaggregation into more specific elements. Staff development activities at the end of the chapter provide more "hands-on" practice with a variety of data sets.

Preparing the Data Report

Before describing methods of deeper data analysis, a review of who should prepare the report of results is necessary. There are tradeoffs between having a principal (or central office assessment person) prepare data tables and bar graphs and present them as a finished report at a staff meeting for discussion versus having teachers make the data tables and bar graphs for a report from individual student data or summarized data. Giving staff a prepared report saves time so that staff can immediately begin describing and interpreting the results. This method is recommended when the staff has been doing data analysis and already feels "ownership of the results." Technology and computer programs can be used to produce elegant tables and graphs. A facilitator may use transparencies or a Microsoft PowerPoint slide show to focus everyone on the summary of results for a team dialogue.

Coming into the data analysis meeting with a "slick report of findings" is not suggested for a staff who has not looked at data tables and bar graphs before or for a staff who has not taken ownership of the results before. The following "preparation steps" are suggested for use with staff whose prior experience with reviewing test data led to their dismissing the test as a "bad test" or to their blaming people and conditions rather than reflecting on the impact of the school's instructional program. This blame reaction negates any inquiry about improving instruction in the school's classrooms, which is the primary target of accountability in the School BUS.

Having teachers participate in the activity of creating the data tables and bar graphs ensures their understanding of tables and graphs and, more importantly, fosters their ownership of the results. The process for creating data tables and graphs discussed in this chapter is no more difficult than that used by elementary school teachers to teach graphing to their students. It is natural for teachers to talk about the results while they create the tables and graphs. In other words, the dialogue begins without prompting by a facilitator. The process of creating a report of findings fosters reflection on the meaning of the results, just as the process of writing a poem, essay, or autobiography fosters deep reflection for students.

Do not create data tables and graphs on transparencies—use poster paper so that finished products can decorate the walls in the staff meeting room. These data tables, graphs, and written strategies about how to improve instruction serve as daily reminders of what can happen when teaching and the staff's commitment to improvement is informed by student results.

Teaching is the Primary Cause and Solution

Before discussing the mechanics of digging deeper into data to make program decisions, it is important to review the guidelines about what types of decisions will be made. The decisions are about actions that are within the control of the school's teachers as a team. Teachers cannot control or change student or parent demographics. Teachers can control how they address the challenges, and they can participate in a culture that continually seeks ways to improve teaching practices. Stories abound of schools that faced enormous challenges and actively engaged in making dramatic success their reality.

Chapter 4 emphasized that teams of teachers are continually exploring ways to improve their professionalism in schools that exemplify learning organizations. Chapter 5 discussed the three components of a school's comprehensive instructional program—core classroom strategies, school interventions, and family and community partnerships. The three components are mentioned in order of importance and sequence of decision-making. Research literature was cited about the importance of many factors, but the quality of teaching in classrooms has the biggest impact on student learning. Chapter 6 discussed a process for school teams to make instructional program decisions based on student achievement results.

Ideas and staff development activities presented in prior chapters as well as other resources can help forge a common belief among teachers that it is their skills as professional educators that matter most in the education of students. Some students pose greater challenges than other students, but all students can learn when high expectations are coupled with effective strategies. Another way to quickly inspire teachers to take primary responsibility for student achievement results is to engage them quickly and empower them in summarizing student data and include them in making instructional program decisions.

Carr has facilitated many school staff meetings about (state) test results in which initial blame for low scores was laid on the test, the students, their friends, their parents, and every other reason except for classroom instruction. Discussing research findings and schools like Reeves' 90/90/90 schools (2000a) can affect some but not all teachers. Movies like *Mr. Holland's Opus* can affect other teachers. Quickly moving from a feeling of powerlessness and hopelessness to an experience of control and capability can turn around many recalcitrant teachers. Sometimes disbelief and avoidance of test results comes from not wanting or not knowing how to change. Giving teachers a quick and simple way to analyze test results and to generate immediate solutions from within the group can be the key to building ownership of student results and a commitment to improvement.

Once staff begins using the data, they begin to build a feeling of shared responsibility for changing student results by changing teaching practices. Once teachers are no longer blamed for poor student results but become empowered to describe and interpret their own results, attitudes shift. Staff begins making data tables and bar graphs of student results for their group's grade level or subject area, describing their group's graph to the rest of the staff, and identifying the area most in need of improvement. They move to the next level to pinpoint one or a very few specific skills that presented the greatest challenge to student learning and identify one or a few specific strategies to address the challenge.

A workshop setting of about three hours might be required, followed by a continuous series of professional development and staff meetings to support change in instructional strategies and to observe impact on student learning. Changing a long history of blaming teachers, of blaming outside forces, and of not having a requirement or effective process for changing how teachers' teach and how students learn is not a one-shot event. A clear process and a leadership that empowers teachers as a team to analyze results in order to inform teaching practices is the first step in a long journey. Sometimes attitude change comes not from talking about attitudes but from doing—using results, making a "do-able" change in teaching, and observing its impact on student learning. Sometimes change comes from pinpointing one small but significant area for change and realizing rapid results, as Schmoker suggested (1999), and then building on that experience to target bigger, long-range change.

Means Versus Percentages

Report achievement results as percentage of students, not as means (also called averages) for any type of test. For example, report the percentage of students at and above the 50th percentile on a norm-referenced test. No recommendation is being made to use the 50th percentile on norm-referenced tests, but this is a widely used cutoff. For a standards-based assessment, report the percentage of students at and above the Proficient level or percentage of students at each performance level.

Traditionally, test publishers redesign an achievement test every seven years and use a "national" sample of students to set percentiles for all students who take the test every year thereafter. For example, Harcourt Brace's Stanford 9 (SAT-9) was normed in 1995 with about 2000 students per grade level. Suppose Andrea, an eleventh grade student, had 69% of the items correct on Total Reading, which converts to the 49th percentile on this test at this grade level. Therefore, Andrea scored higher than 49% of the 1995 eleventh grade norming sample. Since all students in the nation did not take the SAT-9, it is incorrect to say that Andrea scored higher than 49% of students *in the nation*. Norm referenced tests can be used to show gains even though many people wrongly believe that "the curve moves every year." It is possible to track a student's percentiles or a school's average norm curve equivalent scores (NCEs) as they rise or fall over several years until the test is redesigned and renormed.

Problems with Means NCEs

Title I originally but no longer requires the reporting of mean pre- and post-test scores on a norm-referenced test (NRT) for "matched" groups of students receiving Title I services. Matched students were those who had test scores for two consecutive years. Individual student percentiles were converted to NCE scores and the average NCE was reported. Percentiles should not be averaged. Figure 8.1 illustrates the relationship between percentiles and NCEs; both range from 1-99 with a mid-point of 50. An NCE has little meaning as a score; NCEs can be averaged whereas percentiles cannot.

FIGURE 8.1

Comparison of Percentiles to NCEs

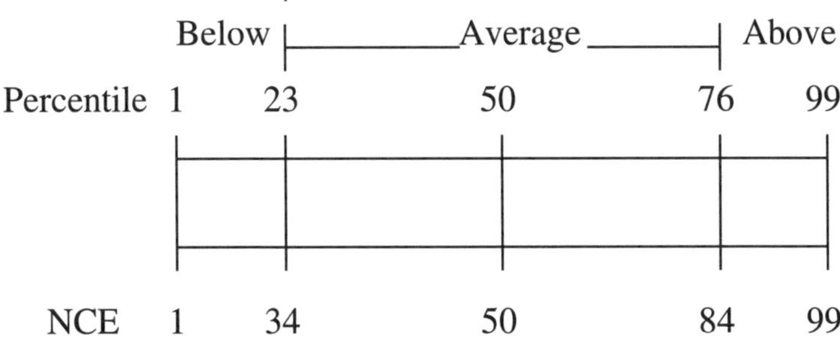

A principle of mathematics states that equidistant scores can be averaged. NCEs are equidistant, percentiles are not equidistant. The number of items a student must get correct to move from the 10th percentile to the 20th percentile is different from the number of items needed to move from the 50th percentile to the 60th percentile. NCEs "stretch out" percentiles near the middle and "squeeze closer" percentiles at the two extremes to make NCE distances equal.

There are three problems with reporting means. The first two are particular to NRT data and concern how mean scores can be incorrectly interpreted. The third problem is general to any type of test and addresses how people often react to a mean score.

First, some schools or districts report mean NCEs on a norm-referenced test but mistakenly explain them as if they were mean percentiles. Consider the case of a district that had a mean NCE of 34 on Total Reading year after year. District administrators wrongly said that the district was at the 34th percentile. They rested on low laurels and did not expect higher achievement from their student population. The next year, the assessment office administrator converted the mean NCE to a percentile. As shown in Figure 8.1, a 34 NCE converts to the 23rd percentile. When it was reported that the "average" student scored at the 23rd percentile—the same NCE as before— the district's sense of accomplishment waned.

Second, instead of correctly saying that the "average" student scored at the 23rd percentile, some people erroneously say that the *school* or *district* scored at the 23rd percentile. The commonly reported percentile refers to the distribution of scores for individual students, not the distribution of mean scores for schools or districts. The distribution of scores for individuals tends to be wider than the distribution of means for schools.

Two students, one at the 1st percentile (1 NCE) and the other at the 99th percentile (99 NCE), yield a mean of 50 for a hypothetical school of two students. A school reporting a mean of 1 would have to have all (or almost all) students scoring at the 1st percentile. The same is true for the 99th percentile. For this reason, the spread of scores for individuals tends to be much wider than the spread of mean scores for schools.

The third problem is how many people "look at" mean scores and how they use them to make instructional decisions. Focusing on a mean score, which is an indication of the performance of the average student, can divert educators' attention away from the distribution of students, especially the performance of students at the top and bottom of the distribution.

The district's assessment administrator must keep in mind how school principals and teachers interpret and use the summary statistics of norm-referenced or standards-based assessments. If reporting mean scores is likely to influence schools to focus on the average learner and to ignore students near the top and bottom, then mean scores should not be reported. Standards-based assessments that report performance levels are becoming more widespread in state and local accountability systems. Using the percentage of students at each performance level is the suggested approach for reporting summary data and using the data to make instructional decisions about students at all levels of achievement.

Use Number or Percentage

For the three reasons stated above, mean scores do not provide information about all students, and the results often lead schools to focus on the average student to the detriment of those above and below. The percentage of students within levels of performance should be reported.

When is it appropriate to report the number of students versus the percentage of students at a performance level? As a rule of thumb, report the number of students when there are 20 or fewer in the group and report percentages when there are over 20. A more cautious approach is not to report results for a group of 20 or fewer students because of the tendency for the group data to be very "unstable," that is, prone to a wild fluctuation if just one student scores very high or very low. Some psychometricians maintain that minimum group sizes for any study should be at least 30 or as many as 100, opting for the larger size when the results are used for high-stakes decisions, but the guiding rule of 20 is sufficient for local decisions in most school contexts.

Let us look at a problem that can occur when reporting numbers instead of percentages. Consider two groups who have taken a math test. In the first group, 40 out of 40 girls passed a math test compared to 40 out of 80 boys on the same test. Obviously, the group of girls outperformed the group of boys. It would be misleading to report that 40 girls and 40 boys passed the test. It would, however, be accurate to report that 100% of girls and 50% of boys passed the test. Percentages are especially appropriate when the sizes of the groups being compared are quite different.

From the Performance Standard to Levels

For a standards-based assessment, report the percentage of students at or above the performance standard (e.g., Proficient or Meets Expectations). This provides a "bird's eye view" of school results. For deeper analysis and to make instructional program decisions, report the percentage of students at each performance level. For a norm-referenced test, a school or district might report, albeit arbitrarily, the percentage of students at and above the 50th percentile.

The intent of reporting a summary of all students' data is to funnel a massive amount of student information down to a few major findings to avoid "drowning in data" and "analysis paralysis." Therefore, report the percentage of students at and above the performance standard, but do not also report the percentage below the standard. If 61% of students were at and above the proficient level, there is no need to also report that 39% were below proficient. If the reader knows half of the story, the reader knows the whole story. Thus, the report of findings is not doubled in size, and "the other half" of students is not ignored in terms of their educational needs.

After reporting the percentage of students at the performance standard for an overall picture of school results, break down the data into the percentage of students at each performance level. In the School BUS, a school staff looks at the percentage of students at each meaningful performance level and uses that information to make instructional program decisions.

For norm-referenced test results, arbitrary performance levels might be used. In this case, report the percentage of students at and above 50th percentile, then at each quarter of percentiles (1-25, 26-50, 51-75, 76-99). When the percentage of students at and above the 50th percentile has been selected for reporting (e.g., by the state), reporting can be slightly modified by using the ranges of 1-25, 26-49, 50-75, and 76-99 to maintain alignment. A variation is the use of five levels, often called quintiles (1-19, 20-39, 40-59, 60-79, 80-99). For standards-based assessments, report the percentage of students at each performance level or summarize further by reporting the percentage at and above the Proficient level.

Describe, Then Interpret

We propose two steps in reporting student results. First, *describe* what the results look like. Second, *interpret* what may be the major causal factor or factors for these results. *Describing* results means identifying any meaningful patterns or differences—in this case, among results for the subject areas for all and each grade level tested. It should not be difficult for a school staff to reach agreement on "what is." *Interpreting* results means offering a plausible reason for the observed pattern or difference.

Sometimes a school staff quickly agrees on the major cause of student results. Sometimes discussion or exploration of alternative causal factors extends over several meetings to identify most likely cause(s). Further exploration might require research to test the validity, or soundness, of each hypothesis, or statement. A school staff may be "too close to their own teaching practices" or have strong mental models that inhibit their ability to "see the causality" or the true relationship between teaching practices and standards and best practices. A school staff may realize that teaching practices need to improve, but no one can offer a reasonable, "research-based" option. In these situations, educators outside the school can be valuable commentators.

Suppose the hypothesis for why high school test results are low is that the textbook is too difficult for many students to read. Students might be asked if not being able to read the textbook is the major hindrance or if there is some other reason. Suppose most students say that a teacher's lecturing for the entire period is boring and shuts down listening. They wish teachers would engage students in thoughtful discussions to derive meaning from textbooks. (This topic of finding corroborating evidence will be discussed fully in a later section of this chapter.)

Staff members should respectfully challenge any interpretation by a colleague that is not plausible or supported by the data. This is part of learning as a team to properly interpret test results. When a student offers a wrong answer during instruction, a good teaching practice is to engage the class in a discussion of alternatives and to use reasoning to arrive at the correct answer without showing disrespect to the initial student. Errors are wonderful opportunities for learning.

Interpretations are disallowed when they stray beyond the influence of classroom practices, school interventions, or, perhaps, curriculum materials. For example, if a teacher says that maturation explains changes in grade level results, that statement should be challenged for two reasons. First, maturation ought to be reflected in a pattern of upward or downward results across grades and perhaps a similar upward or downward pattern for reading, language, and mathematics. Second, maturation is a factor located within the students, outside the control of teachers.

When a school staff analyzes test results, it's focus of interpretation should be on the influence of classroom practices. This is the approach used in the School BUS because staff has limited time for analysis and wants to work on what they can most control—teaching practices. Topics covered during the interpretation process might include school interventions outside the classroom, family and community support strategies, and curriculum materials as long as core classroom practices have been sufficiently addressed first.

A school staff usually has very limited time to analyze assessment results. One hour to three hours in a meeting may be the only time staff has to describe and interpret a variety of data. Describing and interpreting three data tables can take a full three hours. Describing the results with whole staff agreement should be quick so that staff has maximum time to interpret the major causes of the results, the challenges to student learning, and the ways to improve instructional practices so that students will perform much better on the next assessment.

Consider the context of comparing grade levels or subject areas in terms of the percentage of students at or above proficiency on some assessment. How large should a difference be before it is considered a meaningful difference? Sophisticated statistical formulas exist for determining when a difference is significant, but school staff, analyzing their own data in a normal staff meeting during the year, cannot be bogged down with statistical wizardry. The staff needs a user-friendly guide to quickly describe results and move on to interpreting reasonable causality and, most importantly, ways to improve the lowest results.

Figure 8.2 presents Carr's simple guide for describing differences in percentages of students at or above proficiency. His method is a mixture of statistical significance, effect size, and practical significance derived from many years of examining test results in large districts. The comparison could be made among grade levels in a particular subject area (e.g., ninth versus tenth grade on reading), among subjects areas for all grades combined (e.g., reading versus mathematics), or across years (e.g., 1999 to 2000 for all grades combined in reading).

FIGURE 8.2

Guide for Describing Meaningful Differences

	Total Number of Students Being Compared			
Descriptive Difference	50	100	200	500+
	Percentage Points Difference			
None	0-12	0-8	0-5	0-3
Small	13-15	9-11	6-7	4-5
Moderate	16-19	12-14	8-10	6-8
Fairly Large	20-25	15-17	11-13	9-10
Large	26-29	18-24	14-19	11-15
Very Large	30+	25+	20+	16+

Sum the number of students in the two groups being compared—the number of students tested, not just the number of students at and above proficiency. Suppose 100 students were tested in each of two groups, but only 30 students in each group reached proficiency on the test. The sum of the two groups is 200 students. Locate the column in Figure 8.2 closest to the actual sum under the label, "Total Number of Students Being Compared." If comparing essentially the same students across years (e.g., second grade in 1999 and third grade in 2000), use the group of lesser size, not the sum of both groups. Making comparisons across years is a special topic discussed later in this chapter.

Look down the appropriate column in Figure 8.2 at the ranges of differences (differences in percentages of students in two groups or subject areas being compared). The leftmost column shows the adjective to use to describe the difference (e.g., none, small, large). Consider a total group size of 200 and a difference in percentage of